Looking In Reaching Out

a reflective guide

for community

service-learning professionals

Edited by Barbara Jacoby and Pamela Mutascio

Campus Compact

Contents

Table of Worksheets

Foreword

LOOKING IN, REACHING OUT: A REFLECTIVE GUIDE FOR COMMUNITY SERVICE-LEARNING PROFESSIONALS would have been invaluable to me when I began my job as Director of Community Service-Learning at James Madison University (JMU) in 1996. I came to JMU with academic training in counseling and 18 years of experience directing outdoor adventure programs, summer camps, and collegiate leadership programs. This experience gave me a broad understanding of building teams, experiential education, and reflective learning, but I was not prepared for the challenges of running and growing a service-learning office.

Over time I was able to learn the skills and knowledge I needed through strong community and university mentors. Asking questions and, more important, listening to the answers, provided valuable insight and on-the-job training. My development involved much trial and error. This process was vital in building strong relationships with both the university and the larger community; however, it would have been helpful to have some best-practices guidance along the way. Looking back, I realize that many times I was "reinventing the wheel" as I discovered what more experienced service-learning colleagues already knew. Based on conversations with other service-learning professionals, my experience is not unique.

The diverse background of today's service-learning professional is what brings richness and wisdom to the field. It prepares us to see the world in unique ways, by identifying the specialness of difference, while creating paths to build welcoming and inclusive communities. The diversity of our experiences helps us understand that the discomfort created by perplexity is also the spark of transformation. Our challenge is to create a safe and open learning environment that allows this transformation to unfold. Our experiences, both inside and beyond our educational institutions, inform our understanding that the most powerful learning environment is that which partners the community experience with classroom instruction. In turn, this knowledge leads to an awareness that in each experience there are many different ways of seeing and knowing. The true understanding of any experience happens only when these different perspectives are shared and understood by all. Yet, as service-learning professionals, we wonder what the best ways to accomplish our learning goals are. We tire of using the same approaches multiple times and search for new and better ways to facilitate learning. On a more pragmatic note, we seek proven ways of working with faculty, engaging students, building community partnerships, and assessing the success of our work.

Looking In, Reaching Out: A Reflective Guide for Community Service-Learning Professionals serves as a valuable resource to answer these and other questions. It is both engaging and instructive, teaching the reader how to better engage others. It serves as a true, comprehensive "toolkit" for service-learning professionals at any level. Assembled by nationally known practitioners for fellow practitioners, this work addresses innovative ways to facilitate the service-learning process. For the new professional, it offers a service-learning best-practices template. For the more experienced professional, it offers fresh ideas and new "tricks of the trade" around familiar theories. It offers approaches to best capture the transformative power of the service-learning experience.

On first reading, this toolkit inspires new ideas and promotes reflection on how and why we do our work; over time, it will serve as a valuable reference when new ideas are needed in a specific area. Equally important, it stimulates us to think about our work and our relationships with students, faculty, and the community, and challenges us to develop new approaches to strengthening these relationships. For in the end, creating and learning from these relationships is the power of our collective service-leaning work.

Richard Harris
Director of Community Service-Learning
James Madison University

Introduction

Dear Community Service-Learning Colleagues:

We have chosen an extraordinary profession. In the nearly 20 years that I have been involved in community service-learning, I have become convinced that our work has virtually limitless potential to make a tremendous, positive difference in our students, our communities, and our institutions.

As one of my students once told me in reflection, "Service-learning enables students to apply their knowledge 'in real time, in real places, with real people, and with real consequences.'" Another put it this way: "Service-learning takes you to the edge of what you know and who you are."

On the other hand, I and many of our colleagues wonder about what has been called the "dark side" of service-learning. If our students are ill-prepared and our community partnerships are dominated by the power and privilege that institutions of higher education possess, service-learning can, in fact, do harm.

Those of us who labor in the vineyards of service-learning—whether our primary focus is on volunteerism, community service, service-learning, or civic engagement—find ourselves confronted daily with these fears, along with many joys and frustrations. We are thrilled as our students make the leap from charity to social change, when they reach new understandings about themselves and their unique pathways to making the world a better place. We are overwhelmed by the needs and challenges of individuals and communities and by the potential of campus-community partnerships to address them. We are daunted by how much we want to do, the many difficult choices, the resources we lack, and the fundamental problems inherent in the systems within which we work.

We come to community service-learning with varying levels of knowledge and experience and from a wide range of backgrounds, including academic disciplines, student activities, the ministry, the nonprofit sector, and national service. Our varied backgrounds and experiences undoubtedly enrich the field. On the other hand, I suspect that you, like me, sometimes wonder if you are up to the task of leading community service-learning to fulfill its potential for your students, your communities, and your institution. Many conversations I have had with colleagues—both with significantly more and significantly less experience than me—reinforce this suspicion, regardless of the veritable wealth of resources that is available to us in print, on the web, and through conferences and workshops.

These amazing resources offer guidance through principles, benchmarks, best practices, and research findings about how to design, implement, and evaluate service-learning experiences to achieve our desired outcomes for students and community members. While these resources are immensely helpful in enabling us to do our work better, they do not necessarily enable us to become the reflective community service-learning teachers, practitioners, advocates, and leaders that we want to be, that we must be, in order for community service-learning to fulfill its potential.

This volume is different from the many other resources that focus on guiding and enhancing our practice. Its focus is on the practitioner rather than the practice. It is intended for our use in maximizing our potential as leaders of community service-learning so that we may, in turn, maximize its potential. The self-guided approach allows us to explore, at our own pace and in our own order, the various components of what it takes to be "all that we can be" as community service-learning professionals. It provides tools and opportunities to reflect, act, and reflect again, on topics and issues that will enable us to find competence, confidence, support, and balance in our work and our lives.

Recognizing that those in this field use several different terms to describe our work, we have chosen to use the term *community service-learning* in the title of this book. Throughout the text, we use this term and *service-learning* interchangeably. We decided to use the broad term of community service-learning because it keeps the community in the forefront and keeps learning directly connected with service.

The wisdom and diligence of numerous individuals contributed much to this book. My co-editor, Pamela Mutascio, was a joy to work with and is herself a walking encyclopedia of service-learning. A big thanks goes to Dave Donahue for his thoughtful edit. Campus Compact staff members Karen Partridge and Bonnie Grassie-Hughes did terrific work in making the book look the way it does. Campus Compact President Maureen F. Curley has been a tremendous support all along the way. Finally, I thank the chapter authors for so graciously and so generously sharing their knowledge and experience with us.

I hope you find this volume helpful throughout your community service-learning journey. Please share your feedback, joys, and tribulations with me. You will always find a willing and compassionate listener.

Sincerely,

Barbara Jacoby

Senior Scholar
Adele H. Stamp Student Union–Center for Campus Life
University of Maryland, College Park

CHAPTER ONE

Becoming a Reflective Community Service-Learning Professional

Kathleen Rice

WELCOME TO THE FIELD COMPRISING PEOPLE WHO DARE TO WORK on a bold vision: to bridge higher education and communities and to integrate the worlds of scholarship and application in order to strengthen each and transform both in the process. Community service-learning is a breathtaking mission that requires a broad range of skills shaped by sound judgment. It is a challenging leadership role, often masked by administrative and managerial duties and job titles. Enormous opportunities to create purposeful and meaningful work are in your hands; yet, in this emerging field, few of us feel that we are adequately prepared for its surprises and complexities.

This chapter introduces some of the fundamentals, opportunities, tensions, and challenges frequently encountered in this work and offers a framework for reflecting on the many questions that will arise during your development as a community service-learning professional (CSLP). This framework is based on the concept of the *reflective practitioner,* as articulated by Donald A. Schön (1983). By being a reflective practitioner, you can access your own compass—as well as recognize the compasses from which others draw—which can guide you through this often uncharted path you have chosen. You will find questions and exercises throughout this chapter to guide your reflection and assist you in building your knowledge base, your toolkit of strategies, and, most important, your own capacity to ask, sit with, struggle with, and, over time, work though the inevitable questions as a reflective practitioner. Rilke's (1954) call to "love the questions" rather than rush to create premature solutions is a powerful tool for the reflective CSLP:

> I want to beg you, as much as I can, to be patient toward all that is unresolved in your heart; try to love the questions themselves like locked rooms or books that are written in a foreign tongue. Do not now seek the answers; they cannot be given to you now because you would not be able to live them. And the point is to live everything. Live the questions now. You will then gradually, without even noticing it perhaps, live along some day into the answers. (pp. 30–47)

1

The questions you will raise and encounter in this field cannot be answered quickly. Instead, with reflection over time, clarity can emerge on how to institutionalize the values of community service-learning in ways that contribute toward the missions of communities, students, and higher education.

Reflection

What do I mean by reflection, and why is it important to community service-learning work? The community service-learning literature defines reflection in a variety of ways. One that I have found particularly illuminating, because of its recognition that reflection is much more than cognitive analysis, is by Tony Chambers and the National Forum on Higher Education for the Public Good (2002):

> Reflection is a process of seeking clarity about truth . . . truth in experience, thought, beliefs, instincts, and relationships. Reflection can be accomplished independently or as a collective endeavor. Yet, however done, reflection demands consideration of one's internal state (beliefs, feelings, assumptions) and external circumstances (actions, relationships, power dynamics, obstacles). Reflection also demands a self-honesty and humility that will hold its own against affront from any quarter. (inside cover)

Scholars are unanimous in identifying reflection as critical to community service-learning (e.g., Cruz, 1995; Howard, 2001; Porter Honnet & Poulsen, 1989; Sigmon, 1979). Freire (1972) also spoke of the importance of reflection in his discussion of praxis, calling on us neither to act without thought nor to think without acting, but rather to engage in informed action that is linked to certain values. When we explore the act of service in the context of theoretical and other forms of knowledge, coupled with reflection on our perspective and position in the world, we can enhance and transform the quality of the service and of the learning.

Just as reflection is critical for students to link their academic learning with their service experiences (Eyler, Giles, & Schmiede, 1996), so it is critical for CSLPs to engage constantly in reflection for professional reasons, in addition to the obvious personal one—reflection is essential for living a meaningful life. Serving as an effective teacher or guide for others' reflection is difficult if we aren't regularly engaged in our own. Consistent engagement in reflection increases our capacity to be aware of ourselves and our impact on others. This self-awareness is necessary for collaboration, a value and a skill that resides at the heart of community service-learning work. In addition, there is no road map for being an effective CSLP in every higher-education and community context; thus, each of us must chart our own course. Therefore, learning from the successes and challenges in our work requires intentional, ongoing, and honest reflection.

The Reflective Practitioner

What do I mean by *reflective practitioner* and why is it important to community service-learning work? *Reflective practitioner* resists easy definitions, not only because Schön himself does not define it in so many words, but because it is embedded in a larger philosophy of being a professional. For the purpose of this chapter, however, I can give you a sense of what a reflective practitioner is:

It involves a surprise, a response to surprise by thought turning back on itself, thinking about what we're doing as we do it, setting the problem of the situation anew, conducting an action experiment on the spot by which we seek to solve the new problems we've set, an experiment in which we test our new way of seeing the situation, and also try to change that situation for the better. (Schön, 1987a)

According to Schön (1987b), the reflective practitioner participates in a practicum that will help her or him "acquire the kinds of artistry essential to competence in the indeterminate zones of practice" (p. 18). Therefore, developing professional competence in general and the skills of the reflective practitioner in particular requires us to engage in our own practicum or experiential learning process by constantly combining action and reflection in ways that inform each other. The skills of the reflective practitioner will guide us in navigating those "indeterminate zones of practice." To develop these skills, we are called on to figure things out while drawing on our capacities for reflection. Indeed, some CSLPs have described aspects of their jobs as "building the plane while flying it."

Committing to becoming reflective CSLPs comes with challenges. Engaging in reflection is not necessarily an activity understood or sanctioned by the dominant culture in the United States. Few job descriptions list reflection as a required task of the job or include it in the list of required skills and capacities. Time to strengthen our reflection skills and to engage regularly in reflection must be built into our already full job descriptions. Yet, reflecting on our personal views, visions, expectations, hopes, experiences, assumptions, and viewpoints—and how they are similar *and* different from those of our institutions, our institutions' leadership, and our partners—can *save* valuable time. This awareness of where we and others are coming from can provide anchors for engaging in thoughtful action, based on core principles, rather than a (re)action that drifts in response to each competing priority, need, or request. Reflection is also critical for facilitating *quality* learning, service, and partnership.

Reflection on Core Community Service-Learning Principles and Values

One core principle of community service-learning, frequently cited in the literature as a foundation for the frames or lenses from which we approach the work, is: "Service, combined with learning, adds value to each and transforms both" (Porter Honnet & Poulsen, 1989).

This definition identifies some essential elements of community service-learning—service, learning, and mutual transformation. Another way to refer to this mutuality is the concept of *reciprocity,* an essential goal for authentic community service-learning partnerships and, in my experience, a challenging one to achieve in a world fraught with inequities. Reciprocity does not necessarily *expect* something in exchange; rather, it acknowledges that all the partners in the process have wisdom, experience, skills, emotions, and capacities to contribute—that all of us are teachers, learners, servers, served, agents of change, and agents that can be changed by the relationships. Intentionality is required to create authentically reciprocal partnerships, particularly in light of the historical relationships between higher education and communities. Higher education's inequitable history as an ivory tower and as the sole creator of knowledge continues to play itself out today as evidenced by some of the challenges community service-learning partners have identified in working equitably with higher education (Mitchell, 2008; Sandy & Holland, 2006). Reflective CSLPs consistently examine their own beliefs, assumptions, attitudes, expectations, and behaviors in working with community organizations, community members, and community partnerships to identify where this larger historical and social context affects their own ability to engage in genuinely reciprocal relationships.

Another core principle in community service-learning is the importance of determining how community service-learning differs from other forms of service such as volunteerism or community service, as well as how it is different from other forms of experiential learning such as field work and internships. The

> **Reflection Exercise: Your Vision for How Learning and Service Can Add Value to Each and Transform Both**
>
> What do the words "service," "learning," "add value to each," and "transforms both" mean to you? What do they mean on your campus?
>
> Five, ten, twenty years from now, if service and learning were adding value to each and transforming both on your campus and in your community, what would you see? What could the full diversity of students, faculty, staff, community organizations, community staff, community members, and others be doing? What would be different from today? What values would be visible?

work of Robert Sigmon (1979) and Andrew Furco (1996), among others, has helped the field clarify some of these distinctions. Sigmon's typology demonstrates that if all partners are genuinely to benefit from the relationship, they must be intentional about co-creating meaningful service *and* meaningful learning opportunities. He makes the case that SERVICE-LEARNING occurs when there is significant, intentional, and balanced attention to the service and to the learning, and that they are linked to one another, rather than operate as separate processes.

TABLE 1-1: Typology of Service and Learning

service-**LEARNING**	Learning goals primary; service outcomes secondary
SERVICE-learning	Service outcomes primary; learning goals secondary
service learning	Service and learning goals completely separate
SERVICE-LEARNING	Service and learning goals of equal weight; each enhances the other for all participants

---

Source: Sigmon (1979). Used by permission.

The concept of creating a balance between service and learning resonates quickly with CSLPs. Once we begin to put this concept into practice, however, we discover the challenges, complexities, and conflicts inherent within and between service and learning. For example, higher education institutions often place greater priority on student learning than on the benefits of service partnerships with the community. Community-based organizations often place greater priority on ensuring that people who utilize their services genuinely benefit from the involvement of students and faculty. These priorities make sense when we consider the primary missions of each organization. Ensuring that both students and community members benefit equitably is, from my experience, an art crafted through the development of trusting relationships over time.

Sigmon's typology was produced in 1979, and since that time the language of this work has expanded significantly. Campuses and communities use different words to frame their collaborative work. For example, campuses may describe this work as community service, civic engagement, community engagement, community organizing, service-learning, social change, social justice, public service, praxis, activism, community-based teaching and learning, campus-community partnership building, and more.

Stakeholder Assessment

The work of transforming service and transforming learning on your campus is highly dependent on the CSLPs' capacity for effective collaboration. Effective community service-learning programs collaborate with more partners than perhaps any other office on campus or in the community. This collaboration requires CSLPs to have a clear sense of who their stakeholders are. Use the chart on page 6 to brainstorm all the campus and community individuals and groups who might be considered stakeholders of your program. Think broadly. You might include individuals (e.g., campus president, United Way coordinator, multicultural center director) or groups (e.g., community partners, community members, students, faculty members). Indicate with an asterisk the three you think have the *most* impact on your work in community service-learning.

Reflection Exercise: Intentionally Creating Balance between Service and Learning

In reflecting on Sigmon's typology and the concept of intentionally giving balanced attention to service and to learning, what are your initial thoughts?

What is your experience of striving for balance between quality learning and quality service?

What do you see as some of the benefits and challenges of paying attention to the quality of the learning *and* the quality of the service?

What is one area related to this balance you would like to focus more of your energies on in the near future?

Reflection Exercise: The Language of Community Service-Learning

What language is used on your campus to describe this work?

Does your campus have definitions of these words? If so, how were they defined, and by whom?

Do these words and their definitions resonate with you? How do these words and definitions guide your work? Are there challenges with using these particular words or the ways they are defined?

Exploring Your Motivations for Community Service-Learning Work

There is no one path that brings CSLPs to this work. We come from many different professional fields, including but certainly not limited to community-based and/or nonprofit organizations, student development, faculty teaching across the disciplines, community activism, pub-

Stakeholder Definition, Assessment, and Reflection

Stakeholders are those who:

- Are affected by your work;

- Are involved with your institution's other community service-learning or community engagement efforts;

- Participate in community service-learning courses and programs;

- Make decisions about your work;

- Can support your work;

- Can block your work;

- Have information or insight needed for your work; and

- Can partner with you.

Stakeholder Assessment Chart

INDIVIDUALS	GROUPS / DEPARTMENTS / ORGANIZATIONS

Reflection Questions

- What observations do you have about your list? Does anything stand out about it?

- How do you frame your relationship with the three most important individuals or groups you identified? Do you think of them as customers, clients, coworkers, constituencies, stakeholders, supporters, allies, co-educators, or adversaries?

- How does the way you view this relationship affect how you approach and work with each stakeholder?

lic policy, community-based research/evaluation, social work, business, government, national service, religious/spiritual affiliation, K-12 education, and higher education administration. In addition to our diverse professional paths, we come to this work with a variety of life experiences, personal values, and motivations. We have different perspectives on why this work is important, what the goals are, how it should be done, and what we think are the best ways to deepen and broaden the work across campus and throughout our communities. Being aware of our own motivations is important for increasing our capacity to collaborate effectively with others who come to the work with different priorities and motivations, but with whom you share a common vision.

Reflection Exercise: What Brought You to This Work?

What three personal and/or professional experiences (or people) influenced you the most in choosing to do community service-learning work?

What *formal* education has helped prepare you for this work?

What *informal* education has helped prepare you for this work?

For what areas of community service-learning work would you like to better prepare yourself?

Reflection Exercise: Reflecting on Your Cultural Identities

The existence of so many social and institutional "isms" affects each of us on the individual level, whether we want them to or not. Some cultural groups have more access to privilege in the U.S. (e.g., white/European Americans, men, able-bodied people, wealthy and middle class, heterosexuals, native English speakers, U.S. citizens, Christians), while other groups have less access to societal privilege (e.g., Jewish and Muslim people, women, children and elders, people with disabilities, gay, lesbian or transgender people, immigrants, poor people). Our access to privilege often influences how we see ourselves, others, our campuses, and our communities.

How might those identities—and the values, life experiences, and socialization they have generated—helped shape your motivations and approach to engaging in community service-learning?

In recognizing the power imbalances this history of oppression has created, and that we all are affected by today, what do you notice about the ways these inequities play out on your campus, in your community, in your partnerships? How can you as a CSLP create space for dialogue, reflection, and action around these issues that are at the core of much community service-learning work?

How might other power dynamics, such as positional power, affect your relationships with people who supervise you or have more positional or political power at your institution than you do?

(See pages 13–14 for a personal reflection on motivations, identity, privilege and community service-learning work.)

Reflection Exercise: Motivations for Promoting Community Service Learning
(developed by Nadinne Cruz)

Listed in the table below are some reasons people have given for promoting community service-learning in higher education.

1. Read the list and rank the five reasons that are most important to you for promoting community service-learning (1–5) and the five reasons that are least important to you (22–26). If one of your top reasons is not listed, add your own in #27.

2. In columns A–C, identify the three most important individuals or groups that you identified in the Stakeholder Assessment chart on page 6. Rank what you perceive to be the highest and lowest motivations for each of those stakeholders. If possible, ask those stakeholders to complete this worksheet themselves and identify their five most important and five least important motivations.

WHAT IS MY MAIN MOTIVATION FOR PROMOTING COMMUNITY SERVICE-LEARNING IN MY INSTITUTION?	YOUR RANK	STAKEHOLDER RANKS		
		A	B	C
1. Improve campus relationships with neighboring communities.				
2. Fulfill outreach requirements for grant funding.				
3. Provide students with experiences useful for career exploration.				
4. Do the right thing.				
5. Improve teaching and learning.				
6. Promote campus diversity initiatives, teach diversity, and/or improve relationships across differences.				
7. Share campus resources with people who are poor and underserved.				
8. Implement a graduation requirement for undergraduates.				
9. Develop new knowledge.				
10. Improve recruitment and admissions "yield."				
11. Promote the "engaged department/campus."				
12. Make research accessible and useful to the wider public.				
13. Partner with community to co-create mutually beneficial research and broaden what is valued as research.				
14. Implement the institution's mission/vision.				

(continued)

WHAT IS MY MAIN MOTIVATION FOR PROMOTING COMMUNITY SERVICE-LEARNING IN MY INSTITUTION?	YOUR RANK	STAKEHOLDER RANKS		
		A	B	C
15. Strengthen the voluntary sector.				
16. Learn from communities.				
17. Transform higher education.				
18. Promote student development, leadership, and "self-efficacy."				
19. Provide nonprofits with volunteers.				
20. Promote social justice; interrupt institutional racism, sexism, heterosexism, and other forms of discrimination.				
21. Develop a campus culture of community and caring.				
22. Provide or improve practica and internships for professional schools.				
23. Implement a major donor's bequest.				
24. Develop and improve campus-community partnerships.				
25. Nurture social responsibility as an aspect of spirituality.				
26. Help prepare future graduates to be active community members and/or skilled public service staff.				
27. Other				

Reflection Questions

YOUR MOTIVATIONS

- What do you notice about your most motivating reasons? Is there a common thread?

- What is an example of a decision you made or an action you took that reflected your primary motivations? In other words, what has your primary motivation looked like in action?

- Is there an instance when your actions deviated from your primary motivations? What led you to move away from your primary purpose? What was the result?

- What do you notice about your least motivating reasons? Is there a common thread?

YOUR PERCEPTIONS OF STAKEHOLDER MOTIVATIONS

- What do you notice about your perceptions of others' most motivating reasons? Their least motivating reasons?

- How do your motivations and your perceptions of others' motivations compare? How much synchronicity is there?

- Do you have any judgments about what you perceive others might be most motivated by? What is the impact of these judgments on your work together?

- How can your awareness of your perceptions of others' motivations help you in the future?

(continued)

YOUR MOTIVATIONS IN RELATION TO STAKEHOLDER-REPORTED MOTIVATIONS

- How do your motivations and others' motivations compare? How much synchronicity is there?

- What have been the benefits and the challenges of having similar motivations?

- What have been the benefits and challenges of having different motivations?

- Do you have any judgments about what others report they are most motivated by? What is the impact of these judgments on your work together?

- How might your role or position in the institution influence your own motivations? How might others' roles or positions influence their motivations?

- How can your awareness of your own and others' motivations help you in the future?

Where Do Your Motivations Come From?

Not only is it valuable to be grounded in what drives and motivates us in our work as CSLPs, but it is important to have some awareness of the source of these motivations. For each of us, the sources might differ. Our motivations might be shaped by life experiences we have and have not had, our cultural histories and background, books we have read, what we have learned from mentors and role models, family, and communities of origin—and the list goes on. Recognizing the roots of our own motivations can help us understand how others' motivations have their own roots as well.

Infusing Reflection into the Daily Work of the CSLP

Reflection is rarely built into our to-do lists in the same way developing and adjusting budgets, preparing meeting agendas, supporting faculty development, training student leaders, building relationships with community partners, or completing paperwork to manage risk in community service-learning are. How can we integrate ongoing reflection into every aspect of our work, so that it does become an integrated part of our practice and not just something we ask students to do throughout their community service-learning experiences?

Perhaps there are core principles you already weave throughout your work, such as:

- Actively involve students, community partners, faculty, *and* staff as collaborative decision makers in all significant issues;

- Explore the impact of organizational and programmatic decisions on all cultural groups (e.g., women, men, gay, lesbian, bisexual, transgender, younger, older, Asian American, deaf, international, Jewish, able-bodied, white, multi-racial, non-native English speakers).

Consider adding this principle: "Integrate an individual and/or group reflection activity into *every* CSL gathering." These gatherings might include:

- Staff meetings;

- Community forums;

- Academic departmental meetings focusing on community service-learning;

- Faculty development workshops;

- Community-based research symposia; or

- Student leadership program meetings and trainings.

Framework for Reflection Questions

A framework for developing reflection questions may be helpful as you integrate the concept of the *reflective practitioner* into your daily work. There are many methods available, several with interesting similarities. The following table highlights two: the ORID method (used by the Institute for Cultural Affairs) and the "What? So What? Now What?" method of the National Youth Leadership Council. (Note: I and other CSLPs have added a "Gut?" section after "What?" to provide a space for reflection on the emotional content of an experience. I have noticed that skipping this step has made it challenging for people to explore the "So What?" and "Now What?" steps). Both of these methods were derived in part from the work of David Kolb (1984).

I believe that everyone has leadership qualities and that we all have the ability to contribute, inspire, motivate, and stimulate a movement toward change. Your role as a CSLP will call on your strongest leadership qualities and perhaps some that are less developed. Self-awareness is often recognized as a core leadership competency. Reflection is a critical skill for gaining self-awareness. You are part of a movement that is changing how higher education institutions educate and become active members of the community, and how communities become co-educators of students. Reflection sits at the heart of this work.

Throughout this chapter, you have reflected on some of the foundational principles of community service-learning work, on your own motivations for advancing higher education's role in the field, and on how those motivations may shape your philosophy and approach as a leader and agent of change. You also have reflected on your perceptions of the synchronicity between your motivations and those of other key stakeholders, as well as on the impact of that synchronicity. Finally, you were asked to reflect on how your social identities and access to power affect your approach to your work as a CSLP. I invite you to continue your reflections throughout this book and while accomplishing your daily tasks. I hope this frame of the *reflective practitioner* provides you with personal and professional rewards and challenges for years to come.

TABLE 1-2: Framing Key Reflection Questions

OBJECTIVE	WHAT, SO WHAT, NOW WHAT	O.R.I.D.	QUESTIONS
Description	What?	Objective	What happened? What did you see, hear, smell, touch, say? What did we do today? Who utilizes the services? What is a moment or memory that stands out?
Affective Expression	Gut?	Reflective	What surprised you? Frustrated you? Pleased you? Confused you? Disappointed you? Angered you? Where did you struggle? When did you feel affirmed? How did this affect you? What image captures the emotional tone of the experience for you? What range of feelings came up for you during this experience?
Analysis	So what?	Interpretive	What are you learning from this? What difference does that make to you, to your work, to the community? What do you understand differently now? When have you seen something similar before? How does this relate to larger contexts, theories, ideas? What is important about what you have learned? How does this relate to the work of other campus programs?
Application	Now what?	Decisional	What will you do with what you have learned? How does it inform your work with the community? With faculty? With students? What has our group/organization/department learned? What are the implications of what we have done together?

A Personal Reflection on My Cultural Identities, Power Dynamics, and My Motivations for Service

I, like so many in this field, am passionate about the work of supporting people in higher education and in communities in creating collaborative and equitable social change. It is a profession in which I have learned an enormous amount about myself, others, students, institutions, communities, and the joys and struggles of creating a more inclusive and equitable world. At the same time, I recognize that my choice of this career path wasn't totally by chance. Growing up in the late 1970s and early 1980s, I, like many women and girls today, was tracked into a subset of professions. Subtly and not-so-subtly, I was encouraged and expected to be of service to others. I was not conscious of choosing a field that fit within the boundaries of female social norms, but that is what I did. In fact I remember rejecting certain career choices because they were still outside the norm for a woman. I remember choosing not to pursue a career of a television reporter because a man told me, and I believed him, "You won't be able to carry the heavy equipment."

While on one hand I was told, "You won't be able to carry the heavy equipment," I was also told, "If you work hard, you will be successful." As a white person, I saw myself and other people of my race be rewarded, sometimes for what might be considered hard work but often for knowing people in positions of power, often also white, who provided access to opportunities; going to well-resourced schools where the great majority of teachers and principals were also white; or getting a head start in life because neither of my parents had to navigate racial discrimination to go to and graduate from college or buy a home. As I began to learn more about my family's history and that of other racial and cultural groups, I realized the pull-yourself-up-by-your-boot

straps metaphor was a myth. I learned that people who had become successful financially did not do so by themselves but rather with the help of, and often (intentionally or unintentionally) at the expense of, others. I began to learn more about social inequities and the ways our current institutions, created long ago, continue to reinforce that inequity. I also began to learn how I as an individual have reinforced those inequities, often unknowingly, and have had a negative impact on others. I then began to learn that with some work, I could become more aware of how I was reinforcing institutional inequities and build my skills to play a part in interrupting them.

Upon reflection, I can see now how my initial interest in interrupting oppression (a new awareness that, in part, led me to community service-learning work) was to "help people who were oppressed." I remember my surprise when I took Janet Helms' (1990, 1992) assessment of White Racial Identity Development and discovered that my "Pseudo-Independence" was *not* as evolved in terms of developing a positive white racial identity as I had thought. While I did recognize that racism was rampant on the personal, relationship, organizational, and institutional levels, and that I contributed to it and benefited from it, I didn't recognize how my pity and patronizing attitude could actually reinforce the oppression I sought to interrupt. At the time Dr. Helms' work opened my eyes much wider, I was also a graduate assistant promoting co-curricular community service-learning. I began to see how my motivations for "helping" the community were about meeting my need to feel valuable rather than about a shared need for us all to feel whole. Years later, I found myself repeatedly hitting a wall when I tried to make

(continued)

institutional changes from my equity-oriented motivation. My stakeholders and I had not completed the "Motivations for Promoting Community Service-Learning" exercise earlier in this chapter, and I wish I had! I was not aware that my primary motivation was not *everyone's* primary motivation and I had judgments that mine was best, right, and the most noble. Rather than recognizing all our motivations as complementary, I saw them as competing.

For example, I firmly believed that student leaders, community partners, and faculty attending a community service-learning summer institute all brought something critical to the table, that everyone would contribute as both teachers and as learners, and therefore that everyone deserved to be paid the same daily rate that faculty were guaranteed in their contracts. While faculty and community-partner staff had many years of experience and very valuable teaching and community leadership experience, some of the student leaders had the deepest understanding of community service-learning and had life experience that helped them enter and participate in the community with greater awareness and skill than those of us who were not from similar communities.

After several conversations—or, I might more accurately say, after a series of parallel monologues in which the person in the position to make the decision and I were not really hearing each other—we eventually came to agreement. All participants would be paid the same amount. However, on reflection, each of our inability to recognize and validate the others' frames made the process of reaching agreement quite contentious. In the end, while I may have felt *right* by "winning" the argument, in hindsight I also lost the opportunity to engage in true democratic dialogue and strengthen relationships across differences. I can see how my white social conditioning (and perhaps the person I was in conflict with) created this binary perspective of right/wrong or win/lose, when other options were available to us. In this situation, I chose to prioritize my passion for equity over my passion for authentic relationships. I could have paid better attention to both; now I can see that my passion for equity cannot be realized without a commitment to authentic relationships, and my desire for authentic relationships cannot be achieved without a commitment to equity. Had I asked about, listened openly to, and honored these different motivations, along with my own, I might have experienced less difficulty.

While I have focused here on how my socialization (in relation to my gender and race) has impacted my motivations for engaging in community service-learning work (and there is much more, such as how I facilitate and how I have experienced, avoided, and worked with conflict), there has been much to explore about the ways other aspects of my identity (sexual orientation, class, religious upbringing, physical abilities, age, etc.) are also big factors in shaping my motivations for this work.

Acknowledgement

I would like to acknowledge the work of Nadinne Cruz for introducing me to the concept and modeling the practice of the reflective practitioner.

References

Chambers, T. (2002). National leadership dialogues journal [handout]. *National Forum on Higher Education for the Public Good.* Ann Arbor, MI: University of Michigan.

Cruz, N. (1995). Multicultural politics of difference in service-learning. Paper presented at the Council of Independent Colleges National Institute on Learning and Service, St. Charles, IL.

Eyler, J., Giles, D., & Schmiede, A. (1996). *A practitioner's guide to reflection in service-learning.* Nashville: Vanderbilt University.

Freire, P. (1972). *Pedagogy of the oppressed.* London: Penguin.

Furco, A. (1996). Service learning: A balanced approach to experiential education. In *Expanding boundaries: serving and learning* (pp. 2–6). Washington, DC: Corporation for National Service.

Helms, J. E. (1990). *Black and White racial identity: Theory, research, and practice.* New York: Greenwood Press.

Helms, J. E. (1992). *A race is a nice thing to have.* Topeka, KS: Content Communications.

Howard, J. (2001). Principles of good practice in community service-learning pedagogy. *Michigan Journal of Community Service Learning: Service-Learning Course Design Workbook* (pp. 16–19). Ann Arbor, MI: University of Michigan OCSL Press.

Jacoby, B. (2003). Professionalizing the community service/service-learning director role. Available at www.compact.org/wp-content/uploads/media/Professionalization.pdf.

Kolb D. (1984). *Experiential learning: Experience as the source of learning and development.* Englewood Cliffs, NJ: Prentice Hall.

Mintz, S., & Hesser, G. (1996). Principles of good practice in service learning. In B. Jacoby (Ed.), *Service-learning in higher education: Concepts and practices* (pp. 26–52). San Francisco: Jossey-Bass.

Mitchell, T. (2008). Traditional vs. critical service-learning: Engaging the literature to differentiate two models. *Michigan Journal of Community Service Learning, 14*(2), 50–65.

Porter Honnet, E., & Poulsen, S. J. (1989). *Principles of good practice for combining service and learning.* Racine, WI: The Johnson Foundation, Inc.

Rilke, R. M. & Herter, M.D. (translator). (1954). *Letters to a young poet.* New York: Norton.

Sandy, M. & Holland, B.A. (2006). Different worlds and common ground: Community partner perspectives on campus-community partnerships. *Michigan Journal of Community Service Learning, 13*(1), 30–43.

Schön, D. A. (1983). *The reflective practitioner: How professionals think in action.* London: Temple Smith.

Schön, D. A. (1987a). *Educating the reflective practitioner.* Keynote presentation at the American Educational Research Association, Washington, DC. Retrieved from http://educ.queensu.ca/~ar/schon87.htm.

Schön, D. A. (1987b). *Educating the reflective practitioner: Toward a new design for teaching and learning in the professions.* San Francisco: Jossey-Bass.

Sigmon, R. L. (1979). Service-learning: Three principles. *Synergist, 8,* 9–11.

Stanton, T. (1990). Service learning: Groping toward a definition. In J. C. Kendall & Associates, *Combining service and learning: A resource book for community and public service (Volume 1).* Raleigh, NC: National Society for Internships and Experiential Education.

CHAPTER TWO

Navigating the Sea of Definitions

Elaine K. Ikeda, Marie G. Sandy, and David M. Donahue

DESCRIBING THE CONNECTION BETWEEN LANGUAGE AND UNDERSTANDING, Ludwig Wittgenstein said, "The limits of my language are the limits of my mind. All I know is what I have words for." And sometimes the limits of our mind are reflected in the language we use or the meaning we ascribe to words. In the field of service-learning, we suffer no shortage of specialized vocabulary and words to describe concepts and practices considered central to our work. While these terms are meant to convey precise meanings, you may at times have found yourself confused by what someone meant. You are not alone.

In this chapter, we set out some ways to help you navigate through the sea of key terms and concepts in service-learning. To do so, we ask you to think about the associations, values, and beliefs that you bring to understanding these terms. Then we ask you to reconsider these terms from the associations, values, and beliefs of others. Our point is not to come up with a single, definitive definition for any term or concept. This is not a "Build Your Vocabulary in 30 Days" kind of chapter that instructs you to memorize words out of context. Instead, we hope to provide some clarifying questions that you can use when you reflect or talk with others about what you and they really mean. We believe this approach takes advantage of the diversity of opinions and experiences in our field. Indeed, even the Carnegie Foundation's community engagement classification for campuses does not come with hard and fast criteria, but instead supports multiple definitions and diverse approaches. Asking questions about service and learning, therefore, encourages ongoing dialogue that leads to deepening our individual and collective understanding of the complexity of our work and what high-quality service-learning really means to you and those with whom you work. This chapter includes several short exercises throughout the text, as well as longer worksheets at the end to help you complete these exercises.

Commonly Used Terms about Serving and Learning

Words are concepts in actual practice and are part of our greater linguistic and practical context. Philosopher Hans-Georg Gadamer (1975) reminds us that examining our terminology can help us to understand the concepts we currently use to better interpret and therefore act in our present situation. How do you define terms like volunteerism, community service, community-based research, and service-learning? What about community, reciprocity, charity, and change? How do you think your students might define these same terms? How about faculty members and staff members at your institution? How do your community partners define these same terms?

Jerome Bruner (1996) reminds us that human beings act on the basis of their inherent assumptions about how other minds work and how they learn—what Bruner describes as our folk psychology and pedagogies. As service-learning professionals, our practices are based on what we believe service-learning to be, which is tied to how we think others learn, as well as our understanding of the broader purposes of education. Our experiences in service-learning then reinforce our idea of what it is, which further defines our practice. Whether or not we actively verbalize the principles of service-learning to ourselves or others, we most often function on the basis of these implicit definitions. Examining these definitions and their underlying assumptions can shed more light on our practice and help us to become more thoughtful practitioners.

abels in philosophy and cultural discourse…can poison and kill, and they can remedy and cure. We need them to help identify a style, a temperament, a set of common concerns and emphases, or a vision that has determinate shape. But we must also be wary of the ways in which they can blind us or can reify what is fluid and changing."

— *Bernstein, 1992, p. 11*

Defining terms is a slippery business—indeed it is possible to find multiple definitions for each of the terms outlined in this chapter. Subsequent chapters in this book frequently begin by defining terms, perhaps in ways that differ from how you think of these terms. Personal and collective meanings of terms are contested terrain and change over time. While we can certainly strengthen our practice by rendering our personal definitions more explicit, external factors often compel us to clarify these definitions. The push to create succinct definitions is frequently a response to the requirements of foundations and other funding sources, and to varied political pressures on campus. Rigid delineations can serve to limit our practice. Before we provide answers to others, we may need to investigate where these demands originate as well as their accompanying assumptions and frameworks.

Dan Butin writes:

> …[I]t matters just as much WHY we attempt to define SL [service-learning] as HOW we attempt to define SL. The assumptions undergirding our definitions (and desires for definitions) oftentimes reveal much, much more than the definitions themselves. To settle on a definition may in fact be extremely detrimental to the field, for it would seem to settle what SL "really" is… [W]e are much more comfortable with wanting an answer rather than accepting that SL is an exemplary strategy of fostering questions. (personal communication, September 12, 2005, *from the service-learning electronic mailing list).*

We offer the definitions in the following sections not to solidify what is fluid and changing but as a starting point for identifying your own vision, which has determinate shape.

Exercise: Defining "Good"

Before you read these definitions, use a separate 3"x5" index card to write your personal definition of each of the following: a "good" school, a "good" life, a "good" society. We are limiting you to a single index card to get at what's most important, and we've put "good" in quotation marks to acknowledge that *good* can mean very different things. We will return to your index cards at the beginning of the next section.

Volunteerism

Volunteerism refers to activities carried out by individuals, of their own free will, that benefit others and that are not compensated. Safrit, King, and Burcsu (1994) defined volunteerism as "giving time, energies, or talents to any individual or group for which [the individual] is not paid" (p.7). Volunteers' commitment of time and energy can vary widely. A volunteer might serve a few hours once a year at a beach cleanup or mentor a young person on a regular basis over many years. Anyone at any age, with or without a specific institutional affiliation, can usually find someplace to volunteer. Although volunteers learn informally from their experience, the emphasis of volunteerism is placed on service, not learning.

Community Service

Community service is a contribution of time and labor to address human and community needs. It may be based on a mandated requirement or an extrinsic reward. Mandates might include a school's graduation requirements, a court's order in lieu of incarceration or fine, or a government's condition for public assistance. Rewards might include money, workplace leave with pay, career advancement, or opting out of a required paper in school.

Within higher education, community service has a specific definition. *The 1965 Higher Education Act,* as amended by the *Higher Education Amendments of 1992* and the *Higher Education Technical Amendments of 1993,* defines community service as "services which are identified by an institution of higher education, through formal or informal consultation with local nonprofit, governmental, and community-based organizations, as designed to improve the quality of life for community residents, particularly low-income individuals, or to solve particular problems related to their needs." Even within higher education, as with volunteerism, the emphasis in community service is on service over learning.

Community-Based Research

Many higher education campuses have begun to engage more directly in community-based research as a part of their engaged scholarship agenda. Community-based, participatory research usually draws on the expertise of community members themselves to co-construct research agendas, carry out various aspects of the research itself, and define how and when the products of the research will be used. The ethic of reciprocity and mutual benefit, hallmarks of service-learning practice, informs the basic community-based research model, which involves collaborating closely with community partners and integrating classroom learning with social action for the benefit of the community. In community-based, *participatory* research, there is a more explicit emphasis on the fact that neither knowledge nor the research process is ever "neutral."

Service-Learning

An early definition of service-learning described it as "the accomplishment of tasks that meet genuine human needs in combination with conscious educational growth" (Stanton, Giles, & Cruz, 1999). Generally speaking, key themes across definitions of service-learning include collaboration with the community, reflection on service, active learning, explicit connections between service and the curriculum, and the development of students' civic and social responsibility (Ikeda, 1999).

Service-learning is both a pedagogy related to experiential learning (Jacoby, 1996) and a strategy for learning course content, boosting student motivation, and developing social consciousness that has been incorporated in many schools not otherwise committed philosophically to experiential education. More recently, service-learning has been increasingly adapted for online learning environments (Dailey-Hebert, Donnelli-Sallee, & DiPadova, 2008). The term community service-learning is a variation on the term service-learning, highlighting how the community is an explicit and essential component of the process. More discussion of the term *community* follows.

Civic and Political Engagement

While service-learning was initially promoted as a means for learning academic content, more recently it has been seen as a means for promoting students' civic and political engagement. Rather than being treated as collateral to academic learning, for some practitioners and theorists, these outcomes of engagement are the central purposes of service-learning.

The words *civic* and *political* are not without connotation. For some, *civic* conjures up images of high-school civics classes. For others, *political* is a word freighted with negative meaning. We think it is more helpful to think of civic engagement as connecting with and building links among people and institutions in the community to effect desired outcomes. Yet, as the subsequent section examining the wide-ranging definitions of community illustrates, our definition requires still further interrogation. Given the positive connotations attached to the word *community*, though, this endeavor is likely to be engaging and productive.

Similarly, we think political engagement can be framed in positive and engaging ways. The presidential election of 2008 demonstrated that, contrary to portrayals of young people as apathetic and apolitical, college students care greatly about politics and are ready to become involved. That does not mean, however, that service-learning need not play an intentional role in developing knowledge and skills for political engagement (Colby, Beaumont, Ehrlich, & Corngold, 2007; Colby, Ehrlich, Beaumont, & Stephens, 2003).

To understand this role, think back on your last conversation with someone about politics. Perhaps it was only a day or two ago. Now think of your last conversation about politics with someone who held a vastly different political opinion from your own. Chances are it was not as recent. We ask questions across political differences infrequently. Yet service-learning can place students in settings where such bridging conversations take place. Similarly, think about students' reflections on service. Did they connect their service—its need as well as its form—with the political context? Did you prompt such reflections with your own questions? Service always has a political context and outcome. Without intentionally connecting service-learning and politics, service can become an "alternative politics" disconnected from more traditional forms of political participation such as campaigning and voting (Longo, 2004).

Follow-Up:
Examining "Good" and Service-Learning

Look at the definitions you wrote on the index cards before reading the definitions in this chapter.

- First of all, do you find consistencies across your definition of "good" in all three areas?

- What themes strike you as cutting across good in all three areas?

- Looking in particular at the definition of service-learning in this chapter, how does that definition connect or not connect to your themes about a good school, a good life, and a good society?

- In reviewing your 3"x5" cards and how you connect service-learning to ideas about goodness, what assumptions can you find about the goals of education, the role of the individual and the collective in making change, and the role of the instructors, learners, and community partners in creating learning experiences?

A Closer Look at the Meaning of the Definitions

Now that we have laid out starting definitions for what these terms mean, let's return to the question raised earlier by Butin: Why does defining these terms matter?

We have asked you to think about "goodness" because service-learning (as well as volunteerism, community service, and internships) is not a "neutral" phenomenon, despite the technical language of definitions and injunctions from governmental and private funding sources. We give meaning to definitions of service-learning based on our experiences, beliefs, and assumptions. By examining how we give meaning to a term, including meaning in the political and moral dimensions, we can better appreciate the fluid and contested aspects of service-learning. We see these aspects not as a problem but as part of what makes service-learning vital—at least when it acknowledges these fluid and contested areas and provides an opportunity to engage with others to develop deeper understanding and ask new questions. This is particularly important in our ever-changing world of new technologies and global exchanges.

As you think about where your ideas about service-learning and "goodness" come from, consider some of these questions:

- What have been some of your key experiences with volunteerism, community service, internships, and service-learning?

- How do these experiences affect your role as a service-learning professional?

- How do they influence how you teach and how you communicate the mission of service-learning to others?

- Do you prefer one service-learning structure to others? Why? How is this preference translated in your work?

- At the college or university where you work, what are the underlying assumptions that you need to take into consideration when talking to others about service-learning? Are you at a faith-based institution? Does your campus have a social justice mission? How might those contextual factors shape how you talk about service-learning?

- Who might you gather together to discuss the definition of service-learning who would work best on your campus?

Underlying Concepts of Service-Learning

To this point, we have provided an opportunity to think about terms related to service and the connection of service and learning. In the following sections, we ask you to think about the fundamental underlying concepts of service-learning. Again, we do not provide single definitions; rather, we ask you to consider multiple perspectives on these terms to become clearer about what they mean to you and others. We also believe the following sections will help you see how service-learning is not a neutral activity.

Community

No definition of service-learning excludes the word "community." At first consideration, community seems an easy word to define. After all, each one of us lives in community with others.

Your observations about community illustrate ideas articulated by Tonnies (2002), a nineteenth-century German sociologist who defined communities as existing along a spectrum,

---

Exercise: Mapping Your Community

Thinking about the concept of community starts with an examination of your own life. What are the communities to which you belong? A bubble map like the one in Figure 2-1 can help you answer this question. In the middle circle, write your name. Write the name of one community to which you feel you belong in each circle surrounding your name. Feel free to add extra bubbles if needed; similarly, do not worry if you don't fill all the bubbles.

After you've finished filling in the bubbles, try to categorize the communities named in each bubble. What kinds of categories did you notice? No doubt, some communities were geographic in nature— a neighborhood or a city. Others might have been based on shared ideals— NAACP, Amnesty International, or a political party— or affinities and common interests—runners, quilters, or ballroom dancers. Still others might have been based on

characteristics of identity— African American, Jewish, or gay and lesbian communities.

As you look at these various communities, you might also notice that some ties between you and your communities vary in strength.

We recommend that you duplicate the bubble sheet to use with others so that you can name more different communities to generate more categories.

FIGURE 2-1: Mapping your community

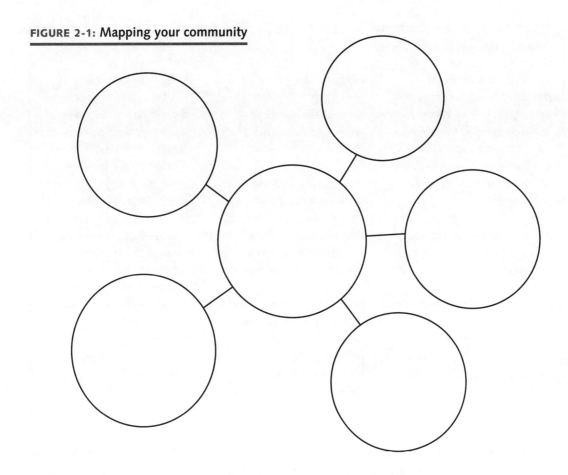

with *gemeinschaft* (community) at one end and *gesselschaft* (society) at the other. *Gemeinschaft* communities are characterized by relationships that are informal, understood, and diffuse, while *gesselschaft* communities are characterized by relationships that are formal, contractual, and specialized. *Gemeinschaft* communities are closer to the imagined ideal of a small village; *gesselschaft* communities to complex organizations. One is not better than the other; both have their advantages and drawbacks. For example, in a *gemeinschaft* community, you might feel cared for, but you might also feel stifled. In a *gesselschaft* community, you might be more anonymous, but your obligations to others might also be spelled out explicitly. The point here is not to valorize community as an unalloyed good. Tonnies noted that communities range from kinship to place to thought, each one having weaker ties than the previous one. More recently, Bellah (1988) and Putnam (1995) have noted that community ties vary from thick to thin. Thinking about the varieties of communities and the nature of community ties can help you be more precise in understanding what you mean when you plan to work in, with, or for the community.

Now that you have thought more about communities in general, it is appropriate to think about specific communities in which you work. One way to understand this is to again start with your own context.

Exercise: Images of Community

Think of a service-learning project of which you are particularly proud and which you feel truly benefits the community. Now imagine you have been assigned to take pictures of the community served by this project.

- What would you photograph? Better yet, don't imagine; take some photos. Or if you have some photographs of the project, dig them up.

- As you look at the photos, whether imagined or real, think about how these images shape your idea of the community. What are some of the words you would use to describe the community?

- Now show your pictures, or share your mental images, with a variety of people in that community. Try to get five different perspectives: a resident or a businessperson, a child or a parent, a lifelong resident or a newcomer. Seek out people whose identity—for example, along lines of race, class, or immigrant status—differs from your own. Ask these "key informants" what they see in your photos and how it compares to what they would photograph if they were taking pictures of the community. What do you see in common? What did they see that you did not? What did you see that they did not? How do their insights into the community confirm or change your original thinking about the community?

(See Worksheet 2-1 on pages 35–36 to complete this exercise.)

Kretzman and McKnight (1993) challenge us to see and work with the strengths and assets of a community, rather than its deficits. Gaining the perspectives of those who see themselves as part of a community can help us value strengths we might not see otherwise, especially if we do not see ourselves as being part of the same community.

Reciprocity

Most definitions of service-learning mention the importance of reciprocal relations among those serving and those served.

Hillman (1999) described how we frequently prefer to think of ourselves as people who give rather than receive service. We construct identities of ourselves as capable people who can help others, rather than people who may feel shame or embarrassment at needing others' assistance. Hillman calls this the "provider-recipient split," an inequality that she describes as habitual rather than inherent and based on perceptions rather than on the requirements of service. This split can stand in the way of building reciprocal relationships in service-learning, where borders between providers and recipients—those "teaching" and those "learning from" each other—are blurred. This kind of mutually beneficial relationship is different from power sharing, where those who have power—the providers—"give up" some of their power, but clearly identifiable and unequal roles remain, with providers quite often attempting to change the values and actions of the receivers to make them more like those of the providers.

Exercise: Reciprocity in Service

To think about reciprocity, first begin by thinking about your best experiences with service.

- Try to list at least a few examples from different times in your life. When you're done, consider the list a piece of data to be analyzed. Look at the list to see how many items came from your experience giving service to others.

- Next, look at the list to see how many items came from your experience receiving service from others.

- If you're like most people, your list consists entirely or almost entirely of experiences giving service. Why is that? We have all received service, whether from a friend helping us out when we had an accident or someone loaning us some tools to complete a project. We have also received service from dedicated teachers, committed environmental activists, and passionate civil rights advocates. So why are we less likely to think of our friends, best teachers, activists, and advocates when assessing our best experiences with service? Why do we think of giving rather than receiving service?

Returning to your best experience with service, were service providers and service recipients clearly identifiable? How might that experience have been changed so you were in a reciprocal, mutually beneficial relationship, rather than in the role of provider or recipient? What would change? For example, serving dinner in a soup kitchen reinforces traditional notions of provider and recipient. But if those serving dinner and those receiving dinner also sat down in a book group to discuss a text that they had all read, then notions of who is giving and who is receiving service become blurred. Those who might have been viewed as "unfortunate" can now display a fortune of knowledge about a book. Those who were seen as "underprivileged" now share in the privilege of teaching as all discuss and learn from each other. The research indicates that while community partners emphasize that they strongly perceive themselves as co-educators of service-learning students, they feel that they are not always treated as equal partners by higher education faculty and staff. Additionally, community partners often believe that there is not enough emphasis on mutuality of benefits for the community partner sites (Sandy & Holland, 2006). Framing a service-learning project as mutually beneficial is most likely to happen when the project is focused on learning as much as, if not more than, service. Some designers of service-learning projects may want to refrain from using the label service-learning with participants because of the unequal power connotations that service has for many.

Charity and Change

In 1996, Westheimer and Kahne used the words "charity" and "change" to describe two different orientations to service-learning across three different domains: the moral, the political, and the intellectual. Since then, these words have been used frequently in service-learning discussions. In Westheimer and Kahne's use, charity and change have precise meanings that can help us understand service-learning. But these terms have also come into common parlance in service-learning, and sometimes they are used as easy labels rather than as tools for analysis. Nevertheless, charity and change have powerful connotations. What is your association with the word *charity*? Chances are it is not positive. Charity has become a pejorative term. We've all felt pity for a "charity case" or heard the indignant phrase, "I don't need your charity." By contrast, *change* sounds positive and hopeful, having associations with justice and renewal. As a result, not surprisingly, most practitioners would like their service-learning projects to be change-oriented. That doesn't mean that you should give up projects at food banks in favor of projects at advocacy organizations to end structural causes of poverty. Instead, think about balancing charity and change on a continuum, rather than making a choice at either end. Hunger won't end tomorrow, and communities must balance immediate needs that can be best met through charity along with long-term structural solutions that can be best met through change.

Balancing charity and change does not have to rely only on a mix of service projects, either. Perhaps charity service brings to your mind soup kitchens, while change brings to mind working at a human-rights organization or lobbying group. We do not see any particular service or organization as being inherently about charity or change; rather, we see much of the charity or change orientation coming from the *reflection* on service, not the service itself. For example, given reflection framed as change, working in a soup kitchen might be the springboard for investigating why hunger exists in a wealthy nation and whether more soup kitchens and shelters are the ultimate answer to questions of poverty. At the other extreme, with little attention to change-oriented reflection, service at an advocacy organization might contribute valuable staff power for needed filing and photocopying but not much else.

Reflection

As mentioned above, reflection is key to what one takes away from a service-learning project and is a central element of service-learning. But reflection is an evanescent phenomenon. Do we even recognize it when we see it? Dewey is the most often cited authority on reflection. In *How We Think* (1933), he defined reflection as the "active, persistent, and careful consideration of any belief or supposed form of knowledge in the light of the grounds that support it, and the further conclusions to which it tends" (p. 6). He also described a

---

Exercise: Analyzing Reflection

- Using students' reflection papers about service-learning projects as data, try filling out a three-column chart. In the first column, list what you want students to understand from reflection. In the next column, record any evidence from the papers that students are meeting those goals. In the third column, make note of what students know well, are confused about, misunderstand, or need more challenging on. What do these data tell you?

- To analyze verbal reflection, try taping a service-learning discussion in class. To think more carefully about whether this conversation was reflective, code the transcript, noting examples of students individually or as a group going through an active, persistent, careful cycle of reflection. Similarly, code the conversation for examples of open-minded, responsible, and wholehearted conversation.

- From your analysis of the written and verbal data, what do you find? What do these written and verbal data tell you about possible changes you might make in creating placements, framing assignments, or structuring reflective conversation and writing?

(See Worksheet 2-2 on page 37 to complete this exercise.)

cycle of reflection that consists of identifying a problem, puzzle, or predicament; turning the problem into a question; forming a hypothesis in answer; applying reason; and forming a conclusion that leads to action. Good reflective questions more often begin with "why" than with "what." (For more on reflection, see Chapter 5.)

As described by Dewey, reflection is not merely a five-step, technical process; it must be open-minded, responsible, and wholehearted. Because it is an internal, mental process, reflection is difficult to "see" and even more difficult to evaluate. Talking and writing are among the best and most common means of reflection and can help us make reflection explicit and visible. We also need to be prepared to use online social media to promote such reflection. We encourage you to use Dewey's ideas as analytical tools for looking at the quality of your students' written and oral reflection.

Voice

> The face and the heart [service-learning office staff] have to educate the faculty, and they are the toughest nuts to crack over there. I had an example this year where the professor changed the syllabus and didn't tell me. I had a string of people coming in and asking for all kinds of things, "I want this, I want press releases, I need this. And after you give me this, I need an hour of your time to answer these questions." And there were 56 students. I wish the faculty had said, "Look, there's a change here." Getting everybody on the same page is an ongoing process, it is this process of navigation. Without a face and a heart, I don't think that would be possible.
>
> —Community partner, quoted in Sandy (2007)

Writers are concerned about developing a voice, an authentic "sound" to the words on every page that comes from each writer's unique experiences. Similarly, in the world of service-learning, you have probably also heard talk about the importance of voice—student voice or community voice, for instance. In the same way that writers ask questions about whether a voice sounds authentic, you too might wonder about the authenticity of voices in the planning, implementation, and reflection of service-learning projects. Probably all of us have had experiences in which we were told that, before a decision was made in a school, organization, or workplace, our opinion would really matter, that we would have input, and that we could have a say on the final results. And just as often we went to those meetings, community forums, or planning sessions and found ourselves presented with a completed plan or decision. The only input that seemed to be valued at that point was our assent to what had already been decided. If that's been the case, you might feel somewhat cynical when you hear someone say, "Your voice matters." So how do we avoid that same illusion in service-learning?

Conclusion: Choosing Words for Your Learning and Serving Context

Words, communities, and even institutions can be understood as processes in flux that evolve over time. While we each harbor our private understandings of the terminology in the community service-learning field, all words derive their existence, meaning, and power by being shared with others. The power of these concepts grows and becomes more valuable as people use these words more frequently, even as their meanings remain contested, fluid entities. Philosopher Hans-Georg Gadamer (1976) reminds us that "words take us back to the beginning" (p.140);

Exercise: Creating Equitable Opportunities for Voice

A tool used by journalists can be helpful to us in seeking authentic voice from our diverse partners. It is based on the "4 Ws and 1H": Who, What, When, Where, and How?

WHO **gets to have a voice in service-learning?** You probably thought of students first. Did you also consider whether various persons in the community, such as agencies and the people being served in a project, have a voice? In addition to thinking about who gets to have a voice, think about whose voices you most often hear. Whom do you most often ask for advice on service-learning projects? Are those persons mostly like you or are they different from you in ways that might be important to conceptualizing and implementing the project?

WHAT **does voice look like in your service-learning projects?** Do you solicit others' opinions but then present them with a plan and expect them to go along after you explain it? If so, that opportunity for "voice" probably does not feel authentic. Think about your planning. Do you try to work out as many details as possible before seeking others' insights? In those cases, others may feel as if they are being presented with *the* plan and that suggestions are not really welcome. Or do you present several possible plans for other people to consider and hold back on sharing your own judgment of the various alternatives? When you take that approach, you avoid the potentially aimless discussion that might happen without any plan, while allowing for real choice. What does voice look like in the reflection process? Are some voices heard more than others? Do participants—whether students or persons from the community—believe that they cannot say some things for any reason? Why might they feel that way?

WHEN **are there opportunities for voice?** Are they limited to only certain times in a project, for example at the beginning when you conduct a needs assessment or at the end when you ask partners to fill out an evaluation of the project? Opportunities for sharing voice can be built into every stage of service-learning experiences.

WHERE **do you invite voice?** Do you expect people to come to you? Do you actively seek other voices by going away from your office and campus to the places where partners might feel like they are in *their* community? Do you go to where community partners might be more comfortable raising their voices?

HOW **do you expect others to voice their ideas?** Do you work in an environment where certain kinds of talk are privileged over others? Is emotional language discouraged to allow for only rational discussion? Whose standards of "appropriate" conversation style dominate? These questions become particularly important when we acknowledge that how people talk is connected to how they identify themselves. If some kinds of talk are not valued, then people who do not fit the mold of appropriate talk will not feel valued, either.

Beyond asking ourselves these questions, we can learn more about voice in our practice by inviting a "process checker" to observe and examine the planning, implementation, and reflection processes for equitable opportunities for voice and equitable outcomes of voice. A process checker can make note of who speaks, how speakers are received, when and where opportunities for voice are presented, and what difference voice does or does not make in the end. An outside process checker can note dynamics that may be invisible to us or difficult to record in the midst of our work. Think of a process checker as a research assistant providing data for further reflection about the role of voice in your work.

they are lived within particular contexts and shared publicly among those who give voice to them.

The terms we have discussed—volunteerism, community service, community-based research, service-learning, charity and change, community, reflection, and voice—are foundations of our professional vocabulary. Colleges and universities, however, differ in how they draw on these concepts and what they value. As a result, it may be more fitting to emphasize one or more of these terms or to draw on a particular aspect of them based on the history, tradition, and mission of your institution. For example, an institution that has a particularly strong civic-engagement mission may find more resonance with activities couched under civic learning than under service-learning alone. Academic departments at the same institution may have vastly divergent notions about the appropriateness of community service in academic settings—even though these departments regularly incorporate internships into their coursework. In some educational institutions, academic course credit might be more forthcoming for a social justice practicum than for an internship experience. In institutions with a strong pedagogical commitment to active learning, it might be helpful to demonstrate service-learning as pedagogy. It is also important to understand the language that resonates with community partners. In some communities, volunteerism may have a longer tradition, while service-learning is still unclear. Or reflection may be less of a concern to them than identifying ways to leverage university resources to effect positive change locally.

Seeking greater clarity in how we use these terms as well as how others define them—seeing the connections among them and coming to some common understandings about how we experience and interpret service-learning—can help us envision the future of service-learning, and is an important part of the reflective process inherent in service-learning itself. Words shape our practice. Practice shapes our words. Kolb and Jensen (2002) emphasize that the health of any conversational community may be characterized more by its ability to allow for divergent opinions and voices, the "interplay of opposites and contradictions" (p.53), than by coherence. You may have responded more strongly to some of the ideas and definitions outlined in this chapter, disagreed with others, and wondered why some definitions were not mentioned at all. How wonderful! Enjoy exploring your own definitions as well as those of your colleagues through ongoing conversations to create more productive and fulfilling learning and serving communities. May our conversations continue for a long time to come!

References
Bellah, R. (1988). *Habits of the heart: Individualism and commitment in American life.* Berkeley, CA: University of California Press.

Bernstein, R. (1992). *The new constellation: Ethical-political horizons of modernity/postmodernity.* Cambridge, MA: MIT Press.

Bruner, J. (1996). *The culture of education.* Cambridge, MA: Harvard University Press.

Colby, A., Beaumont, E., Ehrlich, T., & Corngold, J. (2007). *Educating for democracy: Preparing undergraduates for responsible political engagement.* San Francisco: Jossey-Bass.

Colby, A., Ehrlich, T., Beaumont E., & Stephens, J. (2003). *Educating citizens: Preparing America's undergraduates for lives of moral and civic responsibility.* San Francisco: Jossey-Bass.

Dailey-Hebert, A. Donnelli-Sallee, E., & DiPadova, L. (2008). *Service-learning: Educating for citizenship.* Charlotte, NC: Information Age Publishing, Inc.

Dewey, J. (1933). *How we think.* Boston: D.C. Heath & Co.

Gadamer, H-G. (1975). *Truth and method* (2nd ed.). (Sheed and Ward, Ltd. Trans.). New York: Crossroad Publishing Company. (Original edition published 1960).

Gadamer, H-G. (1976). The universality of the hermeneutical problem. In D. Linge (Ed. & Trans.), *Philosophical hermeneutics* (pp. 3–17). (Original work published 1966). Berkeley and Los Angeles: University of California Press.

Hillman, T. (1999). Dissolving the provider-recipient split. *Academic Exchange, 3*(4), 123–127.

Ikeda, E. (1999). *How does service enhance learning? Toward an understanding of the process.* Unpublished doctoral dissertation, University of California, Los Angeles.

Jacoby, B. (Ed.) (1996). *Service-learning in higher education.* San Francisco: Jossey-Bass.

Kolb D., & Jensen, P. (2002). Conversation as experiential learning. In A. Baker et al. (Eds.), *Conversational learning: An experiential approach to knowledge creation* (pp. 51–66). Westport, CT and London: Quorum Books.

Kozol, J. (1992). *Savage inequalities.* New York: Crown Publishers.

Kretzman, J. & McKnight, J. (1993). *Building communities from the inside out.* Evanston, IL: Asset Based Community Development Institute.

Longo, N. (2004). The new student politics: Listening to the political voice of students. *Journal of Public Affairs, 7,* 61–74.

Putnam, R. (1995). *Bowling alone: The collapse and revival of American community.* New York: A Touchstone Book.

Safrit, R. D., King, J. E., & Burcsu, K. (1994). *A study of volunteerism in Ohio cities and surrounding communities.* Columbus, OH: Department of Agricultural Education, The Ohio State University.

Sandy, M. (2007). *Community voices: A California Campus Compact study on improving partnerships.* San Francisco: California Campus Compact.

Sandy, M., & Holland, B. (2006). Different worlds and common ground: Community partner perspectives in campus-community partnerships. *Michigan Journal of Community Service Learning, 13*(1), 30–43.

Stanton, T., Giles, D. & Cruz, N. (1999). *Service-learning: A movement's pioneers reflect on its origins, practice and future.* San Francisco: Jossey-Bass.

Tonnies, F. (2002). *Community and society.* Mineola, NY: Dover Publications. (Original edition published 1878).

Westheimer, J. & Kahne, J. (1996). In the service of what? *Phi Delta Kappan, 77* (9), 592–600.

Additional Resources

Volunteerism

Astin, A., Sax, L., & Avalos, J. (1999). Long-term effects of volunteerism during the undergraduate years. *The Review of Higher Education, 22*(2), 187–202.

Ellis, S., & Noyes, K. (1990). *By the people: A history of Americans as volunteers: An evaluation report on the student community service program.* Washington, DC: ACTION, Office of Policy Research and Evaluation.

Community Service

Astin, A. (1998). How undergraduates are affected by service participation. *Journal of College Student Development, 39* (3), 251–263.

Coles, R. (1993). *The call of service: A witness to idealism.* New York: Houghton Mifflin.

Cruz, N. (1990). A challenge to the notion of service. In J. Kendall and Associates, *Combining service and learning: A resource book for community and public service.* Raleigh, NC: National Society for Experiential Education.

Cone, R., Kiesa, A., Longo, N. (Eds.) (2006). *Raise your voice: A student guide to making positive social change.* Providence, RI: Campus Compact.

Rhoads, R. (1997). *Community service and higher learning: Explorations of the caring self.* Albany: State University of New York Press.

Community-Based Research

Minkler, M., & Wallerstein, N. (Eds.) (2003). *Community-based participatory research for health.* San Francisco: Jossey-Bass.

Strand, K., Cutforth, N., Stoecker, R., & Marullo, S. (2003). *Community-based research and higher education.* San Francisco: Jossey-Bass.

Stringer, E. (2007). *Action research* (3rd ed.). Thousand Oaks, CA: Sage Publications.

Stoecker, R. (2005). *Research methods for community change: A project-based approach.* Thousand Oaks: Sage Publications.

Service-Learning

Astin, A., Vogelgesang, L., Ikeda, E., & Yee, J. (2000). *How service learning affects students.* Los Angeles: Higher Education Research Institute, University of California, Los Angeles.

Bennet, G., & Green, F. (2001). Promoting service learning via online instruction. *College Student Journal, 35*(1), 491–497.

Butin, D. (2003). Of what use is it? Multiple conceptualizations of service learning within education. *Teachers College Record, 105*(9), 1674–1692.

Butin, D. (2005). *Service-learning in higher education: Critical issues and directions.* New York: Palgrave Macmillan.

Butin, D. (2006). The limits of service-learning in higher education. *The Review of Higher Education, 29*(4), 473–498.

Campus Compact. (2003). *Introduction to service-learning toolkit: Readings and resources for faculty* (2nd ed.). Providence, RI: Campus Compact.

Dailey-Hebert, A., Donnelli-Sallee, E., & DiPadova, L. (2008). *Service-learning: Educating for citizenship.* Charlotte, NC: Information Age Publishing, Inc.

Eyler, J., & Giles, D. (1999). *Where's the learning in service-learning?* San Francisco: Jossey-Bass.

Eyler, J., Giles, D., & Braxton, J. (1997). The impact of service-learning on college students. *Michigan Journal of Community Service Learning, 4,* 5–15.

Eyler, J., Giles, D., & Schmiede, A. (1996). *A practitioner's guide to reflection in service-learning.* Nashville, TN: Vanderbilt University.

Heffernan, K. (2001). *Fundamentals of service-learning course construction.* Providence, RI: Campus Compact.

Kiely, R. (2005). A Transformative learning model for service-learning: A longitudinal case study. *Michigan Journal of Community Service Learning, 12*(1), 5–22.

Metz, S. & Hesser, G. (1996). Principles of good practice in service-learning. In Jacoby, B. (Ed.), *Service-learning in higher education* (pp. 26–52). San Francisco: Jossey-Bass.

Miron, D., & Moely, B. E. (2006). Community agency voice and benefit in service-learning. *Michigan Journal of Community Service Learning,* 12(2), 27–37.

Mitchell, T.D. (2008). Traditional vs. critical service-learning: Engaging the literature to differentiate two models. *Michigan Journal of Community Service Learning, 14*(2), 50–65.

Moely, B. E., Furco, A., & Reed, J. (2008). Charity and social change: The impact of individual preferences on service-learning outcomes. *Michigan Journal of Community Service Learning, 14*(1), 37–48.

Poindexter, S., Arnold, P., & Osterhout, C. (2009). Service-learning from a distance: Partnering multiple universities and local governments in a large-scale initiative. *Michigan Journal of Community Service Learning, 15*(2), 56–67.

Porter Honnet, E., & Poulsen, S. J. (1989). *Principles of good practice for combining service and learning.* Racine, WI: The Johnson Foundation, Inc.

Rhoads, R. A., & Howard, J. (1998). *Academic service learning: A pedagogy of action and reflection.* San Francisco: Jossey-Bass.

Zlotkowski, E. (Ed.). (1998). *Successful service-learning programs: New models of excellence in higher education.* Bolton, MA: Anker Publishing Company, Inc.

History of Service-Learning

Sigmon, R. (1996). A service-learning timeline. In R. Sigmon et al., *Journey to service-learning* (pp. 15–16). Washington, DC: Council of Independent Colleges.

Sigmon, R. (1999). An organizational journey to service-learning. In T. Stanton, D. Giles, & N. Cruz (Eds.), *Service-learning: A movement's pioneers reflect on its origins, practice, and future* (pp. 249–257). San Francisco: Jossey-Bass.

Stanton, T., Giles, D., & Cruz, N. (Eds.). (1999). *Service-learning: A movement's pioneers reflect on its origins, practice, and future.* San Francisco: Jossey-Bass.

Civic Engagement

Battistoni, R. (2002). *Civic engagement across the curriculum: A resource book for service-learning faculty in all disciplines.* Providence, RI: Campus Compact.

Campus Compact. (1999). *The president's declaration on the civic responsibility of higher education.* Providence, RI: Campus Compact.

Campus Compact. (2004). *Essential resources for campus-based service, service-learning and civic engagement.* Providence, RI: Campus Compact.

Colby, A., Ehrlich, T., Beaumont, E., & Stephens, J. (2003). *Educating citizens: Preparing America's undergraduates for lives of moral and civic responsibility.* San Francisco: Jossey-Bass.

Ehrlich, T. (Ed). (2000). *Civic responsibility and higher education.* Washington, DC: American Council on Education.

Gottlieb, K., & Robinson G. (Eds.) (2002). *A practical guide for integrating civic responsibility into the curriculum.* Washington, DC: American Association of Community Colleges.

Jacoby, B. (2009). *Civic engagement in higher education: Concepts and practices.* San Francisco: Jossey-Bass.

Journal of Public Affairs: Supplemental Issue 1: Civic engagement and higher education. (2002). Springfield, MO: Southwest Missouri State University.

Mann, S., & Patrick, J. (2000). *Education for civic engagement in democracy: Service learning and other promising practices.* Bloomington, IN: ERIC Clearinghouse for Social Studies/Social Science Education.

Sandy, M., & Arguelles. (2005). *A testament of no inheritance: Civic and community immersion in the Pitzer College in Ontario Program.* Claremont, CA: Pitzer College. Available from the Pitzer College Office of Public Relations, Avery 105, 1050 N. Mills Ave., Claremont, CA 91711; ph. (909) 621–8219; fax (909) 621–8798.

Web Resources

Association of American Colleges and Universities (http://www.aacu.org/)

Campus Compact (http://www.compact.org)

Carnegie Foundation for the Advancement of Teaching Community Engagement Classification
(http://www.carnegiefoundation.org/classifications/sub.asp?key=1213&subkey=2215)

Center for Democracy and Citizenship (http://www.publicwork.org/)

Center for Information and Research on Civic Learning and Engagement (CIRCLE)
(http://www.civicyouth.org/)

Center for Popular Education and Participatory Research (http://cpepr.info/)

Community-Campus Partnerships for Health (http://depts.washington.edu/ccph/index.html)

Community College National Center for Community Engagement (http://www.mc.maricopa.edu/other/engagement/)

Corporation for National and Community Service (http://www.nationalservice.gov)

Highlander Center's Community-Based Research Resources
(http://www.highlandercenter.org/)

Loka Institute and the Community Research Network (http://www.loka.org/crn.html)

National Service-Learning Clearinghouse (http://www.servicelearning.org)

University of Washington School of Public Health's Community-Based Research Principles
(http://sph.washington.edu/research/community.asp)

U.S. Department of Education Character Education and Civic Engagement Technical Assistance Center (http://www.cetac.org/)

WORKSHEET 2-1: Community Exercise

Think of a service-learning project of which you are particularly proud, which you feel has resulted in good work for the community. Now imagine you have been assigned to take pictures of the community served by this project.

•   What would you photograph?

_____

_____

_____

_____

Or, instead of imagining, take some real photos.

•   As you look at the photos, whether imagined or real, think about how the images shape your idea of the community. What are some of the words you would use to describe the community?

_____

_____

_____

_____

Now show your pictures or share your mental images with various people in that community. Try to get five different perspectives: a resident or a businessperson, a child or a parent, a lifelong resident or a newcomer. Seek people whose identity—for example, along lines of race, class, or immigrant status—differs from your own. Ask these key informants what they see in your photos and how it compares to what they would photograph if they were taking pictures of the community.

•   What do you see in common?

_____

_____

_____

(continued)

WORKSHEET

WORKSHEET

- What did they see that you did not?

_____

_____

_____

_____

- What did you see that they did not?

_____

_____

_____

_____

- How do their insights into the community confirm or change your original thinking about the community?

_____

_____

_____

_____

WORKSHEET 2-2: Analyzing Students' Service-Learning Projects

A. Using students' reflection papers about service-learning projects as data, fill out a three-column chart. In the first column, list what you want students to understand from reflection. In the second column, record any evidence from the papers that students are meeting those goals. In the third column, note what students know well, are confused about, misunderstand, or need to be more challenging. What do these data tell you?

WHAT YOU WANT STUDENTS TO UNDERSTAND FROM REFLECTION	EVIDENCE FROM PAPERS THAT STUDENTS ARE MEETING THEIR GOALS	STATUS OF STUDENTS' KNOWLEDGE ABOUT REFLECTION

B. To analyze verbal reflection, try taping a service-learning discussion in class. To think more carefully about whether the conversation was reflective, code the transcript, noting examples of students who individually or as a group went through an active, persistent, careful cycle of reflection. Similarly, code the conversation for examples of open-minded, responsible, and wholehearted conversation.

C. From your analysis of the written and verbal data, what do you find?

_____

_____

_____

What do these written and verbal data tell you about possible changes you might make in creating placements, framing assignments, or structuring reflective conversation and writing?

_____

_____

_____

WORKSHEET

Establishing and Sustaining a Community Service-Learning Office, Revisited: Top Ten Tips

Barbara Jacoby

S INCE 1992, WHEN I FIRST BECAME INVOLVED with service-learning, the resources offering guidance through principles, benchmarks, best practices, and research findings on how to design, implement, and evaluate service-learning experiences have grown tremendously. While these resources help us to do our work better, they do not necessarily enable us to become the reflective community service-learning professionals (CSLPs) that we must be in order for service-learning to fulfill its potential.

Establishing and Sustaining an Office of Community Service (Campus Compact, 2000), now out of print, served many of us well. Its focus, however, was on the program or office and not on you, whose job is to establish and sustain yourself as an outstanding professional who will, in turn, sustain an outstanding community service-learning program or office.

This book focuses on you. This chapter is coming directly from me to you. I have established and sustained an office and myself as a professional, although it hasn't always been easy. I've been laboring very happily in the community service-learning vineyard since 1992 and have my top ten tips that I'd like to share with you. Throughout this chapter, you will also find quotes from several outstanding colleagues who have generously shared their stories.

Tip #1. Know the History of Service-Learning at Your Institution

If you're not already familiar with the history of service-learning on your campus, lose no time in finding out all about it. Why was service-learning started on your campus? Why was your office or program formed? How? What were the highlights, successes, problems, and failures along the way? This information can be extremely useful, and, even more, you don't want this information to rise up and surprise you at some inopportune time.

Let me use myself as an example by sharing the story of how I became involved in service-learning. In the spring of 1992, while Bill Clinton was campaigning for his first term as president, he talked a lot about having college students participate in community service in exchange for assistance with college expenses—the program that has become AmeriCorps. At the time, more and more colleges and universities were setting up or enhancing community service and service-learning programs.

At the University of Maryland, where I was then director of the Office of Commuter Affairs, the dean of undergraduate studies pointed out to the college president that there was no service-learning program at the university, which is the flagship of the University System of Maryland and a land-grant institution. The president asked my boss at the time, the vice president for student affairs, whether the university should start a program and whether student affairs was the right organizational home for it. The vice president said he would think about it. Shortly after that conversation, he asked me what I thought about student affairs taking responsibility for community service (we weren't using the term service-learning then). He was quite ambivalent about the whole idea. I said, "Sure, it seems like there's a lot of student development to be had from it," although I had no earthly idea where this was taking me. It was not a terribly articulate response, but it had an impact nonetheless. A few days later, my boss called and said, "I want you to take this community service or volunteer 'thing' into your office and make something of it."

Well, I had previously done some community service but knew absolutely nothing about running a program. I immediately got my hands on the few print resources I could find and visited several universities in the area to see what they were doing in community service. That's how I learned the term "service-learning" and the concept of community service in the curriculum.

From the beginning, it quickly became clear to me that at the University of Maryland, we needed to explore the development of both curricular and co-curricular service-learning simultaneously. When I met with my boss to describe this plan, he immediately responded, "Don't go after faculty. They'll sink your ship before you get it out of the harbor."

I realized that I needed to know immediately why my boss felt so strongly about this so I could address his concerns head on. After some digging, I learned that a couple of joint academic affairs–student affairs initiatives had not worked out well in the past. There was some skepticism about embarking on another such partnership. So my staff and I collected as much research as we could that showed the power of course-based service-learning in increasing student learning. We drew on our knowledge of commuter students (then about 75% of our student body). We knew that most of our commuter students worked, many of them full-time and/or at more than one job. Therefore, we formulated the case that it would be much easier for them to engage in service if it were part of a course, rather than just an add-on. Using these arguments, we convinced the vice president for student affairs to allow me to form a faculty advisory board to seek advice and direction for course-based service-learning at the university. Today, service-learning courses have grown significantly in both quantity and quality. (Worksheet 3-1 on pages 49–51 can help you determine the details of the history of service-learning on your campus and how you can use it to move forward.)

Tip #2. Create Your Vision of Success

How will you know if you are successful? Creating a vision of success for service-learning is critical. The vision should be developed in a shared process. (Several websites on developing vision and mission statements are included in the reference and resource sections at the end of this chapter.)

The first steps for developing a vision of success in the context of service-learning are:

- Determine what success means to you personally. What are your values and vision for service-learning? What do *you* want your program's legacy to be for students, the community, the institution, and service-learning in general? (Chapter 1 offers you the opportunity to reflect on these questions.)

- Know what your institution's peers and "aspirational" peers are doing in service-learning. When our current president arrived at the University of Maryland from the University of California-Berkeley, my savvy colleagues and I immediately checked out what Berkeley was doing in our areas of responsibility. You can see the top 25 service-learning programs on the *U.S. News & World Report* website (http://colleges.usnews.rankingsandreviews.com/best-colleges/service-learning-programs), the information source that "we love to hate." Your campus leaders know who's listed and want to be among them. You should know how your institution's program compares to those listed. (Worksheet 3-2 on pages 52–54 can help you identify your institutional peers and priorities and teach you to use that information to advance service-learning.)

- Know your institutional priorities—i.e., the hot issues on campus. Get a copy of your institution's strategic plan. Think constantly about how service-learning relates to it. Is retention an issue? Plenty of data show that students—particularly students of color—are more likely to graduate if they are involved in service-learning (Campus Compact, 2008). Have you told your admissions officers about what service-learning has to offer in the way of recruitment? As more high-school students participate in service-learning, they are asking admissions offices about opportunities to continue and deepen their involvement in college. Diversity is another issue with which your student affairs colleagues are intimately involved. A few years ago, after a spate of hate mail and threats to African-American student leaders on my campus, the president appointed two well-respected faculty members to chair a committee and come up with ways to increase awareness and respect for diversity. Before we explained service-learning to the committee, several faculty members told me they had known nothing about it; they are now among our supporters.

- Know how service-learning can help achieve student learning outcomes. Regional accrediting associations are requiring institutions to clearly state their outcomes for student learning on multiple levels (e.g., course, major, department, college, institution) and how they measure the degree to which students achieve these outcomes. Studies that reveal the benefits of service-learning, such as Eyler and Giles' *Where's the Learning in Service-Learning?* (1999), provide useful information.

- Know, too, the potential "dark sides" of service-learning. If not done well, service-learning can, in fact, do harm to the community and to students (Butin, 2005; Jacoby, 2009).

Unfortunately, community partners have complained about being "used" by colleges and universities, and students complain about wasting time and having their stereotypes reinforced.

- Develop a strategic plan for service-learning. A plan is *strategic* if it serves as a guide for making difficult choices. When deciding whether to expand course-based service-learning in a particular area or start an alternative spring-break program, the vision and strategic plan will help you prioritize options and select those that move toward the vision and goals. (Web resources regarding strategic planning are at the end of this chapter.)

Tip #3. Go for Quality over Quantity

Opt for quality: fewer service-learning courses and fewer student projects done well is the way to go. You don't want to give critics who view service-learning as "soft" or lacking academic rigor any material to work with. Well-organized service projects with clearly defined outcomes and subsequent evaluation of achievements are likely to make students come back for more.

I have learned much from talking to students about quality in service-learning. Maryland public high schools have a 75-hour community-service requirement for graduation. Some students have fabulous, inspiring experiences in which their service work is carefully integrated into the curriculum. Others, however, merely do work that feels aimless, like raking neighbors' leaves, and come away resentful and frustrated. The quality of one service experience can affect a student's interest in doing more. Similarly, course-based service-learning can be of high or low quality. (See the box, "Low- and High-Quality Course-Based Service-Learning," on page 43.)

Another important aspect of quality in service-learning is careful attention to logistics and risk management, which is essential for significantly lowering the probability of a crisis. A crisis can end your program before you even get it off the ground. Learn about the liability and risk-management procedures on your campus; get to know the legal counsel. Know the differences among policies and procedures for credit-bearing experiences, programs organized by your office, and student-organization projects. Learn from other off-campus programs, such as internships, student teaching, and study abroad.

Tip #4. Make the Most of Your Place in the Organization

No matter where your office or program is located organizationally within the institution, service-learning can benefit from partnerships between student affairs and academic affairs. Each has access to knowledge, connections, and resources that enable it to make unique, critical contributions to the development of high-quality service-learning. Academic affairs leadership often results in service-learning being viewed as academically rigorous. Thus, faculty may be more able to secure the support of senior administrators and engage their colleagues in service-learning. Service-learning programs in academic affairs find it easier to modify and implement academic policy that supports service-learning and to create mechanisms that reward faculty participation. Similarly, faculty development for service-learning can be readily integrated into ongoing faculty development programs.

Low- and High-Quality Course-Based Service-Learning

Following are descriptions of a service-learning course before and after the faculty member worked with our office and got some direction and assistance in course design.

Before: Students in a sociology course on popular culture tutored in a local high school. Transportation was arranged for them, but the tutors received little or no direction or feedback on their daily activities with the students. They were also not prepared for the differences between the local high school's population and that of the high schools most of the tutors had attended. The tutors ended up helping with homework, but neither they nor the high school students knew why the tutors were there. As a result, many members of both groups stopped going to the sessions, causing frustration for all, including the school principal.

After: In preparing for the second semester, the sociology course faculty member worked with service-learning office staff to add a clear purpose and more structure to the course. Training and orientation were stepped up. In conjunction with the course focus on popular culture, the tutors planned and organized a poetry slam with the students. Working together, the tutors and the younger students composed poetry and lyrics, planned a public assembly, and compiled a publication of their work. The faculty member tied the project to a course reading about the influence of popular culture and asked students to link the text with their tutoring experiences through class discussions and responses to questions in their journals. In a final activity, the university students and the high-school students discussed similar questions.

Note: This example was drawn from the University of Maryland *Faculty Handbook for Service-Learning,* assembled by Jennifer Pigza (2005).

Student affairs professionals also have much to contribute to service-learning. They know about student development theory and learning styles and have experience with group processes useful in the design and facilitation of reflection. In addition, student affairs professionals are experienced in administration and logistics, including scheduling, transportation, risk management, and conflict mediation. They have networking skills and are experienced at developing relationships. Moreover, they are often known and respected for their seemingly boundless energy.

Community service-learning professionals in both academic and student affairs are usually active members of professional organizations, participants in workshops and listserv discussions, and readers of higher education publications that reflect cutting-edge concepts and practices relating to service-learning. Yet, they generally participate in different organizations and discussions and thus have much to share with one another.

These are some pointers from my own experience:

- No matter which side you're on, take the first step out of the box. For example, let it be known that you are willing to sit on campus-wide committees or teams working on broad campus issues such as retention, diversity, sustainability, global education, institutional assessment, and so on. This involvement can give you a chance to meet others you might not necessarily come in contact with—and they can get to know you and all you have to offer.

- Invest time and energy in getting to know other people. Personal contacts, networks, and the insights and "scoops" from informal relationships are invaluable.

- If you're a student affairs professional, learn "faculty speak." For instance, when I approach new faculty about service-learning's appropriateness for a particular course, I use the analogy of the *text*. I speak of the service experience as a potential text for the course, explaining that students don't get credit for reading the text (that is, doing the service), but for demonstrating their learning from the text (or service). Faculty who worry about giving students credit for something soft then understand that we are, in fact, talking about learning and academic rigor. (Chapters 4 and 6 address this in depth.)

Tip #5. Find Your Allies . . . and Detractors

Whose goals align with yours? Some obvious potential allies are service-learning-friendly faculty members, campus ministers, leadership development educators, and campus activities staff. Think strategically about how service-learning can connect to their goals and challenges. To residence hall staff, for example, service is a way for students to develop a sense of community in their halls and to learn about teamwork. To colleagues in the financial aid office, what matters are regulations requiring that each institution use 7% of its Federal Work-Study funds in wages for students doing community service. And the school of education generally has school-based programs that need volunteers.

Find out who doesn't understand or support your work. For instance, my proposals for institutional funds to support our America Reads program, a mutually beneficial, democratic, sustainable campus-community partnership, kept getting shot down by an influential financial officer because, as he put it, "My church has a reading tutoring program, and it doesn't have any staff or budget." Once I explained that our program involved Maryland students providing individualized reading instruction to children with low reading scores rather than reading stories to them, he seemed to understand. Data showing that Maryland students who served as America Reads tutors scored higher than other students who participated in service-learning in the areas of leadership, diversity, and social responsibility finally convinced him to provide funds for the program. Educate, educate, educate about service-learning by relating its benefits to naysayers or potential naysayers. (See Chapter 10 for further information about evaluation and assessment.)

Tip #6. Numbers Matter

Even if your personal definition of successful service-learning isn't quantitative, you will be asked for numbers. Mere numbers do not reflect the impact of service-learning on students and communities, but numbers do matter. When we reported the number of tons of trash students hauled out of the Anacostia River at our annual Earth Day clean up, administrators and the press took notice.

In another example, many of us served on one of the multiple committees planning for the University of Maryland's 150th anniversary. I was on the Community Outreach Committee, along with several members of the president's staff who knew who I was but knew nothing about the service-learning program. As we were thinking about where to target our community outreach for the anniversary, however, I mentioned that the Office of Community Service-Learning had more than 800 community-based organizations in its database of service opportunities. Suddenly, people sat up in their chairs and asked all about service-learning. Those numbers brought our program into focus for them. Numbers matter; use them in planned as well as serendipitous ways when you can.

Tip #7. Develop Partnerships with Community Organizations
As the editor of *Building Partnerships for Service-Learning* (Jacoby, 2003), I have a few more points from my experiences and from the book's chapter authors:

- Partnerships must be based on the strengths, assets, and capacities of the partnering institutions. Community-based organizations simply may not have the capacity, in terms of staff, space, equipment, and infrastructure, to partner effectively with you. Some community organizations complain of being worn out trying to keep up with the number of students or projects the college or university sends. Similarly, community partners need to realize that colleges and universities are not as infinitely rich as they may seem. Partners need to understand that community colleges, small religious colleges, and large research universities have very different strengths and capacities. And both higher education and community partners need to understand that tough economic times affect everyone. (A good resource on campus-community partnerships for the community partner is Campus Compact's *The Promise of Partnerships: Tapping into the College as a Community Asset* [2005].)

- Partnerships between institutions start as relationships between individuals, as face-to-face meetings, both on campus and in the community. This begins with finding a common language. What does RPT stand for? What's a provost? For those of us in higher education, this means learning the norms and practices of environments very different from ours. We need to know how things work outside our own comfort zone. Get to know each other's norms and basic operating procedures. I remember chairing the first planning meeting for our America Reads program. The task force charged with developing the program consisted of University faculty and administrators as well as teachers and reading specialists from the county school system. We introduced ourselves and then proceeded through the meeting. My colleagues and I, who address each other by our first names, did the same with our potential school system partners. There was also no written agenda for the meeting. I never thought to prepare one, although I had one planned in my mind. After a while I realized something was wrong. School administrators and teachers generally use titles (e.g., Mr., Mrs., Miss, Doctor) in formal settings, and there is *always* a printed agenda.

- According to Judith Ramaley, it is absolutely essential to create "a culture of evidence" (2000). Keep a running record of how well the partnership is working from the viewpoints of all participants, both on campus and in the community. Positional leaders may not have the same views as informal leaders and members of either community. Community-based organization directors may not have the same perspectives as their clients. Also, don't underestimate the power of youth, even young children, to express their hopes, fears, and realities. (*Building Partnerships for Service-Learning* [Jacoby, 2003] has a terrific chapter by Sherril Gelmon about the partnership itself as a unit of analysis.)

Tip #8. Enlist Students as Advocates

Never underestimate the power of students. They are your best advocates. Their stories can be persuasive in situations where you can't be as effective. I have involved students in presentations about service-learning to the president's cabinet, meetings with potential donors (see Chapter 9), as panelists in workshops for faculty, and in many other situations. Possible advocates include leaders of student organizations (both those dedicated to service and others), resident assistants, orientation assistants, admissions tour guides, and students who have taken service-learning courses. These are the students whom administrators know and listen to. And don't forget student reporters for the campus newspapers, radio station, and cable television network, who are always looking for stories. Two publications from Campus Compact (Cone, Kiesa, & Longo, 2006; Zlotkowski, Longo, & Williams, 2006) highlight multiple ways in which students can serve as our colleagues in community service-learning.

Also, collect stories about extraordinary outcomes of service-learning experiences from the students, faculty, and staff involved in service-learning. How can you use these stories to raise the awareness of key stakeholders about the benefits of service-learning?

Tip #9. Use Available Resources

Know what resources are available nationally, in your state, in your local community, and on your campus. For example, at the University of Maryland—and on many other campuses—resident assistants (RAs) are required to plan and implement programs for their residents each semester. They generally have resources to cover nominal costs, but they often need ideas. RAs also take a three-credit course and undergo substantive training sessions. Getting on the agenda to train them in how to design high-quality service projects can enable community service-learning professionals to fill a clear need for programming support and, at the same time, to introduce many students to service-learning and to their offices. On the academic side, there are a new faculty orientation, a summer conference for freshman seminar instructors, and a conference for academic advisers. We use all of these opportunities for workshop sessions and staff information tables, with no cash outlay.

Campus Compact offers annual awards for outstanding student and faculty leadership for service-learning and civic engagement. Nominating students and faculty members on your campus brings recognition to them and to service-learning even if they do not win. When we had a student national award winner on our campus, a news story about the award, the student's biography, and his application essay appeared on the university's home page. The president and public relations people were delighted, and the community service-learning office looked terrific. If your institution is a member of Campus Compact, there are many more resources at your disposal.

Brainstorm about resources available at no cost—on campus, in the local community, in the state, and nationally through higher education and other organizations.

Tip #10. Intentionally Create Sustainable Support Systems
This demanding work and the challenges in our communities can seem overwhelming. Our decisions about what program to support or which community need to address can be very difficult. We worry whether we are up to the challenges and whether we can handle all the competing demands, the long hours, and the hard work. This book is full of strategies, ideas, and stories to help you sustain yourself as a community service-learning professional.

My personal advice is:

- Develop your philosophy of service-learning and know what motivates you. What draws you to the work? What makes it worthwhile for you? Having a personal mission that you can cling to throughout the chaos of your daily life makes a huge difference. Chapter 1 provides great support and scaffolding for doing this reflection.

- Take time to reflect on how you are doing, not just on how the work is going. For many years, on my way home every night, I have asked myself, "What have I done for the students at the University of Maryland today?" The answer can be as simple as emailing a student to tell her about a class, scholarship, or program that might interest her.

- Find peers and colleagues with whom you can regularly share your joys and frustrations. Personal conversations are best, but phone calls are fine. Email and social networking sites like Twitter work well, too, enabling us to check in with each other easily and regularly, albeit asynchronously.

In conclusion, you can do many concrete things, without drawing on financial resources, to establish and sustain your service-learning program by establishing and sustaining yourself as a community service-learning professional. I hope that you will use these ten tips and share them with your service-learning partners.

Acknowledgments
One of the best experiences I've had while writing this chapter has been collecting the quotes from CSLP colleagues who have shared their thoughts and experiences. I sent a list of questions related to this chapter to various listservs and individuals. Some of the same individuals are cited repeatedly. Their insights represent a diversity of levels of experience, institutional types, personal backgrounds, and perspectives. I have erred on the side of quality of responses rather than number of different respondents.

References
Butin, D. W. (Ed.). (2005). *Service-learning in higher education.* New York: Palgrave McMillan.

Campus Compact. (2000). *Establishing and sustaining an office of community service.* Providence, RI: Campus Compact.

Campus Compact. (2005). *The promise of partnerships: Tapping into the college as a community asset.* Providence, RI: Campus Compact.

Campus Compact. (2008). *How can engaged campuses improve student success in college?* Available at www.compact.org/wp-content/uploads/resources/downloads/Retention-Research-Brief.pdf.

Campus Compact. (2007). Earn, learn, and serve: *Getting the most from community service federal work-study.* Providence, RI: Campus Compact. Retrieved from http://www.compact.org/initiatives/federal-work-study.

Cone, R. E., Kiesa, A., & Longo, N. (2006). *Raise your voice: A student guide to making positive social change.* Providence, RI: Campus Compact.

Eyler, J., & Giles, D. (1999). *Where's the learning in service-learning?* San Francisco: Jossey-Bass.

Jacoby, B. (Ed.). (2003). *Building partnerships for service-learning.* San Francisco: Jossey-Bass.

Jacoby, B. (2009). Facing the unsettled questions about service-learning. In J. Strait, & M. Lima, *The future of service-learning: New solutions for sustaining and improving practice.* Sterling, VA: Stylus.

Pigza, J. (2005). *Faculty handbook for service-learning.* College Park, MD: University of Maryland.

Ramaley, J. A. (2000). The perspective of a comprehensive university. In T. Ehrlich (Ed.), *Civic responsibility and higher education* (pp. 227–248). Phoenix, AZ: Oryx.

Zlotkowski, E., Longo, N. V., & Williams, J. R. (2006). *Students as colleagues: Expanding the circle of service-learning leadership.* Providence, RI: Campus Compact.

Additional Resources

Heathfield, S. (2009). *Build a strategic framework: Mission statement, vision, values.* Retrieved from http://humanresources.about.com/cs/strategicplanning1/a/strategicplan.htm.

Howard, J. (2001). *Service-learning course design workbook.* Ann Arbor, MI: Edward Ginsberg Center for Community Service and Learning, University of Michigan.

Inc.com. (2005). *Developing effective vision and mission statements.* Retrieved from http://www.inc.com/resources/startup/articles/20050201/missionstatement.html.

Jacoby, B. (Ed.). (1996). *Service-learning in higher education: Concepts and practices.* San Francisco: Jossey-Bass.

Jacoby, B. (Ed.). (2009). *Civic engagement in higher education: Concepts and practices.* San Francisco: Jossey-Bass.

McNamara, C. (1999a). *Basics of developing mission, vision and values statements.* Retrieved from http://www.managementhelp.org/plan_dec/str_plan/stmnts.htm.

McNamara, C. (1999b). *Strategic planning (in nonprofit and for-profit organizations).* Retrieved from http://www.managementhelp.org/plan_dec/str_plan/str_plan.htm.

Porter Honnet, E., & Poulsen, S. J. (1989). *Principles of good practice for combining service and learning.* Racine, WI: Johnson Foundation.

WORKSHEET 3-1:

Learning About and Using the History of Service-Learning at Your Institution

Refer to documents and interview individuals who were at your institution throughout the development of your service-learning program or office to answer the following questions.

1. Why was service-learning started at your institution?

    _____

    _____

    _____

    _____

2. How was service-learning started?

    _____

    _____

    _____

    _____

3. What terminology has been used to name or describe the program or office?

    _____

    _____

    _____

    _____

4. Who were its advocates and supporters?

    _____

    _____

    _____

    _____

(continued)

W O R K S H E E T

5. Who were the "naysayers"?

_____

_____

_____

_____

6. What were the important milestones in its past?

_____

_____

_____

_____

7. What have been its successes?

_____

_____

_____

_____

8. What have been its problems or failures?

_____

_____

_____

_____

(continued)

Using your responses to the previous questions, list potential action steps (e.g., supporters to recognize and thank, milestones to celebrate, individuals with "ruffled feathers" to smooth, problems to address).

1. _____

_____

2. _____

_____

3. _____

_____

4. _____

_____

5. _____

_____

6. _____

_____

7. _____

_____

8. _____

_____

WORKSHEET 3-2:

Identifying Potential Institutional Factors That Contribute to the Success of Service-Learning

1. What are your institution's peer and aspirational peer institutions?

   _____

   _____

   _____

   _____

2. How do their service-learning programs compare with yours?

   _____

   _____

   _____

   _____

3. What institutions listed in *U.S. News and World Report* as having outstanding service-learning programs are of interest to your campus leaders?

   _____

   _____

   _____

   _____

4. How do their service-learning programs compare with yours?

   _____

   _____

   _____

   _____

(continued)

5. What are your institution's stated priorities?

    _____

    _____

    _____

    _____

    a. What are the current "hot issues" on your campus?

        _____

        _____

        _____

        _____

    b. What sections of your institution's strategic plan relate to service-learning?

        _____

        _____

        _____

        _____

6. Has your institution developed student-learning outcomes?

    _____

    a. What are your regional accrediting association's directives regarding student-learning outcomes?

        _____

        _____

        _____

        _____

(continued)

WORKSHEET

b. What levels of student-learning outcomes exist on your campus (e.g., course, major, department, college, institution)? Are they currently being developed?

_____

_____

_____

_____

c. How can you ensure that service-learning is regarded as a powerful pedagogy for achievement of student-learning outcomes?

_____

_____

_____

_____

CHAPTER FOUR

A Travel Guide on the Culture, Mission, and Politics of Academia to Promote Service-Learning

Marshall Welch

COMMUNITY SERVICE-LEARNING PROFESSIONALS (CSLPs) are on a journey, if not a quest, when attempting to work with faculty and administrators in order to institutionalize service-learning. Although many of us have backgrounds either in the community working with nonprofit agencies or as administrators in student affairs, experiences in these contexts do not always transfer readily to the academic culture of higher education. Thus, we often find ourselves in uncharted territory, where there is always the possibility of getting lost or inadvertently committing a faux pas within a strange, new culture.

This chapter serves as a travel guide to help CSLPs navigate the culture and system of higher education. The interactive nature of activities here will prepare you to conduct what might be considered "academic reconnaissance." You will be able to chart a course through the maze of organizational flowcharts, the terrain of professional turf, and the white-water rapids of intangible cultural variables. When traveling in foreign lands, it's good to have a dictionary or phrase book to help communicate, so I include a glossary of "academese," otherwise known as "facultyspeak." The terms appear in italics throughout the chapter. Reflection passages are dispersed throughout to help you consider the relevance of key points and think strategically. The reflection process includes specific information ("What?" sections) followed by insights ("So What?" sections) to aid you in understanding the importance and relevance of that information. The "Now What?" boxes propose some steps for enriching your understanding of and promoting service-learning in your institution. The activities may require you to do some research or to gather materials. You should reflect on these items and then consider appropriate steps for strategically working with faculty and administrators.

Evolution of Higher Education: What a Long, Strange Trip It's Been
What?

For the first 500 years, universities functioned in a medieval society in which religion, speculation, and superstition influenced the pursuit of knowledge. During the Renaissance, scholars attempted to break from these shackles in pursuit of knowledge and truth. Scholars endeavored to be objective; they were not influenced by other institutions or dogma in their quest for knowledge. As a result, objectivity in *scholarship* is a deeply valued and embedded tenet in higher education (Scott, 2000a).

The notion of *academic freedom* emerged with this search for truth during the Age of Enlightenment. A vital component to academic freedom was the adoption and practice of the scientific method, in which scholars such as John Locke and Thomas Hobbes established a hypothesis and then tested it through analysis of experiments. Academic freedom is the right of scholars to teach, conduct research, and publish without control or restraint from any institution, be it the academy or any political or religious entity. Therefore, the essence of academic freedom is the idea that truth can best be discovered through the open, objective exploration of information.

These deeply rooted tenets of objectivity and academic freedom have a direct impact on the values and behaviors of faculty today, especially with regard to what and how they teach. First and foremost is the sense of obligation to remain objective. Faculty members have a legitimate concern that their teaching and research could be influenced by some constituency. Second, the process of discovery is generally an autonomous process in which faculty work alone. Third, faculty work hard to control factors outside the laboratory or classroom that might influence or contaminate the scientific inquiry or results of the experience. Finally, faculty view themselves—and rightly so, to an extent—as knowledgeable experts on a given topic. Thus, they are creating new knowledge and a way of understanding what we know, otherwise known as *epistemology*. They might, therefore, see the notion of co-creating knowledge with non-experts such as students and community partners as a rather far-fetched idea, contrary to academic tradition and culture.

These combined factors create a general reluctance on the part of faculty to engage in any type of *scholarship* or teaching that could be perceived as a threat to objectivity and academic freedom. CSLPs should consider these factors and perceptions in the context of service-learning. The notion of faculty actually working with a community partner can seem somewhat aversive. After all, that community agency is likely to have a particular mission or even agenda that could potentially have an impact on objectivity and academic freedom. Likewise, the notion of collaborating outside of academia impinges on the culture of faculty autonomy. Scholarly work is by nature autonomous, and faculty rarely interact with colleagues down the hall, let alone with "strangers" in the community. Similarly, a faculty member has no control over what students might learn beyond the classroom. While faculty may recognize the experience of community agency representatives, those individuals may not necessarily have scholarly expertise. Oftentimes, the tenets of faculty work do not account for the other logistical challenges of establishing partnerships with community agencies and coordinating student placements and evaluating their learning. All these demand time and energy that faculty believe may distract them from their traditional notion of what constitutes their work and the role of higher education.

HIGHER EDUCATION IN THE UNITED STATES

The primary purpose of the first U.S. colleges and universities was the development of students' character (historically limited to young, white men) and intellect (Colby, Erlich, Beaumont, & Stephens, 2000). By the 1900s, innovative institutions such as Cornell, Harvard, Yale, the University of Chicago, and the University of Wisconsin had borrowed the concept of research from European schools and integrated it with the American emphasis on teaching and the formation of citizens (Sullivan, 2000).

Harkavy (2005) notes that higher education's current preoccupation with research is a recent phenomenon that arose from the ashes of World War II. At that time, American society as a whole was preoccupied with the Cold War and competition with the Soviet Union. Consequently, universities became entrepreneurial in their quest for government-funded research grants. With those funds came income and prestige with which faculty members were rewarded as they obtained grants. This, in turn, resulted in a change in faculty reward structures that reinforced research over teaching, especially at universities. As Rice (1996) documented, the role of faculty began to shift from one of service to one of science. Faculty began to develop knowledge not only for its own sake rather than social benefit, but also because they were extrinsically rewarded with promotion and tenure when they engaged in research. The charge to create "new knowledge" became paramount.

Thus, faculty members are impelled to be productive, not only in terms of producing new knowledge but in producing new research dollars. The result is what Benson and Harkavy (2002) call the "commodification" of higher education. As we will see later, however, not all faculty members are subject to this expectation, because of the varying missions of higher education institutions.

A NATIONAL RESPONSE

By the 1980s, society at large and scholars within academia began to sense that higher education was not effectively nurturing students' sense of civic responsibility (Sax, 2000). In 1985, the Carnegie Foundation for the Advancement of Teaching released a report entitled *Higher Education and the American Resurgence,* which stated, "If there is a crisis in education in the United States today, it is less that test scores have declined than it is that we have failed to provide the education for citizenship that is still the most important responsibility of the nation's schools and colleges" (Newman, 1985, p. 31). Likewise, the National Commission on Civic Renewal (1998) focused on higher education's "civic *dis*-engagement."

As a response to this indictment, a growing national movement called for colleges and universities to become civically engaged, evidenced by an increasing number of reports, books, articles, conferences, and action taken by higher education. In 1999, the Kellogg Commission on the Future of State and Land-grant Universities published a report, *Returning to our Roots: The Engaged Institution,* which defines engaged institutions as those "that have redesigned their teaching, research, and extension and service functions to become even more sympathetically and productively involved with their communities" (p. 9).

So What?

Service-learning is one way to promote civic engagement (Billig & Welch, 2005), which explains much of the sudden interest and growth of service-learning since the late 1980s and early 1990s. Many presidents of colleges and universities have embraced service-learning not only as a viable form of teaching and learning but also as an effective public relations tool to counter negative public sentiment. Conversely, many faculty members who do not necessarily understand service-learning are dubious about this method and question whether it is really part of the institution's mission. And while presidents, foundations, and scholars have begun to recognize the importance of civic engagement, most faculty remain oblivious to it and misunderstand what it is or how to promote it. Most believe that their identity is inextricably tied to their discipline.

Mission Possible: Understanding Your Institution and Its Mission
What?/So What?

Each type of higher education institution has its own history, traditions, and mission. The historical context of your institution is likely to have an impact on the development and implementation of service-learning.

COMMUNITY COLLEGES

The American Association of Community Colleges, founded in 1920, charts the emergence and phenomenal growth of community colleges in the mid-twentieth century as a response to an increasing demand in the workforce for college-educated employees. Many potential college students were either unable or unwilling to leave their homes to attend college in the traditional sense of living on campus and earning a degree. The community college was appealing to many underserved or underrepresented groups that needed some technical training rather than a bachelor's degree. At the beginning of the twenty-first century, there are more than 1,100 community colleges with over 11.6 million students. Most are women and come from underrepresented groups; their average age is 29. Nearly two-thirds of these students attend part-time. Most are employed; many work full time or at more than one job.

Tuition at community colleges is usually not as expensive as at four-year institutions, and courses are often taught at nontraditional hours such as evenings or weekends. Over time, community colleges have enabled students to make an easier transition from high school to four-year institutions. Students can take introductory courses (in smaller-class settings) that meet the requirements of baccalaureate-granting colleges and universities.

Now What?

Identify some faculty members or administrators whom you know well and ask them what their role is. Do they mention civic engagement in their responses?

Ask faculty or administrators what academic freedom is and what it means to them. Do their responses reflect a culture of autonomy? Do their answers include preparing students to be good citizens through partnerships with the community? Their responses will reflect faculty members' opinions about civic engagement and hint at their understanding of the role of service-learning.

Because community colleges focus on teaching rather than research, faculty may be interested in exploring service-learning as a *pedagogy*. Many community-college instructors, however, are employed off campus in other professions and teach only one or two courses. Most part-time instructors feel that they don't have the time or resources for service-learning activities that create additional work outside the classroom. Yet, there are many innovative service-learning programs and courses at community colleges. Some focus on developing the technical skills students seek by working in the community, and others enable students to count the experiences they are already involved in, such as PTAs and youth organizations.

LAND-GRANT INSTITUTIONS

The Morrill Act was signed into law by President Lincoln in 1862 to promote the "liberal and practical education of the industrial classes in the several pursuits and professions of life" (Boyte & Kari, 2000, p. 47). The act was instrumental in creating what are known as land-grant institutions. Part of the reconstruction of the nation following the Civil War included the development of usable knowledge for rebuilding the industrial democracy, resulting in the creation of land-grant colleges to provide technical assistance to communities (Boyte & Kari, 2000). Therefore, the Morrill Act articulated a mission of teaching agriculture, military tactics, and the mechanical arts, as well as classical studies, so that members of the working classes could obtain a liberal, practical education.

In essence, the act led to the rapid development of new kinds of institutions with a very practical mission. The mission was manifested immediately through agricultural extension programs, literally extending the knowledge from the institution out into the fields. In 1887, the Hatch Act allocated federal funds to create experiment stations and extension programs. To this day, most land-grant institutions have extension offices readily accessible to farmers and ranchers throughout their respective states.

This history is important to understand because, although the mission of outreach lends itself nicely to service-learning, the emphasis on the development of technology related to agriculture has also promoted a greater focus on research. Therefore, many faculty members at land-grant institutions are expected to engage in extensive grant-funded research activities and teaching courses. As we will see later, this demand can be a challenge to faculty, making them reluctant to consider creating and teaching service-learning courses.

LIBERAL ARTS INSTITUTIONS

The Association of American Colleges and Universities (AAC&U) was established in 1915 to promote liberal education as a philosophy of education that empowers individuals, liberates the mind from ignorance, and cultivates social responsibility (AAC&U, 2005). Service-learning fits well with this mission. Liberal arts institutions are typically smaller and often private. Their missions focus on teaching students to be well-rounded individuals, professionals, and citizens. Most faculty members take great pride in teaching students to be critical thinkers and rely heavily on theoretical constructs or models in their teaching. In many cases, tension between the college and community has developed—sometimes referred to as *town and gown*—because the intellectual emphasis on learning is perceived as impractical at best or elitist at worst.

Teaching is the primary role and responsibility of faculty at a liberal arts institution; research is not considered as essential as it is in research institutions. Initially, it might seem that faculty at a liberal arts college would be receptive to service-learning. Yet, instructors may teach up to three or four different courses a semester. Managing that many courses, which may meet twice or three times a week, plus designing lesson plans and grading papers, takes considerable time and effort. Consequently, the additional logistical challenges associated with service-learning courses may seem daunting.

FAITH-BASED INSTITUTIONS

The U.S. Department of Education estimates that of the nearly 4,000 colleges and universities in this country, approximately 900 identify themselves as religiously affiliated. Faith-based institutions are either directly operated by or affiliated with a specific religion. They have traditionally focused on students' spiritual growth and response to moral issues. Like land-grant colleges, the mission of faith-based institutions often explicitly articulates the value of service to others, or "social justice." This mission often encourages service-learning that addresses academic as well as spiritual goals. The Council for Christian Colleges and Universities (CCCU) was founded in 1976 with a mission to advance the cause of Christ-centered higher education and to help institutions transform lives by relating scholarship and service to biblical teachings.

HISTORICALLY BLACK COLLEGES AND UNIVERSITIES

Historically black colleges and universities (HBCUs) were created to provide an education to African Americans, but they also enroll students from other racial groups. Most of the 105 HBCUs emerged after the U.S. Civil War, although the oldest dates to 1837. Of these, 17 are land-grant institutions, while others are private, public, liberal arts, or community colleges. About 214,000, or 16%, of all African-American higher education students in the United States are enrolled at HBCUs, which comprise 3% of all colleges and universities nationwide. The National Association for Equal Opportunity in Higher Education (NAFEO) is a professional association that represents the nation's HBCUs.

Scott (2000b), who provides a comprehensive examination of HBCUs' role in civic engagement, comments: "The experience of historically black colleges and universities in preparing students for civic engagement is inextricably bound to the missions of the institutions" (p. 264). These institutions provide a college education for historically underrepresented students, while creating a sense of community for educated African Americans who can nurture the political, social, and economic welfare of the black community. This historical mission lays an excellent foundation from which to build service-learning courses and programs.

TRIBAL COLLEGES AND UNIVERSITIES

Out of the civil rights movement emerged tribal colleges and universities (TCUs) to promote Native American students' self-determination, while maintaining and strengthening tribal culture (Fann, 2003). The American Indian Higher Education Consortium, formed in 1972, consists of over 30 institutions in the United States and Canada. TCUs are typically located in isolated areas and therefore provide much-needed resources to the Native American community. Most students attending TCUs live at home and have jobs outside school. These demographics present unique challenges to promoting service-learning, although the historical mission of serving the tribal community has a strong connection to service-learning.

RESEARCH INSTITUTIONS

A research university is exactly what its name implies—an institution where research is valued and extensively practiced. There are several subcategories of research institutions. Some have doctoral programs in which advanced graduate students, many of whom anticipate a career in higher education, learn how to conduct research. Others have graduate programs only at the master's level.

Faculty members at research institutions are expected to engage in research and publish their findings. In this way, they are creating and disseminating new knowledge. Research expectations also often include writing and securing grants. Some faculty are explicitly required to write grants to bring in funds to the institution.

Many public institutions are receiving less and less support from state legislatures, forcing them to look elsewhere for fiscal assistance. In most major grants, research institutions obtain fiscal resources above and beyond dollars that actually fund the grant project. These funds are often called indirect costs and essentially help pay for the operation and management of the institution itself, right down to paying utility bills. The indirect costs often represent 50% of the grant funding. This competitive process demands a great deal of time and effort. Once a grant is successfully obtained, it requires oversight and management, which helps explain the reluctance of faculty to engage in any type of work that might distract them from these expectations. Both faculty and administrators are keenly aware of the amount of time and energy that service-learning requires. Consequently, depending on the title and role of a faculty member at a research university (described later), some instructors may have little interest in service-learning. I do not imply, however, that researchers cannot or do not teach service-learning courses.

Unlike at faith-based institutions, the term *social justice* will often not resonate at a public research institution. In fact, the term can be aversive, a perception tracing back to the history I described earlier in which academia has traditionally embraced objectivity and eschewed any moral stance as a reaction against religious dogma. The term *civic engagement* seems to be less emotionally charged and thus appears to be perceived as more secular, although most faculty members would not necessarily know what it means or entails.

> **Now What?**
>
> Determine how your institution identifies itself (liberal arts, research, etc.). The introductory section of a course catalogue or a website will probably include a section on the institution's history and mission.
>
> Obtain a copy of your institution's mission statement. Search for explicit language that supports service-learning or civic engagement. How can you use that language in your discussions with faculty and administrators?
>
> Find out more about the national professional associations for your type of institution and see what resources and information on service-learning or civic engagement they can provide.

The type of institution and its expectations for its faculty have an impact on faculty receptivity to teaching service-learning classes. Theoret-ically, service and outreach has traditionally been part of the mission and purpose of land-grant and faith-based institutions. Dialogue with faculty at these types of institutions should tap into that history. Conversely, CSLPs need to recognize the expectations of faculty at other types of institutions and be prepared for resistance. At the same time, specific types of institutions appeal to certain demographic profiles of students. That student profile may or may not lend itself easily to service-learning courses.

Faculty Rank and Role
What? / So What?

So, an instructor is an instructor, right? Wrong. The old saying "semantics is everything" couldn't more accurately reflect the importance of understanding the many different titles and roles for faculty. These differences may matter more at some types of institutions than at others. In general, there are five broad faculty categories, all of which may have some overlap: tenure-track, instructor, adjunct, lecturer, and clinical.

TENURE-TRACK FACULTY

Tenure-track faculty is a descriptive title literally meaning, "this faculty member is on a path or track working toward *tenure,*" which is described in more detail later. In short, a faculty member on this path must meet strict criteria outlining roles and expectations to earn a life-long appointment. Conducting research and publishing are typical expectations for tenure-track faculty at a research institution. Therefore, a tenure-track faculty member without tenure is more likely to be focused on research and publishing than on teaching. Tenured faculty may admonish them to "publish or perish" (see the section on "Retention/ Promotion/Tenure").

Conversely, tenured faculty members are often free to pursue scholarly interests that may include service-learning. There is an ongoing debate about whether faculty should engage in service-learning before or after tenure. I have explained to faculty and their department chairs that service-learning can be a catalyst or impediment to achieving tenure. It depends on whether the faculty member is meeting the department's criteria. The potential danger is the amount of time and work that goes into developing and implementing a service-learning class, because it could detract from other scholarly work such as research and publishing. Faculty members, however, are more likely to achieve tenure if they integrate their teaching and research. This includes conducting research in a way that is related to their service-learning course, such as community-based research. This is an important talking point when working with tenure-track faculty.

INSTRUCTOR

An instructor is a faculty member whose primary role is teaching, so he or she is not expected to conduct and publish research. You would think, then, that service-learning would immediately appeal to an instructor, but many instructors teach several courses with a large enrollment. Developing and successfully implementing a service-learning course is much more challenging than teaching a traditional course, which may be a negative factor to an instructor.

ADJUNCT INSTRUCTOR

An adjunct instructor's primary employment is generally outside the institution. For example, a practicing attorney may be hired to teach a course on contract law. Often, adjunct instructors teach for the love of teaching and may be interested in service-learning as an innovative pedagogy. Service-learning may appeal to them as a practical way to use knowledge. In addition, because of their positions in the community, they might also be potential community partners.

LECTURER

A lecturer is a faculty member who is hired expressly for teaching and is not expected to conduct research. Lecturers may teach part-time or full-time. They are not on a tenure track, so they may be called non-tenure-track faculty. Like adjuncts, they may be employed elsewhere; many teach at more than one college. Because they are not on the tenure track, they may be prime targets for service-learning. Other characteristics of adjunct instructors, described above, may also apply.

CLINICAL FACULTY

Clinical faculty members supervise students in professional settings outside the institution. They may teach a class or seminar tied to experiential education, but they are generally not expected to conduct research. Typically, the experiential education is referred to as a practicum, clinical, internship, or in the case of education, student teaching. This approach is very common within professional disciplines such as education, social work, and nursing. Many applied sciences such as pharmacy and even engineering require some type of field-based learning

---

Now What?

- Obtain a list and description of the faculty categories at your institution.

- List the faculty who currently teach service-learning and determine their titles. Are they tenure-track and, if so, do they already have tenure? Or are they clinical faculty?

- Identify whom you might target for discussions about service-learning, based on their title and expectations.

- Review the course catalogue. Identify existing classes and instructors for which service-learning might be a practical option.

- Do title and role matter at your institution? Why or why not?

- Do faculty see service-learning and internships as identical? If so, what is your role in clarifying the differences?

- When working with tenure-track faculty, prepare a list of ideas for how they might publish an article or make a conference presentation about their service-learning course. Likewise, think about how a faculty member might conduct research about his or her service-learning class, comparing it to traditional courses with pre- and post-measures.

- Compile a list of journals and conferences in the field of a tenure-track professor to help him or her consider venues for integrating service-learning teaching and research.

experience that needs coordination and supervision. Because clinical faculty are already working with students in community settings, they may be more likely to understand the objective of service-learning. Conversely, clinical faculty members are also more likely to confuse service-learning with internships or to think they are already doing service-learning, when, in fact, they are not incorporating reflection into their classes.

Retention/Promotion/Tenure
What? / So What?

Tenure-track faculty must go through a review process that assesses their scholarly productivity to determine if they are *retained, promoted, or tenured* (RPT). Unsuccessful review can result in the termination of a faculty member's appointment, which is sometimes seen as professional suicide. "Publish or perish" aptly describes the survival mode in which some faculty members find themselves, especially at research institutions. Therefore, CSLPs should understand and appreciate the RPT process. You should expect the review to have an impact on faculty members' decisions about their involvement in service-learning. Understanding the process will enable you to have meaningful conversations with faculty as well as to support those who do engage in service-learning.

The RPT process is intended to maintain quality. It is generally quite arduous and stressful for faculty. The review is conducted by their peers as well as administrators within and often outside the institution. The review process is usually conducted for three distinct yet related stages of a faculty member's career. The steps and time frames vary across institutions and even within institutions. What follows is a general description of the RPT stages and process.

The first stage is for retention. Faculty members are initially contracted as assistant professors for a probation period, usually two years. During this time, an instructor is expected to adhere to a set of criteria in various activities that typically include teaching, research, and service. Peers within the department and/or college use formal criteria to review and assess the faculty member's work. If deemed acceptable, that faculty member is retained for another specified period of time, typically another two to three years.

The second stage of review is for promotion and tenure, and is usually conducted at the fifth year of an assistant professor's appointment. Another review process determines if the faculty member has demonstrated competency to earn tenure, which means his or her appointment is assured, essentially for life. This may occur around the seventh year of an appointment. If a faculty member earns tenure, he or she is promoted to the rank of associate professor.

Another, third review stage occurs in order to earn promotion to a higher level, such as professor, which indicates the faculty member is an established, competent scholar and teacher. The standards are high, and the rank affords a degree of prestige, some privilege, and sometimes significant financial advancement. The timeline varies considerably. Some faculty are content at the associate-professor level and never attempt to go higher; others apply for promotion and are denied. Their tenure is not affected.

CRITERIA AND CATEGORIES

Each department or institution establishes criteria for what constitutes quality and an acceptable level of productivity in various academic activities, typically the *academic trilogy* of research, teaching, and service. The degree of specificity of the criteria varies greatly. The criteria also include a ranking system with the following ratings: excellent, satisfactory, marginal, and unsatisfactory. The criteria are designed to maintain objectivity as well as to minimize the political or theoretical conflicts that often occur in academia.

In the context of research, some criteria focus on the number of articles published in peer-reviewed journals and the prestige of the journals. Other products may be valued, depending on the discipline. For example, many disciplines rank a book higher than an article. Likewise, the fine arts or architecture programs may emphasize creative works. Large research institutions may expect the successful acquisition of large grants.

In teaching, there may be multiple criteria, including not only the quality and innovative approaches to instruction but also the number of courses taught and the number of students enrolled in each course. Student and peer teaching evaluations may also be factors.

Service in the academic world of faculty is different from what most students or community partners envision. It is typically concentrated in two areas. Governance, such as serving on various committees at the department, college, or institutional level, might include a curriculum committee or an admissions committee. The other form of service focuses on the professional organizations of a faculty member's discipline and might include serving as a reviewer on the editorial board of a journal or on the governing body of a professional association.

REVIEW PROCESS

The review process is complicated, requiring considerable time and effort. Faculty members generally create a portfolio that includes a personal statement, a *curriculum vita* (CV), and samples of their scholarly work, course syllabi, and evaluations. The personal statement articulates their scholarly interests and professional goals and includes a statement of their philosophical approach to research and teaching, as well as the theoretical framework they employ for their work. A CV is similar to a résumé that documents productivity in research, teaching, and service; it lists publications, presentations at conferences, grants awarded, courses taught, graduate student advisory committees on which they serve, and other service activities. A faculty member often must include copies of scholarly work such as journal articles or book chapters.

Documentation of teaching includes copies of course syllabi and sometimes the results of evaluations by students or faculty peers. Reviewers look for evidence of rigor in teaching, including readings, assignments, assessment procedures, and innovative instructional approaches. Here is where service-learning often comes in: the documentation process allows faculty members to describe in detail how they developed and implemented their service-learning courses.

So who exactly is doing all this reviewing? Again, it varies by department, college, and institution, but there is a general chain of events and cast of characters. The first step is usually at the department level. Colleagues review the faculty member's portfolio, using the established criteria. They then rank the faculty candidate's performance and forward a recommendation for retention, promotion, or tenure up the chain of command. The next link in the chain is the department chair, who either validates or challenges the results and recommendation of the faculty colleagues. Next, faculty within the college review the portfolio and also forward a ranking and recommendation. The dean of the college receives this growing file and continues the process. Eventually, the portfolio and the accumulated results may reach the desk of a vice president or even the president of the college or university. But wait, there's more!

Many institutions include an external review of the portfolio. The faculty member submits a list of recognized scholars at the state, national, or international level. A committee or department chair then selects two to three of these experts, requesting that they review the portfolio using the appropriate criteria. Their report is then included in the portfolio.

> **Now What?**
>
> • Return to your institution's mission statement and determine the relative value of teaching, and service-learning in particular, compared with other scholarly expectations such as research. Is the institution likely to embrace the concept of service-learning?
>
> • Obtain a copy or copies of various RPT criteria and procedures. Examine the nature of expectations and the benchmarks for assessing faculty productivity. Is service-learning explicitly recognized and valued? Where is it listed—under teaching or service? If it is not listed, how might you initiate a discussion about including it?
>
> • Talk with a faculty member, department chair, or dean about the RPT experience. Gain insight into the process as well as the emotional and political dynamics associated with it. Try to probe their understanding of how and where service-learning fits in the process.
>
> • Look at a faculty member's portfolio to see what it consists of.

So what does all of this mean to a CSLP? First, it is absolutely essential to understand and appreciate the RPT process in order to promote service-learning effectively to faculty at your institution. Second, you can assist a faculty member in preparing for the review by working with him or her to describe service-learning as an innovative pedagogy. In your role as service-learning advocate, anticipate that faculty review committees, department chairs, and others involved in the review process may have preconceived notions of what service-learning is (or isn't). If they perceive service-learning as a "touchy-feely service project" that does not reflect academic rigor, they are likely to dismiss it and possibly penalize an instructor who is engaged in service-learning.

Academic Chain of Command
What?
Higher education is a bureaucracy. It is important for CSLPs to understand the chain of command and how it often dictates what gets done, how, and by whom. I will begin with faculty. Depending on the culture of the department or institution, the power of a faculty member directly depends on rank. In some cultures, this ranking system is essentially a caste system in

which lower-ranked faculty members have little or no say or influence in major policy decision making. For instance, clinical or adjunct faculty may have no voice in any decisions regarding the hiring of a new tenure-track faculty member. Similarly, lower-ranked tenure-track faculty members often do not have a role in the review of their colleagues with higher rank. Meanwhile, assistant professors trying to earn tenure must maintain a delicate balance among their research, teaching, and service. Typically, they are eager to please and will often say yes to many things, such as taking on a service-learning course. But higher-ranking colleagues may counsel them to refrain from activities such as service-learning until they have tenure.

Faculty members—even those with the highest tenure status—report directly to a department chair. The chair has considerable power and responsibility as the fiscal manager of the department and as the person who also makes teaching assignments. Ideally, the chair is a mentor to all faculty, especially new non-tenured professors. As mentioned earlier, non-tenured faculty often show considerable energy and enthusiasm in trying to make their mark in the department and will agree to take on new, exciting challenges. Consequently, a department chair might dissuade a non-tenured professor from taking on the additional challenges of a service-learning course early in his or her career. The department chair also serves as the liaison or representative to other entities within the college and institution as well as the local community. Therefore, the chair is also interested in the public-relations image of the department. In addition, the department chair plays a significant role in the promotion and tenure review process. Therefore, it is important that a chair fully understand and appreciate what service-learning is. The chair might see service-learning as either an important contribution or a detriment to the department's image.

Department chairs report directly to a dean, who oversees all of the academic departments within a college. Depending on the size of the institution and college, there may be associate deans responsible for coordinating various administrative duties. For example, in a university setting, an associate dean in a college might oversee research, while another associate dean coordinates the educational programs. The dean is the fiscal manager of the college. Like the chair, the dean plays a critical role in the performance-review process. Unlike the chair, however, the dean is often somewhat removed from direct interaction with students or faculty. Consequently, the role of the dean has often been described as lonely or even "squeezed," because the position is between department chairs, who are still in the trenches, and upper-level administrators involved with larger policy issues.

Deans are under the supervision of a chief academic officer or provost. At large universities, there might be an associate vice president of undergraduate education and one for graduate education. In many ways, the vice presidents actually run the day-to-day administrative functions of the university. Their administrative actions must reflect the philosophy and policy of the president or chancellor.

As the face of the institution, the president or chancellor represents the university to all external stakeholders, including government officials, donors, alumni, and the community at large, by bridging *town and gown*. This top-level administrator generally sets the tone of the institution and communicates its mission. For example, a president with a hands-off approach may incorporate a decentralized governance of the institution in which policy and decision making are carried out at the departmental or college level. In contrast, some presidents are highly centralized, with a top-down approach. The president is often consumed with policy and budgetary matters. He or she typically assembles and regularly meets with an advisory group, including the vice presidents, to take the pulse of the institution and get input on important policy matters. Given the huge public relations aspect of the president's role, service-learning is often viewed favorably because it depicts the institution as a "good citizen" to the community.

And don't forget the board of trustees or board of regents! All institutions of higher education have a governing board that oversees the educational mission and financial administration of the school. The board essentially acts as a body of accountability to ensure that the entire academy, from the faculty to the president, is serving as a good steward of the resources allocated to the institution. Public institutions have additional accountability to the state legislature.

So What?

A faculty member's decision to engage in service-learning is influenced by an array of complex cultural, political, financial, and professional factors from peers and administrators. Yet, instructors are generally focused on what constitutes good teaching and learning (Welch, Liese, Bergerson, & Stephenson, 2004), which serves as a way for CSLPs to get their foot in the door to talk about service-learning. At the same time, a CSLP must be mindful of these factors and explore ways in which service-learning can be either a catalyst or a deterrent to promotion and tenure.

Chairs and deans are consumed by a preoccupation with infrastructure issues such as resources and budgets (Welch et al., 2004). When they are approached with a new idea such as service-learning, they will ask bottom-line questions, such as, "How much will it cost?" and "What are its benefits to the department or the college?" They also look out for faculty to ensure they are not distracted from their work. Why does any of this matter to you as a CSLP? Chairs and deans won't embrace service-learning if they don't understand it or if it costs too much in time and money. A CSLP must highlight the important pedagogical role of service-learning and demonstrate how service is tied to instructional objectives. You must provide the technical and financial assistance.

Now What?

- Learn who's in the chain of command by studying the organizational chart of your institution.

- Schedule a one-on-one meeting with a department chair, dean, and vice president. Ask them to describe their roles and priorities. Describe how service-learning fits within their roles and priorities and how you can assist them.

- Create a one-page or tri-fold brochure of talking points about service-learning and its benefits to share with faculty and administrators when you have one-on-one meetings.

- Give your president talking points on a regular basis so he or she can use them with donors, alumni, and legislators to illustrate the impact and value of service-learning.

A vice president's support of service-learning depends on his or her understanding of it. Your job is to articulate the instructional dimensions of service-learning, coupled with the value-added components of good public relations. A president is likely to be especially interested in how service-learning will appeal to alumni, donors, and the legislature. Arming yourself with testimonials from students and community partners, impact data, and research will help you articulate the value of service-learning.

Conclusion

Understanding the customs presented in this tour guide and the culture's language in the accompanying glossary will help you enjoy the journey through the sometimes confusing world of academia and minimize any faux pas. The "Now What?" sections will assist in preparing you for your interactions with professionals in this unique culture.

In conversations with academicians, ask them to describe the mission of the department or institution and their role in meeting that mission. Ask about the type and rank of faculty within a department as well as their roles and responsibilities in research, teaching, and service. Ask about the RPT process. Conduct these conversations at various rungs of the institutional ladder. Engaging in these dialogues will serve three important purposes. First, you will demonstrate your basic understanding of the cultural and political organization of the institution, which establishes your credibility. Second, you will demonstrate an interest in their work and the challenges associated with their roles and responsibilities. Establishing a relationship is absolutely essential to promoting and incorporating service-learning. Finally, the valuable information you glean from the conversations and your understanding of the institution will help you to strategically promote and implement service-learning.

"Acadamese" or "Facultyspeak" Glossary

Academic freedom: A deeply embedded and highly valued tenet within academic culture in which faculty are free to engage in a search for intellectual truth, without the influence of politics, religion, superstition, or other institutions. Faculty members are afforded freedom in their teaching in terms of what and how it is taught. Hence, they are often initially cautious of forming partnerships with community agencies to teach service-learning because it might be construed as an impingement on their academic freedom.

Academic trilogy: Faculty and administrators typically engage in three scholarly activities—teaching, research, and service—to varying degrees, as stipulated in retention-promotion-tenure (RPT) criteria.

Curriculum vita: Similar to a résumé, it is a detailed list of a faculty member's scholarly activity, usually in teaching, research, and service.

Epistemology: This impressive, intimidating word means "the intellectual process of understanding the world," using theory or experience to understand how the world works or how one behaves in the world. For example, people often subconsciously refer to how their parents modeled money management in order to manage their own. That experience defines how things are done. Academically, faculty use theoretical models to teach students how to construct their understanding of the field or world as a whole.

Pedagogy: Simply, a way or method of teaching and learning. Service-learning is a form of pedagogy.

RPT: Retention, promotion, and tenure. Every institution has a process and criteria that faculty members must complete to be retained for their appointment, promoted in rank, or to achieve tenure.

Scholarship: The topical area of faculty's teaching or research efforts and interests, scholarship typically takes the form of writing articles, books, chapters, and grants, or teaching courses. Students and community partners often erroneously think of this term as referring exclusively to a financial grant or award for tuition or expenses associated with college.

Service: Faculty must participate in various activities within the institution or profession. Institutional service often takes the form of serving on governance committees such as a curriculum committee. Professional service can include serving on an editorial review board for a scholarly journal or an advisory board of a professional association. Within academic culture, service is generally regarded as having less status because committee work takes time from research or teaching. Faculty or administrators often confuse service-learning with academic service or service projects (e.g., food drives) and view it with disdain. Service means something very different to community agency partners and students.

Tenure: The earned right of faculty members who have demonstrated their scholarly competence to retain their appointment indefinitely. Tenured faculty are periodically reviewed by their colleagues to assess their productivity.

Tenure-track: A faculty member who is working toward tenure is on a tenure-track.

Town and gown: Refers to the historical separation and tension between the community and the perceived elitism of institutions of higher education.

References

Association of American Colleges and Universities (AAC&U). (2005). Retrieved from http://www.aacu.org/about.

Benson, L., & Harkavy, I. (2002). Democratization over commodification!: An action-oriented strategy to overcome the contradictory legacy of American higher education. *Journal of Public Affairs, 6,* 19–38.

Billig, S. H., & Welch, M. (2005). Service-learning as civically engaged scholarship: Challenges and strategies in higher education and K-12 settings. In M. Welch & S. H. Billig (Eds.), *New perspectives in service-learning: Research to advance the field* (pp. 221–242). Greenwich, CT: IAP Publishing.

Boyte, H., & Kari, N. (2000). Renewing the democratic spirit in American colleges and universities: Higher education as public work. In T. Ehrlich (Ed.), *Civic responsibility and higher education* (pp. 37–60). Phoenix, AZ: Oryx Press.

Colby, A., Ehrlich, T., Beaumont, E., Rosner, J., & Stephens, J. (2000). Introduction. In T. Ehrlich (Ed.), *Civic responsibility and higher education* (pp. xxi–xxiii). Phoenix, AZ: Oryx Press.

Fann, A. (2003). *Tribal colleges: An overview.* Los Angeles, CA: ERIC Clearinghouse for Community Colleges. Retrieved from http://purl.access.gpo.gov/GPO/LPS43173.

Harkavy, I. (2005). Service-learning and development of democratic universities, democratic schools, and democratic good societies in the 21st century. In M. Welch & S. H. Billig (Eds.), *New perspectives in service-learning: Research to advance the field* (pp. 3–22). Greenwich, CT: IAP Publishing.

Kellogg Commission on the Future of State and Land-grant Universities (1999). *Returning to our roots: The engaged institution.* Washington, DC: National Association of State Universities and Land Grant Colleges.

National Commission on Civic Renewal. (1998). *Nation of spectators: How civic disengagement weakens America and what we can do about it.* College Park, MD: University of Maryland.

Newman, F. (1985). *Higher education and the American resurgence.* Princeton, NJ: Carnegie Foundation for the Advancement of Teaching.

Rice, R. E. (1996). Making a place for the new American scholar. Working paper series: Inquiry #1. Washington, DC: American Association of Higher Education.

Sax, L. J. (2000). Citizenship development and the American college student. In T. Ehrlich (Ed.), *Civic responsibility and higher education* (pp. 3–18). Phoenix, AZ: Oryx Press.

Scott, D. K. (2000a). Spirituality in an integrative age. In V. H. Kazanjian & P. L. Laurence (Eds.), *Education as transformation: Religious pluralism, spirituality, and a new vision for higher education in America* (pp. 23–36). New York: Peter Lang.

Scott, G. D. R. (2000b). A historically black college perspective. In T. Ehrlich (Ed.), *Civic responsibility and higher education* (pp. 249–262). Phoenix, AZ: Oryx Press.

Sullivan, W. M. (2000). Institutional identity and social responsibility in higher education. In T. Ehrlich (Ed.), *Civic responsibility and higher education* (pp. 19–36). Phoenix, AZ: Oryx Press.

Welch, M., Liese, L., Bergerson, A., & Stephenson, M. (2004). A qualitative assessment project comparing and contrasting faculty and administrators' perspectives of service-learning. *Journal of Higher Education Outreach and Engagement, 9*(2), 23–42.

Campus Compact Resources
Indicators of Engagement
(http://www.compact.org/category/resources/service-learning-resources/indicators-of-engagement-project/)

Resources from a three-year project, funded by the Carnegie Foundation for the Advancement of Teaching, to combine documentation and dissemination of best practices of the engaged campus with an organizing effort to help campuses achieve broader institutionalization of civic engagement.

Service-Learning Syllabi Project (http://www.compact.org/category/syllabi)

The Service-Learning Syllabi Project contains over 300 exemplary service-learning syllabi across a wide variety of disciplines.

Publishing Outlets for Service-Learning and Community-Based Research (http://www.compact.org/category/resources/service-learning-resources/publishing-outlets-for-service-learning-and-community-based-research/)

A dynamic list of print and online publishing outlets.

Additional Resources

Association of Public and Land-grant Universities. (2009). Retrieved from http://www.aplu.org.

Frye, N. (1967). The knowledge of good and evil. In N. Frye, S. Hampshire, & C. C. O'Brien (Eds.), *The morality of scholarship* (pp. 1–28). Ithaca, NY: Cornell University Press.

O'Meara, K., & Rice, R. E. (2005). *Faculty priorities reconsidered: Rewarding multiple forms of scholarship.* San Francisco: Jossey-Bass.

CHAPTER FIVE

Developing Your Ability to Foster Student Learning and Development through Reflection

Jennifer M. Pigza

"Giving money to a homeless person can be service. It has to do with how you approach people, how much time you spend with them. Do you recognize their humanity? Do you attempt to make a connection? Is what you feel compassion or pity? Do you look into their eyes?"

IN THE QUOTATION ABOVE, Alberto, one of my students, describes his experience helping homeless men and women obtain public aid. He and other students were discussing whether particular actions represent community service or perhaps something else, like charity or activism. Alberto brought the discussion to another level when he talked about relationship, compassion, and responsibility. In the words of Keith Morton (1995), Alberto was showing us a "thick" experience of mutual recognition with a homeless person, rather than a "thin" exchange of a furtive or distracted glance. As a teacher and facilitator, I am sometimes graced with moments like this, which remind me of the wisdom of our students, the leadership and challenge they offer their peers (and me), and what a privilege it is to share the world with them.

Which components of Alberto's course-based and co-curricular service-learning experiences provide a foundation for his learning and development? Preparation, action, reflection, and evaluation—surely the quality of *all* these key components of a service-learning experience influences students' learning and development. Poor planning causes frustration; paternalistic attitudes jeopardize reciprocity; and limited training can place students in situations in which they are unprepared for the people and places they may encounter.

This chapter focuses on high-quality reflection and its role in student learning and development in community service-learning. The first section explores the multiple meanings and connotations of reflection. From this initial place of understanding, the chapter reviews the larger lens of student learning and development theories and their connection to planning and facilitating service-learning reflection. The third and fourth sections delve into the practical details of conceptualizing and actualizing reflection. The closing comments remind us of the balance between intention and serendipity in working with students, community partners, and ourselves.

To Reflect Is To Respect

Alberto's comments about *seeing* homeless men and women and *looking* into their eyes provide a great opening for reflection. Many community service-learning professionals (CSLPs) know of the reflection exercise called "Mirror, Microscope, Binoculars" (e.g., see Hamilton College's Project SHINE, 2009). The exercise asks students to view a community service-learning experience at three levels. What does this experience reveal about me? How does it challenge me? How am I coming to know the people, issues, dynamics, and challenges at the community site? How do I see the larger, complex web of socio-cultural issues in this situation, and how might they play out in the future?

The mirror-microscope-binoculars exercise invites different perspectives of an experience through the metaphor of seeing. To reflect is to re-see, to respect. Respect is a continuous process of seeing a changing landscape of people, ideas, problems, and solutions; it is also participation in a community of others who are also considering their own roles in society.

Complicating Assumptions about Reflection

The notion of reflecting as respecting complicates common assumptions about reflection and service-learning. Reflection is *not:*

- A didactic retelling of the events at a service site, although this is a first step to understanding the meaning of actions, context, or academic content;

- Simply an emotional outlet for feeling good about doing service, or for feeling guilty about not doing more, although considerations of our emotional responses to service are often useful (and necessary);

- A time for soapbox opinions, although learning how to express our political, moral, and civic passions in the public square is important; or

- A tidy exercise that closes an experience; reflection is ongoing, often messy, and provides more openings than closings.

Particularly for faculty, the notion of reflection suggests a navel-gazing activity that is both limited and non-academic. On many campuses, the word *reflection* itself is a death knell to conversation about the value of service-learning or experiential learning of any kind. CSLPs quickly learn what specific language opens and closes conversations on a particular campus and perhaps among different departments. "Critical thinking," "integrating knowledge," and "theory-to-practice" are among the phrases that resonate with faculty and student affairs colleagues when CSLPs describe the concept of reflection in community service-learning. As you identify service-learning allies across campus, ask them what language they believe is the most effective in your setting. I typically ground my own conversations about reflection by using the term *critical reflection*.

Critical Reflection

There are many reasons that the phrase *critical reflection* is an appropriate, useful way to talk about reflection in community service-learning. At first, the phrase reminds us that reflection is a *critical element* of a service-learning experience. Reflection is essential, vital, and irreplaceable. That reflection be done—and that it be done well—is essential. Critical reflection also links *critical thinking* to reflection. In the midst of critical reflection, students become constructive critics of themselves, society, policies, and course content. They can learn how to ask and explore important questions. Critical thinking also links to the language of faculty and student affairs professionals.

Another related term is *critical questions,* which challenge us to recognize complexity in an issue that may seem straightforward. Community service-learning educators pose questions to students and recognize the questions that students seem to pose to themselves. For example, when I was a student, I participated in an international service-immersion experience. I met families who lived in garbage dumps and subsisted on what they salvaged from the debris. They lived in abject poverty, yet they smiled and welcomed me to their village. I was invited to consider questions like these: How can someone be both poor and happy? Aren't these incongruous conditions? What does it mean to be welcoming?

By designating service-learning reflection as critical reflection, I also show a philosophical grounding of *critical pedagogy,* of teaching for social justice. In some settings, such as campus ministry or African-American studies, the notion of teaching for social justice is a welcome connection. In other settings, such as an economics department or a college's AmeriCorps program, a foundation of critical pedagogy may not resonate as well and consequently may hamper your efforts to foster quality reflection.

Finally, the phrase critical reflection serves as a reminder of who is essential to the reflection process. Reflection is not a one-way task just for students; everyone must participate. Faculty and facilitators learn side-by-side with their students. Community partners should be welcome collaborators in the critical reflection process. They can offer issue education, skills training, and conversations about public service and vocation. Invite community representatives onto campus and acknowledge their expertise to students.

Along with other chapter authors in this book, I urge you to be a reflective practitioner in the development of your community service-learning program. Successful CSLPs know how they personally name and know reflection. They also develop a language of service and reflection that resonates with the culture and language of their college, administrative division, department, and local community. For example, in private circles, you may talk about transformative learning, but with campus administrators you may describe service-learning and reflection in terms of theory-to-practice and critical thinking. This naming and translating of service and reflection is an ongoing process, with a constant respect for teaching and learning in community service-learning.

Student Learning and Development

Faculty and facilitators of community service-learning often consider questions such as: Why do my students expect me to have all the answers? Why do so many students hesitate to claim a position on an issue? How can I encourage them to see socio-cultural and economic issues with more complexity?

Theories of Learning and Development

There are many theories that can help faculty and facilitators better understand students. Depending on the course content or the goals of a student organization or alternative spring break, you might want to consult one theory over another. For example, Kohlberg's (1975) theory of moral development can help you understand why some students see very limited options in a particular situation when others see many. Or exploring the notion of multidimensional identity development may help you understand the ways students might respond when interacting in the community and with each other.

McEwen (1996) offers an excellent review of the connections between student learning and development theories and the aims of community service-learning. These theories and frameworks are useful references for curricular and co-curricular settings, which can inform all aspects of the design and implementation of community service-learning. Table 5-1 is based largely on McEwen's work and serves as a beginning point for further study.

We need not be experts in these theories to be effective service-learning educators or to facilitate quality critical reflection. Perhaps you can use one family of theories or a particular article for faculty and staff development; everyone can learn together. Contact campus colleagues familiar with these ideas and discuss over lunch. You might also talk with students (privately or in small groups) about what they encounter in themselves and others when engaging in service. By saying, "Teach me" to students, we show that we care about them and that we are all teachers and learners at different times.

Worksheet 5-1 ("Intellectual and Moral Development") and Worksheet 5-2 ("Who Are Teachers and Learners? What Is Knowledge?"), at the end of the chapter, are invitations to faculty, facilitators, and CSLPs to connect quality service-learning experiences and reflection with models of student learning and development. Worksheet 5-1 briefly reviews Perry's (1970) intellectual and moral development theory and asks that you think about the students in a particular program or course. How might this information inform your planning and critical reflection?

Worksheet 5-2 presents Baxter Magolda's (1992) model for epistemological reflection, a model that explains *how* we know what we know. Baxter Magolda posits differing roles for the learner, peers, and the instructor or facilitator across four ways of knowing. This is particularly applicable to service-learning because the hierarchy of teachers, advisers, and students is somewhat flattened in this type of co-learning experience. Reviewing this grid may help you understand your own students and their expectations about teaching and learning. With this knowledge, you can establish reasonable goals for your students within a particular experience.

Learning and Development Linked with Service-Learning

Many aspects of students' environments have an impact on their learning and development: family and friends, academic courses, living situations, co-curricular activities, and work, to name a few. Community service-learning is a powerful forum for inviting students to learn and develop. Eyler and Giles (1999) report that service-learning benefits students in the following areas:

TABLE 5-1: Student Learning and Development

FAMILY OF THEORIES	EXAMPLES OF THEORIES
Cognitive Development Help to understand the processes of students' thinking: *how* we think, not *what* we think; build from Piaget	• Intellectual and ethical development (Perry, 1970) • Women's ways of knowing (Belenky, Clinchy, Goldberger, & Tarule, 1986) • Gender-related patterns in intellectual development (Baxter Magolda, 1992) • Moral development (Kohlberg, 1975) • Ethic of care (Gilligan, 1982) • Spiritual development (Fowler, 1981; Parks, 1986, 2000)
Learning Style Models Describe differences in how people learn and interact with their environment	• Experiential learning and learning styles (Kolb, 1984)
Psychosocial Development Describe issues and developmental tasks students face	• Seven vectors (Chickering & Reisser, 1993)
Identity Development Understand how people perceive the various elements of their own identity (race, class, gender, sexual orientation, ability, etc.)	• White racial identity development (Helms, 1990) • Minority identity–general (Atkinson, Morten, & Sue, 1993) • Multidimensional identity (Jones & McEwen, 2000) • Multiracial identity (Wijeysinghe, 2001) • Latino identity (Ferdman & Gallegos, 2001) • Sexual orientation (Evans & Wall, 1991; Fassinger, 1991)
Career Development Focus on how people make vocational choices	• Career decision making (Krumboltz, Mitchell, & Jones, 1976) • Five types of career theories (Osipow, 1983)

- Academic learning;

- Understanding and applying knowledge;

- Stereotyping and tolerance;

- Personal development;

- Interpersonal development; and

- Community and college connections

The various stakeholders of service-learning are often interested in these learning outcomes to differing degrees. For instance, an accounting faculty member may be focused on academic learning and applying knowledge. The coordinator of a tutoring program, on the other hand, may be interested in stereotyping and tolerance as well as interpersonal team development.

Critical Reflection in Action

The three levels of reflection described in Table 5-2 do not follow a learning or development model *per se*, but they reflect a progression you might see in students and in their interactions with you and their peers (Bradley, 1995). The three levels were first posed as a way to assess students' written reflection, but they are also compass points that can help you assess the depth and complexity of students' reflections.

A description of each level of reflection is matched with students' fictional comments and ways an educator might invite the student to delve more deeply into critical reflection. The examples draw from education-related service, both academic and co-curricular.

TABLE 5-2: Levels of Reflection

Level One	
- Gives examples of observed behaviors or characteristics of the client or setting, but provides no insight into reasons behind the observation; observations tend to be one-dimensional and conventional or unassimilated repetitions of what has been heard in class or from peers.	*Student:* "When his mother dropped off Stewart today, she seemed to quickly leave him at the door. She didn't help him with his coat and lunch or make sure he saw one of the teachers. Maybe her parenting is making his disability worse."
- Tends to focus on just one aspect of the situation.	*Faculty member:* "How might you learn more about this particular child or rules about how children are dropped off? Which of our readings might help you distinguish between the physiological
- Uses unsupported personal beliefs as frequently as hard evidence.	and cognitive components of disability and environmental influences?"
- May acknowledge differences of perspective but does not discriminate effectively among them.	*(continued)*

TABLE 5-2: Levels of Reflection (cont.)

Level Two

- Observations are fairly thorough and nuanced, although they tend not to be placed in a broader context.

- Provides a cogent critique from one perspective, but fails to see the broader system in which the aspect is embedded and other factors that may make change difficult.

- Uses unsupported personal beliefs and evidence but is beginning to be able to differentiate between them.

- Perceives legitimate differences of viewpoint.

- Demonstrates a beginning ability to interpret evidence.

Student: "Today I worked with the older students—18- to 21-year-olds who are developmentally disabled. I helped a girl learn to put tools together so that she might get a job. I'm not sure if she will ever be able to live on her own; maybe a group home is best."

Big Buddies facilitator: "Tell me more about what you think adulthood means. What are our dominant social values about work, and how does that affect what you (and others) expect of this student?"

Level Three

- Views things from multiple perspectives; able to observe multiple aspects of the situation and place them in context.

- Perceives conflicting goals within and among the individuals involved in a situation and recognizes that the differences can be evaluated.

- Recognizes that actions must be situationally dependent and understands many of the factors that affect their choice.

- Makes appropriate judgments based on reasoning and evidence.

- Has a reasonable assessment of the importance of the decisions facing clients and of his or her responsibility as a part of the clients' lives.

Student: "I attended a staff meeting today and realized that most of the staff is white, while most of our students are black. Although the staff seems to work well with the children and families, the role of race and power in the school can't be ignored. What does it mean for me to be a white woman who wants to work in a community where most of my students might be black? The local school system is much more racially diverse than our school. Now I see the concrete results of biased diagnosis. What is my role as a teacher in helping students be appropriately diagnosed and placed?"

Service-Learning Internship Mentor: "You have clearly identified important questions of power and ethical responsibilities. I encourage you to bring this up in the group as well as with your supervisor at the school."

The Rhythms of Reflection

The "Four Cs of Reflection" have long guided community service-learning planning and implementation. Reflection must be continuous, connected, challenging, and contextualized (Eyler, Giles, & Schmiede, 1996):

- *Continuous.* For the greatest learning outcome over time, critical reflection must be an ongoing component of a student's entire education and service involvement. In the context of a particular course or program, "continuous" implies that reflection must occur before, during, and after the service-learning experience. Pre-reflection assists in preparing students for the agency, neighborhood, task, and relevant issues. Reflection during service occurs through problem solving onsite. Post-service reflection invites an evaluation of the service experience itself, integrating newly gained experiential knowledge with existing knowledge.

- *Connected.* Service-learning reflection must connect experience with the other areas of students' learning and development. Service can make theories real, turn statistics into people and situations, and pose questions in ways that might not happen in a non-experiential context. In turn, through service, students develop their own models to explain what they experienced through service. Connected reflection bridges classroom learning, personal reflections, and firsthand experiences.

- *Challenging.* Challenging reflection poses old questions in new ways, reveals new information and perspectives that require thought and investigation, and raises new questions. Sanford's (1966) notion of balancing challenge and support is key to this component of reflection.

- *Contextualized.* When designed with context in mind, reflection provides the link between thinking and doing, and preparing for doing again. The context of the service-learning experience helps guide your choices about reflection—its process, content, and location. Reflection may be designed as an informal conversation, a structured journal, or small group interaction (for instance) and may occur in the classroom, a workshop, or a community center, with community partners, or individually.

The Four Cs are applicable to both curricular and co-curricular community service-learning. A faculty member may use them to review the ways that reflection occurs throughout a syllabus or particular unit. A student volunteer manager can be encouraged to use them in planning meetings and conversations with students. A facilitator may turn to the Four Cs in developing the curriculum for a week-long service immersion. A community partner might be able to employ them in the training and orientation offered to volunteers and in the supervision offered to staff and student interns.

Circles, Cycles, and Labyrinths

The inherent rhythm of community service-learning is circular in nature (see Figure 5-1).

The process of action and reflection that can produce change is called *praxis,* another term often seen in service-learning and education literature. Reflection begins with the preparation

FIGURE 5-1: Kolb's Experiential Learning Cycle

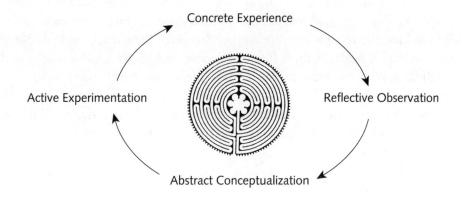

Source: Kolb, David A: *Experiential Learning: Experience as a Source of Learning and Development,* ©1984. Reprinted with the permission of Pearson Education, Inc., Upper Saddle River, NJ.

you offer students before their service experience. Pre-reflection might include a conversation about students' expectations of the people and place they will serve. This lays a foundation for the service, questions students' assumptions, and provides a platform for sharing reactions, thoughts, and theories as the service and reflection continue.

While praxis and the Kolb learning cycle engage us in a continuous circle of action and reflection, the rhythm of reflection also resembles a labyrinth, a finely devised pathway from outside the circle to the inmost region. As you trace the pathway, you appear to approach the center of the labyrinth, only to make a turn and double back along a similar yet different route. If critical reflection is an ongoing element of community service-learning, then questions, conversations, activities, readings, and musings will bring you and your students back and forth across seemingly familiar territory but with new insights, questions, and planned actions at each turn. And if you feel lost, trust the process of teaching and learning. The way out can be as head-turning as the way in.

Margaret's Journey

Margaret, a student who was beginning a year-long commitment to work ten hours a week in an after-school program for formerly homeless children, sent me a quick email describing her first weeks as "astounding." When I asked her to explain, she answered:

> What I mean by *astounding* is that I am amazed at how the children here are very optimistic about their situations. They do not take things for granted. The youth that I work with have a very close-knit relationship. They have welcomed me with open arms, and they refer to me as teacher. When they did this, I was so awestruck that I could not respond. To have someone look up to you and want you to guide them to the right path and help them be the best they can is such an honor.

Margaret enters the labyrinth and experiences a surprised response to and from her students. She is astounded, and I ask her to tell me what that means. I join her as she takes the first turn in the journey. She tells me more about the children and the honor and responsibility of the work. Margaret and I exchange emails from time to time, and we see each other every other week. I ask about teaching and community. We journey forward, double back, and rest along the way. The conversation we began in these first emails continues in private discussions and group reflection activities. We go back and forth between understanding and questioning, commitment and challenge, desolation and consolation. A portion of this journey is Margaret's alone. Another portion she shares with the children and mentor at her agency, another with me, and yet another with her friends and colleagues in the service and leadership development program in which she participates.

A Critical Reflection Toolbox
Reflection Tips

The images of the experiential learning cycle and the labyrinth are helpful to a point. The reality of facilitating a quality service-learning experience requires attention at every turn in the cycle or the labyrinth. Here are some practical tips for planning and sustaining critical reflection:

- When encouraging faculty to strengthen the critical reflection components of their academic service-learning, identify a thread of engaged teaching and learning in that discipline. Follow this thread to its source and back again. When you speak to a faculty member, draw on this language for assistance and validation. For example, a chemist can be encouraged to explore with students the common benefits of scientific discovery; an economist might invite students to consider non-capitalistic frameworks for economic development.

- Identify colleagues on your campus, another campus, or in your community who are service-learning or community development professionals and call on their expertise. Meet with them, visit their offices, observe their classes and programs, and borrow their materials.

- Identify colleagues who are skilled facilitators and teachers. Even if they are unfamiliar with community service-learning, they are committed to student learning and development, whether inside or outside of the classroom. Observe their facilitation, ask them for facilitation tips and guides, or offer to do a workshop with them so that you might practice your skills.

- Call on student leaders and community partners to lead reflection conversations and activities. The shared leadership will be refreshing for students, reinforce the value and wisdom of community members, and give you some time to observe and reflect on your own work.

- Scan for professional development opportunities focused on student learning and development, "train the trainer" models, teaching workshops, service-learning within specific disciplines, and group facilitation.

- Develop your own notebook or electronic file of reflection activities and course assignments. The service-learning community generously shares reflection ideas; however, cite the source on your written materials. Not only is this professional but it also enables participants to seek additional information and resources by the same author or publisher.

- Be patient with yourself and your colleagues as you develop your skills of critical reflection. Some of us are better at crafting written assignments or conceptualizing the curriculum of a program or class, some are proficient in group facilitation, and others are better at coaching students to be peer leaders of service and reflection.

- Engage in your own service-learning experiences. This will place you in your students' position as a learner and give you practice and insight into the process of critical reflection. And you might find it professionally rewarding to step out of a leadership role and simply immerse yourself in a service experience.

Reflection Resources

Some of my favorite, most effective and engaging reflection activities appear in Worksheet 5-3. Sometimes, however, my commitment to engaged teaching and learning meets the real limitations of my creativity. The well-worn bag of tricks is insufficient, and my brain is blocked. Have no fear! There is an unending source of service-learning reflection and engaged teaching literature both on the Web and in print. Wander through them with curious abandon or search with a specific intent in mind. Selected resources are listed at the end of this chapter.

Intention and Serendipity in Student Learning and Development

Any of us involved in teaching, advising, managing, and leading understand that intention and knowledge provide guidance to planning but take us only so far. Student learning and development happen in moments that are planned, unplanned, and absolutely chaotic. As CSLPs, we learn to create flexible plans, welcome the unexpected, and relinquish control. Serendipity is a powerful force in service and critical reflection. Open-ended questions lead us into unknown territory, new experiences tap into new ideas and feelings, and learning from a child, a client, or a homeless person may be an unexpected gift for our students. We, our students, and our community partners share a journey of respecting the world and harvesting the learning that can grow from the experience.

I think of Alberto and his comments about working with homeless men and women. Alberto's ability to wade into the complexity of service and community is only the most recent evidence of a lifelong process that began in his youth and continues in college. One semester before I met him, Alberto took a service-learning course, "Building the Good Society." Now he is quick to tell fellow students, and me, "That class changed my life." In that moment, Alberto says that a course changed *his* life. In a future moment, perhaps he will see that he can foster change in the men and women he works with and that he and his peers can co-create change in the life of their community on campus and beyond.

Students perceive our experience, our knowledge, and our passions; all three draw them into learning and being with us. Alberto says, "That class changed my life"; I say that working with students like Alberto changes mine. Teaching and learning with students in community service-learning is a joyous responsibility that I reflect on just about every day.

Acknowledgment

Portions of this chapter appear in the service-learning handbooks she composed for the University of Maryland and American University.

References

Adams, M., Bell, L.A., & Griffin, P. (Eds.) (1997.) *Teaching for diversity and social justice.* New York: Routledge.

Angelo, T. A., & Cross, K. P. (1993). *Classroom assessment techniques: A handbook for college teachers.* San Francisco: Jossey-Bass.

Atkinson, D. R., Morten, G., & Sue, D. W. (1993). *Counseling American minorities: A cross-cultural perspective* (4th ed.). Dubuque, IA: W. C. Brown and Benchmark.

Baxter Magolda, M. B. (1992). *Knowing and reasoning in college: Gender-related patterns in students' intellectual development.* San Francisco: Jossey-Bass.

Belenky, M., Clinchy, B., Goldberger, N., & Tarule, J. (1986). *Women's ways of knowing.* New York: Basic Books.

Boyte, H. C., & Farr, J. (1997). The work of citizenship and the problem of service-learning. In R. M. Battistoni & W. E. Hudson (Eds.), *Experiencing citizenship: Concepts and models for service-learning in political science* (pp. 35–48). Washington, DC: American Association of Higher Education.

Bradley, J. (1995). A model for evaluating student learning in academically based service. In M. Troppe (Ed.), *Connecting cognition and action: Evaluation of student performance in service-learning courses* (pp. 13–26). Providence, RI: Campus Compact.

Chickering, A. W., & Reisser, L. (1993). *Education and identity* (2nd ed.). San Francisco: Jossey-Bass.

Evans, B. J., & Wall, V. A. (Eds.). (1991). *Beyond tolerance: Gays, lesbians and bisexuals on campus.* Washington, DC: American College Personnel Association.

Eyler, J., & Giles, D. E. (1999). *Where's the learning in service-learning?* San Francisco: Jossey-Bass.

Eyler, J., Giles, D. E., & Schmiede, A. (1996). *A practitioner's guide to reflection in service-learning: Student voices and reflections.* Nashville, TN: Vanderbilt University.

Fassinger, R. E. (1991). The hidden minority: Issues and challenges in working with lesbian women and gay men. *Counseling Psychologist, 19,* 157–176.

Ferdman, B. M., & Gallegos, P. I. (2001). Racial identity development and Latinos in the United States. In C. L. Wijeyesinghe & B. W. Jackson, III (Eds.), *New perspectives on racial identity development: A theoretical and practical anthology* (pp. 32–66). New York: New York University Press.

Fowler, J. W. (1981). *Stages in faith: The psychology of human development and the quest for meaning.* San Francisco: Harper San Francisco.

Gilligan, C. (1982). *In a different voice.* Cambridge, MA: Harvard University Press.

Hamilton College. (2009). Project SHINE. Retrieved from http://www.hamilton.edu/levitt/SHINE.

Helms, J. E. (1990). Toward a model of white racial identity development. In J. E. Helms (Ed.), *Black and white racial identity: Theory, research, and practice* (pp. 49–66). Westport, CT: Greenwood Press.

Jones, S. R., & McEwen, M. K. (2000). A conceptual model of multiple dimensions of identity. *Journal of College Student Development, 41*(4), 405–414.

Kohlberg, L. (1975). The cognitive-developmental approach to moral education. *Phi Delta Kappan, 56,* 670–677.

Kolb, D. A. (1984). *Experimental learning.* Englewood Cliffs, NJ: Prentice Hall.

Krumboltz, J. D., Mitchell, A. M., & Jones, G. B. (1976). A social learning theory of career selection. *Counseling Psychologist, 6*(1), 71–81.

McEwen, M. (1996). Enhancing student learning and development through service-learning. In B. Jacoby (Ed.), *Service-learning in higher education: Concepts and practices* (pp. 53–91). San Francisco: Jossey-Bass.

Morton, K. (1995). The irony of service: Charity, project and social change in service-learning. *Michigan Journal of Community Service Learning, 2,* 19–32.

Osipow, S. H. (1983). *Theories of career development* (3rd ed.). Englewood Cliffs, NJ: Prentice Hall.

Parks, S. (1986). *The critical years: The young adult search for a faith to live by.* New York: Harper Collins.

Parks, S. (2000). *Big questions, worthy dreams: Mentoring young adults in their search for meaning, purpose, and faith.* San Francisco: Jossey-Bass.

Perry, W. G. (1970). *Forms of intellectual and ethical development in the college years: A scheme.* Austin, TX: Holt, Rinehart and Winston.

Reed, J., & Koliba, C. (2003). *Facilitating reflection: A manual for leaders and educators.* Retrieved from http://www.uvm.edu/~dewey/reflection_manual/index.html.

Sanford, N. (1966). *Self and society: Social change and individual development.* New York: Atherton.

Wijeyesinghe, C. L. (2001). Racial identity in multiracial people: An alternative paradigm. In B. W. Jackson, III & C.L. Wijeyesinghe (Eds.), *New perspectives on racial identity development: A theoretical and practical anthology* (pp.129–152). New York: New York University Press.

Additional Resources
Service-Learning Theory and Practice
AAHE. *Concepts and models for service-learning in the disciplines.* (20-volume series; now available from Stylus Publishing.)

Battistoni, R. M. (2002). *Civic engagement across the curriculum: A resource book for service-learning faculty in all disciplines.* Providence, RI: Campus Compact.

Howard, J. (2001). *Service-learning course design workbook.* Ann Arbor, MI: OCSL Press.

Jacoby, B. (Ed.). (1996). *Service-learning in higher education: Concepts and practices.* San Francisco: Jossey-Bass.

O'Grady, C. R. (Ed.). (2000). *Integrating service-learning and multicultural education in colleges and universities.* Mahwah, NJ: Lawrence Erlbaum Associates.

Rhoads, R. A., & Howard, J.P.F. (Eds.). (1998). *Academic service learning: A pedagogy of action and reflection.* San Francisco: Jossey-Bass.

Teaching and Reflection
Barkely, E. F., Cross, K. P., & Major, C. H. (2005). *Collaborative learning techniques: A handbook for college faculty.* San Francisco: Jossey Bass.

Campus Compact. (2000). *Introduction to service-learning toolkit: Readings and resources for faculty.* Providence, RI: Campus Compact.

Campus Compact. (2001). *Service-learning: Using structured reflection to enhance learning from service.* Retrieved from http://www.compact.org/disciplines/reflection/.

Idealist on Campus. *Civic education curriculum.* Retrieved from http://www.idealistoncampus.org/ioc/learn/curriculum/index.html.

National Service-Learning Clearinghouse: http://www.servicelearning.org.

Student Learning and Development
Broido, E. (2000). The development of social justice allies during college: A phenomenological investigation. *Journal of College Student Development, 41,* 3–18.

Jones, S. R., & Hill, K. (2000). Crossing High Street: Understanding diversity through community service-learning. *Journal of College Student Development, 42,* 204–216.

Mezirow, J. (2000). *Learning as transformation: Critical perspectives on a theory in progress.* San Francisco: Jossey-Bass.

Perry, W. G. (1970). *Forms of intellectual and ethical development in the college years: A scheme.* Austin, TX: Holt, Rinehart and Winston.

Rhoads, R. A. (1997). *Community service and higher learning: Explorations of the caring self.* Albany: State University of New York Press.

WORKSHEET 5-1: Intellectual and Moral Development

Perry's (1970) theory of intellectual and moral development asserts that:

- Learning is ego-threatening and involves affective and cognitive challenges;

- Learning moves from concrete and simple thought processes to ones that are more complex;

- As we think with more complexity, moral and ethical skills and attributes come in to play;

- There are nine positions of moral and intellectual development that are repeated throughout our entire lives with different issues, knowledge, and experiences (people are not positions);

- The true work of development occurs as people bridge between positions; and

- The loss and grief involved with development must be honored.

Use the third column to write characteristics of your students that might fit the different positions. How does this information help you think about developing students' critical thinking?

POSITIONS	SUMMARY	YOUR STUDENTS
Dualism Positions 1 & 2	In dualism, a student moves from experiencing no diversity of opinion to a stage where there is definitive right and wrong in opinions. Teachers, parents, peers, and books are experts.	
Multiplicity Positions 3 & 4	In position 3, opinions are seen as right, wrong, or unknown. The student focuses on the process to acquire the "right" information and on fairness. The student is also becoming more comfortable with multiple perspectives. In position 4, the student accepts multiple understandings of knowledge: known, unknown, can be known, will remain unknowable. Emphasis is on either the rightness of one way of thinking or on the equal validity of all ways of thinking.	
Contextual Relativism Positions 5 & 6	In position 5, the student begins to understand that some opinions/knowledge are better than others and that knowledge is developed within a context. "Good" knowledge has the proper context, evidence, support, and justification. As the student moves to 6, he or she begins to understand the need to make a commitment to certain opinions/knowledge.	
Commitment to Relativism Positions 7–9	The student makes initial commitments to an aspect of self or attitude or belief and begins to understand the ramifications of the decision. As commitments deepen and increase in number, additional implications are felt and understood.	

WORKSHEET 5-2: Who Are Teachers and Learners? What Is Knowledge?: A Summary of Baxter Magolda's (1992) Epistemological Reflection Model

Three important elements of educational experiences:

- Confirmation—affirms and supports student learning.

- Contradiction—offers challenges.

- Continuity—provides a familiar base and community for learning.

	ABSOLUTE KNOWING	TRANSITIONAL KNOWING	INDEPENDENT KNOWING	CONTEXTUAL KNOWING
Role of Learner	• Obtain knowledge	• Understand knowledge	• Think for oneself • Share views with others • Create own perspective	• Exchange and compare perspectives • Integrate and apply knowledge
Role of Peers	• Share materials • Explain what they have learned	• Provide active exchanges	• Share views • Serve as a source of knowledge	• Enhance learning via quality contributions
Role of Instructor	• Communicate knowledge • Ensure that students understand knowledge	• Use methods aimed at understanding • Employ methods that help apply knowledge	• Promote independent thinking • Promote exchange of ideas	• Promote application of knowledge in context • Student and teacher critique each other
Nature of Knowledge	• Is certain and absolute	• Is partially certain and partially uncertain	• Is uncertain—everyone has beliefs	• Is contextual—judge on basis of evidence in context

Questions for Facilitators' Consideration

- How would you describe the role of learner, peers, instructor, and knowledge in the programs and courses you facilitate? With which type of learning are these roles most associated?

- How would your students describe their role as learners, and the roles of their peers, instructor, and knowledge for your class or program?

- How do the answers to these two questions help you understand your students and the challenges you hope to create in the learning environment?

WORKSHEET 5-3: Building a Critical Reflection Toolkit: Sample Activities and Assignments

Intentionally planning for reflection and critical thinking in service-learning courses helps faculty broaden their teaching techniques overall. As you read these examples, you may find applications to your courses and programs. The following sample assignments and activities are drawn from a number of resources; see this chapter's reference list for full citations of those that are available.

Several assignments and activities in this section are developed from *Classroom Assessment Techniques* (Angelo & Cross, 1993). *Classroom Assessment Techniques* provides faculty resources and tools for gauging students' level of understanding and engagement in a course. In addition to offering 50 activities and assignments, it includes a self-scored survey designed for faculty to assess their desired learning goals for a specific course. In the examples below, the teaching tool template is applied to a situation specific to service-learning.

Artistic Reflection (Eyler, Giles, & Schmiede, 1996)
The process of artistic reflection challenges students to think metaphorically, conceptually, visually, and through color and line about their service-learning experiences. While artistic expression may be challenging for some students, it allows different learning styles a place in intellectual pursuit. Students may be asked to write a poem, select a song or photo, or draw something that reflects their response to service-learning.

> *Example.* Students have been working with the local food bank to produce public relations projects; additionally, they have performed several hours of direct service at the agency. A photo gallery of this experience might include photos of a truck laden with donations, raw hands from sorting canned goods, or the doorway to a classroom-size walk-in freezer. Students would then explain why these photos are significant. The gallery might be installed at the agency, in the communication department, or in a common area on campus.

Continuous Journal
The continuous journal engages students in crafting a common journal of their service-learning experiences and challenges them to engage each other in questioning. This journal exercise is useful in a virtual or physical space. It might also be adapted into a traveling journal that would be passed among students from week to week. The first journal entry is a question or musing from one person. At the end of the person's entry, he or she poses a question for the next person to answer. Both faculty and students can participate in this journal. At the end of a period of time, faculty might copy the continuous journal and ask students to synthesize their collective learning and reflections.

> *Example.* Opening question: Why is theater a vehicle for social change? The first student answers the question and then ends his/her entry by posing a new question.

(continued)

WORKSHEET

Double-Entry Journal (developed from Angelo & Cross, 1993)
This technique provides detailed feedback to faculty about how students read, analyze, and synthesize the course content and the service-learning/community-based research (CBR) experience. The journal is written on a page that is divided into two vertical columns. There are four steps in this process:

1. Select a short passage that is relatively provocative, or have students recall a specific incident/conversation/experience from the community site.

2. In the left column, ask students to copy short excerpts from the reading or summarize the community experience.

3. In the right column, ask students to explain why they chose the excerpts/experience. They should also comment on their reactions, disagreements, agreements, confusions, and extant questions.

4. Faculty provide feedback on the writing assignment. In the process, faculty learn about what is compelling to students, what texts/experiences they are drawing from for meaning-making, and how well they can integrate course content.

Essay or Journal
Written assignments can be fruitful ways for students to begin to link their service with their learning. The key is to provide enough structure to the assignment to enable students to move beyond "here's what we did and how I felt" to more complex and nuanced understandings and connections.

Original Essay: Write a two-page reflection about your first two weeks of doing service at Food and Friends.

Revised Essay. Write a two-page reflection about the first two weeks of your service in the kitchen and/or with meal deliveries at Food and Friends. Briefly (one paragraph) describe your particular service activities. Spend the remainder of the reflection on the following questions: What questions does this raise for you about the root causes of poverty? What policy frameworks that we have reviewed might help you answer the question?

Everyday Ethical Dilemma (developed from Angelo & Cross, 1993)
Gather a current news article that addresses the course's focus of concern. Ask students to identify the conflicting values at play in the article and how their experiences in service and the classroom readings help them understand the issue.

(continued)

Example. Your students are working in a community family health clinic and are bringing up issues about health care access, information, and affordability. In order to bring a global dimension to the discussion, you might copy a recent newspaper article that explores U.S. federal policy and actions to stem the spread of HIV in Africa. The conversation might then explore different vocations within medicine, the conflicting attitudes about sexuality in multiple cultures, and the connections between providing health care and health care policies.

Gathering Field Data (Eyler, Giles, & Schmiede, 1996)
Data gathering at the service-learning site can be designed as an introduction to the site or neighborhood, a critical piece of ongoing research, or a way for students to apply the theories learned in class to real-life situations.

Example. A project can be created that engages students in observation and conversation with leaders at their service-learning/community-based research sites. The class's collective work becomes a synthesis project that helps students to link ideas about community development/nonprofit management/specific issues with real people and course content.

Gallery Experience (developed from Adams, Bell & Griffin, 1997)
The gallery experience poses a series of questions/statements around the room related to a topic of interest. Ideally, the questions work together to bridge theory and practice and allow for musings about what is known and unknown. Participants are invited to take a place in front of a posted question and are given a period of time to respond. The facilitator then instructs the group to move around the room to answer another question. This round robin continues until all people have the opportunity to respond to all questions. The facilitator asks one person to read the responses on each paper. The group then steps back and discusses the questions and responses of most interest.

Example. Students have been exploring social stratification and simultaneously working in agencies that serve people who are homeless. The questions in the gallery might be:

- Homeless people are…

- What words describe your thoughts about your experience at the agencies?

- What words describe your feelings about your experience at the agencies?

- Why does homelessness exist?

- What role does socioeconomic stratification play in America?

(continued)

WORKSHEET

Invented Dialogue (developed from Angelo & Cross, 1993)
This activity encourages students to integrate the perspectives and knowledge of a variety of sources. Invented dialogues can take place as role-plays or as written papers or journals.

> *Example.* Craft a dialogue about a proposed urban stadium project between a mayor, a city council representative, a business owner who will be displaced by the stadium, and a low-income resident of the city. Their topic of discussion is the development of a stadium for the local national football team—such as the multiple benefits and losses (and for whom), conflicting values, the role of government in private enterprise, and developing the soul of a city.

Letter to the Editor
As a way of formulating an argumentative essay and to model participation in public dialogue, ask students to write a letter to the editor about an issue that links their service experiences with the course content. This may be an academic exercise, or students may be invited to submit their letters for publication.

> *Example.* You and your students have been discussing obstacles non-English speakers encounter in seeking employment. You are also working with adults and children at a local organization that serves a largely Mexican and Mexican-American community. Ask students to write a letter to the editor of two newspapers: your city's mainline newspaper and your Latino-focused newspaper. Invite students to write a commentary about the funding, organization, availability, etc., of English for speakers of other languages (ESOL) education in your community. They may be pro or con any particular aspect; however, the letter must link their experience to the readings of the course.

Misconception/Preconception Check (developed from Angelo & Cross, 1993)
This pre-service activity is a great way to begin to understand what students know and don't know about the issue, people, or environment that will be explored. It also provides the opportunity to engage in an asset-based conversation about the area and population that are the focus of the course. The instructor can engage in conversation about misconceptions/preconceptions, or the exercise might be a quiz created by the instructor, community partners, and/or students.

> *Example.* An instructor whose course includes service-learning or CBR might have students develop a quiz about Oakland/California/etc., education and income levels across the city or state, racial/ethnic demographics, and other items of particular interest, including students' attitudes or experiences of the neighborhood.

(continued)

One-Word Journal (developed from Angelo & Cross, 1993)
In this in-person exercise, students are invited to answer a question using just one word. Students write their one-word response on a sheet of paper. They are then asked to write a paragraph or two that explains why they chose that particular word. Students share their answers in pairs, small groups, or with the entire class.

> *Example.* "Why do most governmental jurisdictions not adopt a living wage policy for hourly employees?" Students write their one-word answer. "Now, write a paragraph or two about why you choose this word."

Pro-Con Grid (developed from Angelo & Cross, 1993)
This activity challenges students to integrate the ideas of several sources and to make initial judgments about the validity and strength of those ideas. The course content as well as service-learning experiences inform the evaluation.

> *Example.* In an article addressing the connections between service-learning and civic engagement, Boyte and Farr (1997) propose three types of citizenship. The pro-con assignment might read: "Using the three conceptions of citizenship presented by Boyte and Farr, construct a matrix that explores the pros and cons of each type of citizenship. Given the pros and cons, what type of citizenship do you think you were taught, either implicitly or explicitly? What type of citizens and citizenship does society need?"

Three-Minute Speeches (from David Sawyer, as cited in Reed and Koliba, 2003)
This exercise invites students to use their own words, stories, and very selves to speak to an issue or experience that is important to them. It also builds a sense of community and encourages deep listening. The instructor poses a common question to the entire group and allows at least 30 minutes for preparation. During the speeches, one person will serve as a timer and give one-minute warnings. When the speaker is done, another student takes the stage. The instructor should ask students to self-identify to be the next speaker based on how their speech "speaks to" the speech that was just given; therefore, the series of speeches combine to produce a threaded narrative. The facilitator should provide appropriate closing remarks at the end of the speeches.

> *Example:* Invite students to craft a three-minute speech on the following question: "What is the key reason you are involved in service work?" Tell students they can relate a story about an event, circumstance, or person who has influenced them, or describe other reasons for doing this work.

CHAPTER SIX

Working with Faculty: Designing Customized Developmental Strategies

Patti H. Clayton and Billy O'Steen

RESISTANCE. SKEPTICISM. CAUTION. CURIOSITY. ENTHUSIASM. Commitment. Faculty members come to professional development related to teaching in general and to civic engagement and service-learning in particular at points all along this spectrum (Ramaley, 2000). They may be interested in implementing service-learning in their teaching, conducting community-based research, mentoring students on co-curricular alternative spring-break trips, advancing engagement within their departments, revising or creating new minors or majors with a civic engagement thread, or collaborating on a publication related to community-engaged teaching and learning. They may work with undergraduates or graduate students, be involved with communities locally or abroad, teach in classroom settings or online. They may come as individuals or as interdisciplinary teams or as departmental cohorts.

In all cases, however, the task of a community service-learning professional (CSLP) is to meet faculty members where they are and to support them in learning what they want and need to learn, often by collaborating with them and learning right along with them. Helping faculty see service-learning's potential for strengthening connections among the various dimensions of their work (e.g., teaching, research, and service) is no simple task, but taking it on can be extraordinarily empowering for everyone involved. Given the pedagogy's extraordinary ability to engage a wide range of constituents, your work with faculty in the context of service-learning and civic engagement will, in turn, touch the people they work with and the structures they work within in significant ways.

In this chapter, we examine our own experiences as service-learning faculty and faculty developers to explore patterns in the dynamics of working with faculty. We share some of our most significant learning through recommendations and questions. As we reflect on our own experiences, we also ask you to engage in a similar analysis of your own faculty, program, and institution. Your reflections on your own story as a CSLP (from Chapter 1) will be helpful here. Through this process, you will both begin to make some of the choices involved in developing your own approaches to working with faculty and come to better understand the choices facing faculty as they integrate service-learning and civic engagement into their courses and research. Ideally, the design of *your* strategies will be shaped by your understanding of the issues at stake in the design of *theirs*.

The anticipated outcomes of this chapter hinge on one primary realization: working effectively with faculty and teaching effectively with service-learning involve *designing customized developmental strategies*. The choices that inform the design require careful consideration of constraints, objectives, and context. Neither CSLPs nor faculty members have complete control over these variables. What we do have, however, is the power to make intentional choices, to adopt an experimental mind-set, to observe outcomes and compare them to objectives, and to revisit and revise our choices. In other words, we need to bring a scholarly mind-set to this work by turning the tasks of working with faculty and teaching with service-learning into opportunities for ongoing learning—ours and theirs. Such intentional design work is key to maximizing the potential of these processes and to ensuring that the quality of our work improves over time.

Each reader of this chapter—like each faculty member you work with—will design customized approaches, suited to your institutional setting and evolving to take advantage of the ever-changing opportunities of that context. While grounded in an understanding of principles of good practice, the strategies that you design for working with faculty and that they, in turn, design for teaching with service-learning should be sensitive to the place, people, and history comprising your context. As Chapter 4 describes, the culture of a land-grant institution is different from that of a research university, an HBCU, or a liberal arts college. A small campus operates differently from a large campus, a rural campus from an urban campus, a residential campus from a commuter campus. Students in engineering, English, or social work bring different skills, backgrounds, questions, and ways of thinking. Tenure-track faculty bring different objectives than tenured or non–tenure-track faculty, just as faculty experienced with non-traditional pedagogies bring different questions than do new faculty. Each service-learning program has grown from unique roots, which shape its evolution in particular ways. Designing a customized process for working with faculty includes allowing for creativity and always being aware of emerging opportunities. The best strategies for working with faculty are intentionally designed yet organic.

Although explicit in the term, it is easily overlooked that faculty development at its best is developmental—for the faculty members who participate and for their curricula and departments. It is also developmental for you as the CSLP and for your service-learning program. To take it one step further, it can be developmental for your institution and even for the academy as a whole. Faculty members are the lifeblood of institutions of higher learning, and as their assumptions, practices, and commitments change, so too does the institution and the academy as a whole—slowly and reluctantly at times, but change it does. Few initiatives have the power to touch an institution at all levels and across all units as thoroughly as service-learning and civic engagement do. We believe that this process of developing self, others, programs, departments, and institutions has tremendous transformative potential.

We have defined your task as designing customized developmental strategies for working with faculty. Our task is to support you in examining some of the most important elements of the journey you are undertaking with your faculty and in applying guiding principles to your work. Accordingly, this chapter is organized into four sections, each of which addresses a question that we have found to be important in our own experiences as service-learning faculty who have also become faculty developers. Each section opens with a reflective vignette from our experiences, offers some analysis of the vignette and considers the implications for designing your strategy for working with faculty, and closes with an opportunity for you to reflect on the content in terms of its application to your own situation.

Before you delve further, we encourage you to recognize that while your work with faculty is influenced by many factors, one of the most important variables is *you*. Who you are, your past experiences, the meaning you have made from those experiences, your skills and convictions, and your priorities will—and we believe, should—affect your choices as you design a strategy for working with faculty. Understanding the interplay between you and your context makes you a more aware, scholarly, and effective designer. Therefore, we suggest that you refer to your reflections from Chapter 1 as you proceed through this chapter. Before examining our first vignette below, please spend a few moments reflecting on the context in which you and your faculty work (see Worksheet 6-1, "Reflection on Your Context," beginning on page 114).

How Can We Best Engage Faculty—Self-Selection, Training the Converted, the Hard Sell, or All of the Above?

BILLY'S REFLECTION: As I sat through the first session of my New Faculty Orientation Day at NC State University, I began to feel somewhat lost and disconnected. I had been an instructor at a community college with 100 faculty members. The sheer size and sprawl of my new institution (33,000 students and 2,000 faculty members) was starting to settle in. The provost facilitated a brief introductory activity that provided me with some names and faces of the 100 or so other new faculty members, but I felt as if I were in freshman orientation again. I knew that the likelihood of getting to know many, if any, of these folks was slim. Thus, it was with this discomfort, disorientation, and a desire for connection that I entered the next phase of our orientation, a "tradeshow" of campus programs related to teaching and learning.

Having done some work in community service in my role as director of an experiential middle school and as site director of an alternative spring break trip in graduate school, I was familiar with the idea of involvement in the community as an educational opportunity. I did not explicitly have any plans to pursue such activities in the teacher education courses I was to offer in the College of Education at NC State, but I was open to the idea. Thus, my ending up at the service-learning display table could be described as intentional serendipity. In a short conversation with the program director, I learned about the range of courses supported by the program and the opportunities for faculty development and support. I came to understand the program's efforts to establish a learning community around this pedagogy. I left the tradeshow with a slightly improved feeling of connecting to someone or something on this large campus.

During the first weeks of classes, while getting used to a new city and a new campus, I accepted an invitation to participate in service-learning faculty training. Although the requirements of the training were not strenuous (one two-hour meeting per week for seven weeks in addition to a service-learning experience on a Saturday), I had been cautioned many times throughout my induction as a new faculty member not to commit to anything that did not directly contribute to my research agenda. At the time, I (and perhaps my colleagues) did not see any potential connections between service-learning and research, as it appeared to be a professional development opportunity focused on teaching. Nonetheless, I began the training believing that I could use service-learning in my work with pre-service and in-service teachers. The most important apparent benefit at the time of the training, however, was the opportunity to connect with faculty members outside of my immediate program—a challenge inherent to a university as large as NC State but common on campuses of all sizes.

When Billy first came to campus as a new faculty member, he had a range of previous experiences that converged to make curricular service-learning an intriguing option. Your faculty, too, will likely come to this work with some relevant background, on your own campus or others, or in their experience as students. Faculty members may be aware of service as a co-curricular activity but not as familiar with its role as pedagogy and scholarship. Their previous experiences will shape their assumptions and expectations and will influence their responsiveness to any particular outreach approach you use. Billy's path to the service-learning program at NC State was a combination of self-selection, training the converted, and selling. Each approach can stand alone, but they also work well in combination, as in Billy's case.

While Billy's personal interest in exploring new teaching philosophies and practices was a critical reason for his participation in professional development and subsequent use of service-learning in his classes, that interest had to be met and nurtured by a faculty development program. For self-selection to work as a method for engaging faculty in service-learning, the program must be visible and must connect with faculty at the right time, when they are receptive and able to invest in learning about it. One particularly good time is when new faculty members are looking for places to connect on their campus and are not yet feeling overwhelmed or overcommitted. Faculty members may also be particularly ready to connect with a community service-learning program when they are approaching review for reappointment, promotion, and tenure, especially if that program supports them in implementing service-learning as a scholarship of teaching and learning (SoTL) or scholarship of engagement activity. Service-learning can contribute to faculty members' portfolios in all their areas of responsibility (teaching, research, and service) and can also help them integrate work across these various arenas; the self-selected may be particularly ready to become involved when they have two or more years to conduct solid work before adding it to their portfolios for review.

Beyond the visibility of a flashy banner or brochures at a tradeshow, the *sharing of products* from other faculty members' involvement with service-learning provides points of entry for "converted" faculty members who don't need a "sell job" but who do need concrete reasons for participating in the face of other demands on their time and attention. Structure opportunities for faculty to learn about their colleagues' involvement—ideally directly from these colleagues (e.g., presenting with experienced faculty members at their own department meeting, or hosting discipline-clustered gatherings with poster or panel presentations by these experienced faculty). When faculty encounter service-learning and civic engagement in the context of their own discipline, their interest and receptivity are often strengthened. Both new and experienced faculty often have a strong desire to connect their various roles and responsibilities. Through a sharing of teaching, research, and service products, CSLPs can effectively recruit the converted by emphasizing the integrative potential of professional development, collaborative research, and cross-departmental collaboration.

No matter how visible your community service-learning program is or how clear the benefits of faculty involvement are (e.g., see Astin, et al., 2000; Eyler et al., 2001; and Eyler & Giles, 1999), some faculty members still need convincing. In some cases, they may even be skeptical or actively resistant. Become familiar with the research on motivations and deterrents, and design your strategy for working with faculty accordingly. One key finding, for example, is that most non-practitioners do not understand the rationale for service-learning (Abes, Jackson, & Jones, 2002). In the same way that training the converted may require you to define and express your program's benefits in new ways, selling service-learning calls for *understanding a faculty member's context* and then explaining how involvement with your program connects to that context.

A very effective way to achieve an intimate knowledge of faculty members' context is simple yet labor-intensive: spend time with them. Get to know faculty members—their interests, concerns, prior experiences, and current objectives—and how they and their departments interpret the appropriate mix of their teaching, research, and service responsibilities. Once you understand their context, you can create ways for your program to support them and, in turn, to support colleagues within and beyond their department. Learning from their colleagues may help to overcome resistance. In addition, help faculty members see you as an educator, scholar, and colleague working alongside them, rather than as an external administrator whom they perceive as disconnected from their daily work.

Remember that it is unreasonable to expect your program to connect meaningfully with every faculty member on your campus. Many who are resistant will likely remain so, despite your best efforts; and you may not be able to identify and support all who are interested. Think strategically about whether there are individual faculty members you especially want to reach out to, because of their influence among their peers, their ability to champion the work among administrators, or the unique experience or perspective they might bring to your program.

Pause here to reflect on the questions of why and how faculty come to service-learning and how your program can support them in doing so on Worksheet 6-2, beginning on page 120.

Once You've Connected with Them, How Can You Best Provide Professional Development and Support to Faculty Members—a Gradual Wade In, an Immersion in the Deep End, or Somewhere in Between?

BILLY'S REFLECTION: "The outer cage is for us to run into in case one of our big cats gets loose," explained the volunteer coordinator. As I shoveled the concrete mixture into a trench to shore up the foundation for this outer cage, the statement made our work particularly relevant—if not for us, then for other less fortunate visitors to the facility. Our work that morning at the unique compound dedicated to preserving endangered species of carnivores, including leopards and tigers, did not entail any dramatic dashes away from a big cat. What it did entail was an opportunity to provide much-needed service to a community organization, while serving simultaneously as a vehicle both for probing, firsthand, the topic of ethics and building community by working with a team of previously unfamiliar faculty colleagues. What resulted was a strong conviction about the power of service-learning.

After a brief introduction to key concepts in environmental ethics and a pre-service reflection on our expectations about the facility after perusing the Web page, colleagues from the College of Engineering and the College of Agriculture and Life Sciences as well as from Student Health Services joined me for this morning of service in our local community, followed by an afternoon of reflection on campus. My team's work at this volunteer-run organization brought to life what had only existed as isolated and somewhat simplistic academic concepts in ethical theory in a way that classroom lecture and discussion could not. By performing necessary repair work so the organization could be designated by the U.S. Department of Agriculture as an educational institution and could gain opportunities for much-needed funding, I experienced firsthand the direct impact of individual efforts on resource-limited community organizations.

From the stories of tigers that had been illegally imported and then abandoned on the streets of our country's largest cities, I saw the links between individual choices and large-scale social and ecological issues. In debating cage size versus the number of animals housed at the compound, I struggled with the trade-offs and hard choices that characterize ethical decision-making. And through the eyes of a snow leopard whose natural habitat is not central North Carolina but rather the high mountains of Nepal, I saw the links between resource consumption and habitat destruction and the injustices inflicted on humans and non-humans alike.

During the afternoon reflection session, I became more empathetic and understanding of my teammates' views (often quite different from my own). I realized that a colleague with vastly different expectations and experiences with zoo-like facilities could reach and defend entirely different conclusions regarding appropriate trade-offs in the treatment of the animals. Thus, the progression of the day—academic content, pre-service reflection, service experience, and post-service reflection—led me to a better understanding of my larger community, my teammates, ethics, and my own values and convictions.

This service-learning immersion experience was a component of the semester-long faculty development workshop series. The immersion experience that launched this training confirmed the power of a well-crafted service-learning experience, helped me to better understand the type of process I was inviting my students to participate in and how it would challenge them, and grounded my syllabus redesign work in the subsequent workshops with a concrete example of the dynamics of service-learning pedagogy.

Billy's experience represents one particularly dramatic approach to service-learning faculty development, but it is not the only one. One way to think of the range of approaches is along a continuum of intensity levels of such variables as:

- Time required of participants and facilitator(s);

- Financial expenses;

- Number and type of people involved in planning and implementation (students? community members? administrators? experienced faculty? program staff?);

- Depth and breadth of learning outcomes; and

- Prerequisite level of experience desired for participants.

The following box, "A Continuum of Approaches to Faculty Development," illustrates a wide range of faculty development activities, from lower to higher levels of intensity.

A Continuum of Approaches to Faculty Development

- An email message to faculty with links to online information on service-learning.

- A one-on-one conversation with a faculty member in your or his/her office.

- A 30-minute presentation at a departmental meeting.

- A set of materials on your webpage for faculty to download.

- A one-hour workshop, "Introduction to Service-Learning" or "Service-Learning in Your Discipline."

- A small resource library with books for faculty to borrow.

- A luncheon with an informative program for faculty and community partners.

- A three-hour workshop, "Designing a Service-Learning–Enhanced Course," "Designing Reflection in Service-Learning for Civic Learning," or "Establishing and Maintaining Community Partnerships."

- A half-day workshop, "Service-Learning 101" or "Community-Based Research 101."

- A three-hour van trip, visiting several community organizations.

- A full-day immersion in a service-learning process (as in Billy's vignette).

- A semester-long series of brown-bag lunches, in which faculty gather to discuss a set of readings and their own experiences as service-learning instructors and/or community-based researchers.

- A semester-long workshop series, or a three-day retreat, during which faculty revise a syllabus or write a grant proposal for a new collaborative research project.

- A year-long learning community process, in which faculty work together on a common project such as redesigning their departmental curriculum for cross-course sequencing of service-learning.

- An ongoing scholarship of teaching and learning (SoTL) project, in which faculty co-author articles, present at conferences, conduct research with colleagues on their own or other campuses, and/or develop new professional development opportunities and implement them among their own colleagues.

How intensive an approach is possible and appropriate depends on many factors, including the priorities, financial resources, and staffing of your service-learning program. For some programs, faculty development is the central focus, and a range of opportunities is regularly offered by experienced faculty or staff. Others focus primarily on placing students in the community and offer little support to faculty in developing courses or otherwise engaging with service-learning and civic engagement as scholars. Even in this latter case, however, you can work with faculty in a meaningful way: you can help them to better understand good practices for managing placements, to develop ways to evaluate the quality of the experience with community partners, or to move from placements to true partnerships, for example. Regardless of a program's historical focus, we suggest that faculty development be a part of the mission of the CSLP, because it is key to effective implementation of the pedagogy and to the affiliated institutional change processes. Even if supporting faculty in integrating service-learning into their courses is not your core mission, your work with faculty can accomplish other goals, such as nurturing a campus culture of civic engagement and increasing the general level of awareness of service-learning.

The approach, or mix of approaches, most appropriate for a particular faculty member or group of faculty members is also determined partly by the level and nature of their interest. In this way, the range of intensity and interest levels is linked to the developmental possibilities of working with faculty, with less intense approaches often better suited to faculty with low levels of experience or interest, and more intense approaches often most appropriate for those with greater experience and interest in investing in service-learning. We often think in terms of supporting *a developmental journey* among our faculty members—meeting them where they are and offering them ever-more intense opportunities for involvement—and we realize and accept that fewer and fewer faculty will move on through each increasingly intense stage of the journey.

For example, if you have an opportunity to speak to a general audience or to a departmental meeting for a short time, then designing a 30-minute introductory presentation, with examples from disciplines represented in the audience, may be the best approach. If some in the audience express interest in learning more, you can follow up by inviting them to your website or resource library. If you have access to more of their time, you could offer a two- or three-hour workshop or even a full-day immersion that builds on the initial presentation. If some participants become seriously interested in integrating service-learning into their courses—or if a department is interested in curricular revision—then a retreat or workshop series may best meet their goals. Once faculty have taught with service-learning, then an advanced workshop, a faculty learning community process, or a SoTL project can help them take their implementation to new levels; and leadership roles through which these experienced faculty members help recruit colleagues and co-facilitate professional development activities can bring their journey full circle as they enable others to journey with them.

Remember that the task here is to design customized developmental processes for working with faculty (see Worksheet 6-3, "Reflection on Process Design," beginning on page 123). This involves making choices that are driven by the particulars of a given context, including a range of variables, only some of which are under your control: Who are your faculty members and what do they bring to the process? Who are you and what do you bring? What are the goals—yours, theirs, the institution's, the community's? What are the constraints under which your design must operate? What are the most salient issues for this particular individual or group at this particular time in their professional development—definitions, course design, reflection, partnerships, assessment, mentoring, scholarship, or other issues?

Regardless of the approach you design for a particular faculty development opportunity, there are some best practices to use across approaches. We describe two here.

Inviting Faculty into Roles as Learners

Billy's experience was a powerful approach to faculty development because he and his colleagues were immersed in the service-learning process as students themselves, which clarified some of the challenges and opportunities in the pedagogy. In this case, faculty participants attended an initial introductory workshop, undertook the immersion experience (which included academic material, relevant service, reflection, and a debriefing of the process as a microcosm of service-learning), and then completed a series of six additional workshops before presenting their revised syllabi to one another and to the facilitators for feedback. The immersion served to ground the rest of the training process, giving participants firsthand exposure to the implications of their various design choices and concrete examples of the issues to consider (such as reflection and working with community partners). Immersion can take many forms and can target different learning objectives, some requiring less than a full-day experience. For example, the first hour of a three-hour workshop can be devoted to giving faculty a task designed to raise key elements of the session's content, followed by reflection on that task. Such an approach enables faculty members to experience activities that they can adapt for their own uses. It also reminds them what it is like to be a student in an unfamiliar learning environment and sensitizes them to the challenges their students may face.

Modeling the Pedagogy

Designing a workshop to include reflection on an experience as a way of inductively raising content-related issues is an example of modeling the pedagogy, a best practice in faculty development. It is helpful to design a professional development activity in a way that parallels the course design process and to make this process visible to the participants. As a designer and facilitator of a learning process, ask yourself in advance (and perhaps ask the participants as well):

- What are our learning goals?

- How do these goals translate into assessable objectives?

- What teaching and learning strategies are well matched to these objectives, and how can we best implement them in this context?

- How will we assess learning? What other outcomes are we going to assess?

- How will I reflect on the workshop in order to improve my own practice as a facilitator in the future?

Modeling this process for faculty participants can encourage them to do the same with their service-learning–enhanced courses. Any well-designed faculty development program, and any attempt to implement a new pedagogy in the classroom, offers opportunities for experiential learning by faculty. Therefore, another dimension of modeling the pedagogy is to facilitate participants' careful reflection on their experiences, in accordance with the learning goals, and to enable them to identify specific implications for changes in their future teaching (see Clayton & Ash, 2005).

This use of reflection to support ongoing learning and improvement in the faculty development process is applicable with faculty at any stage, new or experienced. It is one of many ways in which faculty development can be structured in accordance with Kolb's learning cycle (described in Chapter 5) and thus embody the same understanding of learning that is at the heart of service-learning and other civically engaged pedagogies (see Bringle, Hatcher, Jones, & Plater, 2006). In designing your strategy for working with faculty, think carefully about how best to meet them where they are—in terms of experience, interest, learning style—and how to create opportunities for them to expand and deepen their involvement over time. Like students, faculty are at different levels of readiness and have different objectives. Our approaches to faculty development, therefore, should be targeted, to the extent feasible, specifically to the developmental level of the particular faculty member. Given that resources for this work are often scarce, you may be unable to work continuously and equally with groups of faculty across the developmental spectrum. New programs may direct more effort toward introducing new faculty to service-learning as a pedagogy, while more established programs may evolve with their faculty and focus more attention on the scholarship of teaching and learning and/or the scholarship of engagement.

Using Worksheet 6-4, beginning on page 125, take some time to reflect on this discussion of the spectrum of approaches to faculty development as it applies to your own situation.

Now That Faculty Are at the Table, What Is It They Most Want and Need to Learn?

PATTI'S REFLECTION: About a month into the semester, at an evening tutorial, I was sitting with a group of students in my course on the relationships among science, technology, and society. My heart broke as I saw tears of frustration on their faces and heard confusion and disempowerment in their voices. I had just given them my feedback on their first round of reflection products and their first drafts of group progress reports. My injunction to revisit some of their assumptions and to rewrite accordingly pushed them over the edge. They concluded that they didn't understand what we were doing in the class, and worse, they thought they couldn't do it. Over the next several days, we talked, one-on-one and as a class. We re-read what they had written and processed my feedback. We went back to the fundamentals of service-learning. And together we had an epiphany of sorts: service-learning was confronting all of us with the need to teach, learn, and serve in different, unaccustomed ways. We had to learn new ways of thinking and acting.

The students listed the ways in which service-learning was different from their more traditional classroom experiences. They were accustomed to instructors telling them what they needed to know; here they were being asked to articulate their own learning. They were used to being fairly passive and reactive in class; here they were as responsible for making class discussions productive as I was. They were used to objectives and methods that were determined for them; here they were asked to co-create a shared understanding of goals and strategies. They were accustomed to an instructor evaluating their progress; here they also needed to evaluate their own progress—individually and as a team—and to initiate necessary changes. They were used to writing what they had already learned and submitting it for a grade; I was asking them to continue learning through the process of writing and rewriting.

Their list grew and grew as the semester progressed, until at the end they proposed turning their thinking into an activity at our end-of-year Celebration of Service-Learning. They wanted to stimulate other instructors and students to think about their own service-learning experiences in light of the challenges presented by their non-traditional nature. These students launched a project focused on examining what they called "shifts in perspective and practice required for and fostered by service-learning," and they gave some preliminary suggestions for how we might prepare ourselves to make these shifts in our classrooms and in our faculty development processes. From the night my heart broke to the afternoon at the end of the semester when it swelled with pride in my students and a greater sense of community than I had ever felt with students before, my journey has made me a much more effective service-learning instructor and CSLP.

Patti's story suggests an underlying dynamic that faculty need to be aware of as they begin to teach with service-learning: whatever the nature of the faculty development they have undertaken in order to prepare themselves, *teaching with service-learning will itself be their most significant opportunity to learn about the pedagogy and how to implement it effectively.* They need to be open to this possibility and to be as reflective on their teaching experience as they ask their students to be in their service-learning experiences.

Patti also learned the importance of *making visible to our students the nature of, and rationale for, service-learning,* which requires much more than an introductory reading or presentation during the first week of class. It demands revisiting the nature of service-learning as the semester unfolds and students encounter more aspects of the process.

Perhaps the single most important characteristic of service-learning that needs to be visible—to students but also to faculty—is its non-traditional, *"counter-normative"* nature (Howard, 1998). Remember your own undergraduate experience, or ask students to tell you about theirs. When asked to identify the defining elements of traditional teaching and learning, many of us will generate similar lists that include students as passive receptacles of information, knowledge as residing in textbooks and in the mind of the instructor, and learning as memorization evaluated by regurgitation. Service-learning violates these norms in subtle and not so subtle ways. Students are producers rather than merely consumers of knowledge. Knowledge resides in the community and in the students as well as in books and in the minds of instructors. Learning is accomplished through critical reflection on experience, not only by listening and reading. Learning is less about facts and more about connections among ideas, application, and making informed judgments. Teaching is less about sharing expertise than about designing contexts within which certain types of experiences occur and facilitating the collective making of meaning.

Because most instructors and students come to service-learning with traditional expectations and norms, they need to develop different perspectives (or understandings) and practices (or behaviors). They need to build their own and each other's capacities to teach, learn, and serve in new ways. Doing so will help them be more successful in undertaking service-learning and help them fully maximize the transformational potential of the pedagogy: to become self-directed learners, critical thinkers, effective citizens, and skilled professionals (Clayton & Ash, 2004).

What important principles of teaching with service-learning should you share as part of your strategy for working with faculty, given that they will be challenged to teach—and to think about their teaching—in different ways? We discuss six key ideas for faculty to be aware of as they begin teaching with service-learning:

1. The service-learning component of a course—whether short-term or semester-long—must be carefully *integrated* into the rest of the course, not added on. Regardless of its intensity (e.g., number of service hours or degree of student responsibility), the students' experience in the community is to serve as a text, similar to readings or other sources of information. Service-learning is generally combined with other pedagogies, such as interactive lectures, library or Internet research, class discussions, interviews, or other data collection. Thus, a new service-learning instructor will likely appreciate your support in weaving the various elements of the course together into a seamless learning process. We believe this process of integration is driven by the same questions we pose in Worksheet 6-3 (about objectives, constraints, etc.). In guiding faculty through these design choices, you can help them view service-learning as an alternative way of accomplishing some of the same objectives as their current approaches, and you can support them in making any associated trade-offs (such as giving up some readings to allow room for the service experience or replacing a research paper with an intensive, guided journal that draws on readings, research, and the service experience).

2. Service-learning is *academically grounded.* Just as credit is not given for reading a book but rather for the quality of analysis demonstrated in an essay, credit is given not for service but rather for the demonstration of learning through reflection on the service. Faculty often need support in making close connections between their course content and the service-learning experiences they design for students. The more explicit they are in their academic learning objectives and the more involved they are with community partners and students in designing service-learning activities accordingly, the better able they will be to make such connections.

3. By definition, service-learning is oriented toward *civic learning* as well as mastery of course material. Disciplines and their practitioners have public purposes; they connect in meaningful ways with societal issues and concerns. Faculty members need to be clear, in their own minds and with their students, that academic learning is connected to civic learning and that developing the knowledge, skills, dispositions, and behaviors of citizens and civic-minded professionals is an important objective of service-learning (Saltmarsh, 2005). The topic of civic learning and engagement is further addressed in Chapter 11.

4. Faculty need to understand and *use reflection as a rigorous teaching and learning strategy.* Many may dismiss or minimize this element of service-learning because they may not feel confident in facilitating or evaluating it or because they associate it with a "touchy-feely," stream-of-consciousness diary. The key to integrating service-learning into a course and to generating powerful academic and civic learning is well-structured reflection (Ash, Clayton, & Moses, 2009; Ash, Clayton, & Atkinson, 2005; Ash & Clayton, 2004; Hatcher, Bringle, & Muthiah, 2004; Eyler & Giles, 1999; Eyler, Giles, & Schmiede, 1996). Your own use of reflection in faculty development, therefore, becomes important in helping faculty see the possible outcomes of reflection and think creatively about appropri-

ate ways to implement it. Connecting reflection with assessment can help faculty realize that reflection generates, deepens, and documents learning and therefore is the vehicle for improving the quality of both learning and service (Ash, Clayton, & Moses, 2009; Ash, Clayton, & Atkinson, 2005; Clayton et al, 2005; Ash & Clayton, 2004). See Chapter 5 for a more extensive discussion of reflection.

5. *Bringing other voices into the work* of educating students may be unfamiliar and uncomfortable for some faculty. Service-learning is a partnership process, and at its best it positions students, faculty/staff, and community members as co-educators, co-learners, and co-generators of knowledge (see Chapter 8 for a discussion of community partnerships). The extent to which faculty members invest in the creation and maintenance of relationships with community members and collaborate with them in the design and delivery of their courses varies widely. Some faculty you work with will already have research or other projects underway in the community and may therefore be receptive to and capable of bringing their students into these relationships. Others will want to rely heavily on you to handle this part of the service-learning process for them. One of the most difficult aspects of your work with faculty may be crafting an appropriate balance between providing support for the partnering process and ensuring the necessary level of faculty involvement in the process (Clayton & Moses, 2006). A second important issue here is the role of student voice and student leadership. Part of your work with faculty is to help them see students as colleagues who bring their own objectives for learning and service to the service-learning classroom and who, as peer leaders, can add unique and valuable features to the design and delivery of service-learning courses and community engaged scholarship (Zlotkowski, Longo, & Williams, 2006).

6. *Faculty need to build their students' capacities to undertake service-learning successfully.* Appropriately designed activities on the first day of class can help prepare students for the non-traditional nature of the service-learning classroom, for the challenges of collaborating with others, and for dealing with ambiguity in problem and role definition (Ash, Clayton, & Moses, 2009; Clayton & Moses, 2006). Research into issues facing their community partners and structured onsite orientations can help students become more effective in interacting with the population they seek to serve. Reflection on group dynamics can help them to anticipate and deal with some of the obstacles they may face in project management. Role-playing can sensitize them to the importance of a thoughtfully designed entry into and exit from the community. Helping faculty who are new to the pedagogy design these and other capacity-building activities into their syllabus will make their initial implementations of service-learning more successful for everyone. You can help them see connections between their own efforts to teach in an unfamiliar, non-traditional way and their students' need to learn and serve in equally unfamiliar ways (Clayton & Ash, 2004).

To help apply these principles of designing and implementing service-learning to your own work with faculty on your campus, see Worksheet 6-5, beginning on page 128.

How Can You Help Faculty Refine Their Service-Learning and Civic Engagement Work through Integration of Their Teaching, Research, and Service?

BILLY'S REFLECTION: Service-learning has been quite a journey for me, having started as a new faculty member who came to a large research university and early on began to find a sense of community through service-learning and now having become a faculty developer who creates communities for and with faculty engaged in a variety of pedagogies. The journey has certainly been central to my growth as an educator, scholar, and citizen.

During one part of that journey, the rain loudly struck the metal roof of our sheltered platform in the middle of the Appalachian Mountains, and I began the familiar process of facilitating a small-group reflection session as I had learned it from the NC State Service-Learning Program. That I used this process during my work with primary-school, middle-school, high-school, and university teachers on their eight-day Outward Bound professional development course was a testament to the level at which service-learning philosophy and practice, like the soaking summer rain around us, had come to permeate my life as an educator. However, as a faculty member at a research-focused university, a development in my teaching could—and indeed, had to, if I were to succeed professionally—also serve me in my other roles.

In another part of the journey, I left the bright, warm sunshine of a Florida afternoon and reluctantly entered the dark, cool convention center to prepare for my presentation at an academic conference on staff development. The artificial climate of the meeting room was slowly transformed into warmer, authentic space as the participants engaged in the activities I was facilitating. Their engagement stemmed from both the interactivity of the group exercises and the content we began to discuss, which focused on my research on sustaining faculty interest in service-learning over time. The participants at this conference, most of whom were staff developers, addressed a key question on how to maintain interest in any pedagogical innovation.

My findings from this research were later applied to my work with colleagues in the College of Education as a Service-Learning Program Faculty Fellow. I recruited a group to participate in a special workshop series, offered exclusively to these faculty and emphasizing examples from middle-school teacher education. During those few weeks, my colleagues and I thought about how we might use the vertical integration of service-learning to better connect the range of curricular and co-curricular experiences pre-service teachers must undertake. Through this integration of teaching, research, and service, I learned much about the challenges facing faculty developers and CSLPs, all of which is serving me well in my current role in the University Centre for Teaching and Learning at the University of Canterbury in New Zealand.

Beyond the pedagogical benefits Billy gained from adopting the principles of service-learning in his teaching, his position as a tenure-track faculty member prompted him to seek further integration of civic engagement into his research. For Billy, this *progression from engaging with service-learning as an instructor to engaging with it as a scholar* was realized through opportunities to do research for and with the Service-Learning Program as a Faculty Fellow. The program offered a range of faculty development opportunities, structured along a developmental trajectory so that instructors had ever more intensive and more highly responsible ways to work in the arena of civic engagement. As his example illustrates, faculty members who have taught with service-learning and want not only to refine their implementation but also to connect the pedagogy to their roles as scholars can come together to form a learning community or community of practice and/or take on positions with a service-learning program as Faculty Fellows or Senior Scholars or Faculty Liaisons (or whatever title is most appropriate for your program and their responsibilities). They can provide leadership to your program (e.g., co-facilitating faculty training, serving as liaisons to their academic units, participating in strategic planning) and conduct research at the interface of their professional interests and the program's needs (e.g., for assessment data). In summary, you might choose to structure your work with experienced faculty in order to support their ongoing learning and growth. Not only will the faculty member benefit from such an arrangement but you may find this to be a way in which your program can become more scholarly in orientation.

You can also broadly support faculty in connecting their work as teachers to their work as scholars by: (1) helping them find opportunities to publish and present their work; (2) helping them partner with colleagues doing similar work in other departments on campus and at other universities in a process that produces and disseminates scholarly products; and (3) creating opportunities on your own campus (e.g., forums, mini-conferences, poster sessions) for them to learn about and present their work as the scholarship of teaching and learning and the scholarship of engagement. As an example, for Patti, her students' "shifts in perspective and practice" project became one of her program's SoTL projects, generating an article in a peer-reviewed journal, several conference presentations, and an ongoing research agenda; in conjunction with the program's focus on critical reflection, this "shifts" project led to the development and dissemination of a capacity-building tutorial on reflection and associated faculty development workshops and inter-institutional research projects. Sharing examples such as this with your faculty and structuring opportunities for them to undertake their own unique versions of civic engagement as scholarship will help them to envision possibilities for themselves and for your program. Use Worksheet 6-6 (beginning on page 131) to brainstorm such potential enhancements, followed by Worksheet 6-7 (beginning on page 134) as a final reflection on all six exercises in this chapter; keep in mind the key ideas from the discussion in this chapter, in the box on the following page, as you turn to Worksheet 6-7.

Conclusion

PATTI'S REFLECTION: Almost a decade ago, one of my students remarked, "It never occurred to me to talk to a professor about my life. Students and professors are not on the same side." I now realize that this comment, which reflected the student's perception of the university as an uncaring community—actually, not as a community at all— was a seminal moment for me. It led me not only in the direction of service-learning but also to an approach to working with students and faculty that has community building at its core. From its inception, the program I led was conceived as an intentional attempt to nurture a sense of community and an awareness of shared goals and shared responsibility. At its heart, it entwined faculty development and student leadership development.

The primary vehicle for development on both fronts was a mentoring community in which students and faculty came together to learn more about and advance service-learning. The word we came to use to express this fundamental orientation is co-creation. Our courses, our training processes, and our scholarship were co-created—from origination of ideas, to development and implementation, through evaluation and revision—by students and faculty (and, to a lesser extent, by community partners). Several years into our program, I worked with three student leaders to co-author a book chapter on their "developmental journey" with service-learning (Whitney, McClure, Respet, & Clayton, 2007). These students speak of myriad collaborations with faculty, staff, and other students as their engagement with service-learning evolved, and conclude that:

Key Points

1. Working with faculty involves designing customized, developmental processes.

2. Key in connecting with faculty are:
   - Having a visible program;
   - Choosing the "right" timing for faculty members;
   - Sharing their colleagues' work as examples;
   - Attending to the faculty member's context; and
   - Positioning yourself as their colleague rather than as an outside administrator.

3. You have a wide range of faculty development activities to choose from as you design your strategy, informed by the nature of your program and the level of interest of faculty members.

4. Two good practices in working with faculty are:
   - Invite them to become learners; and
   - Model the pedagogy.

5. Important messages you can share with faculty include:
   - Teaching reflectively with service-learning will itself be their most significant opportunity to learn about the pedagogy.
   - Make visible to students the nature of and rationale for service-learning.
   - Take advantage of and build capacity for the counter-normative nature of service-learning.

6. Characteristics of service-learning at its best that you should share include:
   - Integration of service and learning;
   - Academically grounded;
   - Oriented toward civic as well as academic learning;
   - Reflection as a rigorous teaching and learning strategy; and
   - Integration of multiple voices (including students and community members).

7. With your support, faculty can undertake a developmental journey, progressing from engaging with service-learning as instructors to engaging with it as scholars.

8. Key implications for you as a CSLP:
   - You yourself are a key variable in your work with faculty.
   - Your own growth is as much at stake as is that of the faculty you work with.
   - Through your work with faculty you can help transform your program, your institution, and higher education as a whole.

Each step along the way was supported in important ways by a network of relationships. We have each mentored and been mentored, challenged others and been challenged in our turn, given and received support. The growth of one has therefore been intimately linked to—indeed, interdependent with—the growth of another. Thus, in our experience, tapping the developmental potential of service-learning involves not only a journey through increasing levels of contribution, investment, responsibility, and ownership but a *shared* journey. (p. 194)

My work as a CSLP has been strongly oriented toward modeling such collaboration and supporting students and faculty in experimenting with and fully realizing its transformative potential. If nothing else, we know that not only are we "on the same side," but in fact there are no "sides" in this work: there is a community of learning and mentoring. And as we expand and deepen that community, students, faculty, staff, and community members grow together in our capacities as co-educators, co-learners, and co-generators of knowledge.

Within any collaborative endeavor—teaching a workshop on literature analysis to undergraduates, advising a doctoral dissertation, or educating faculty members about civic engagement and service-learning—authentic interaction and shared ownership must be created and sustained. Thus, perhaps the most important dimension of your work with faculty is to support the formation of a learning community, one that embodies and in turn enables the fundamental democratic orientation of service-learning. You may find, as we have, that defining your work with faculty as focused on community building and shared voice and mutual transformation is both a successful strategy for building your program and a rewarding approach to your role. Bringle et al. (2006) suggest that faculty development be "coordinated with other institutional activities such as curricular reform (e.g., learning communities, capstone courses, honors program), institutional assessment and accreditation, budgeting, revising campus mission statement, strategic planning, and developing interdisciplinary approaches to civic engagement." In summary, the CSLP need not be alone in the effort to nurture a culture of civic engagement through work with faculty.

As service-learning educators who work with both students and faculty, our energy is often focused on spreading the word about the value we see in using the tenets of service-learning pedagogy. So it is challenging and frustrating when some of our faculty colleagues don't seem to hear the same clarion call that we do. Although working with faculty in the developmental and contextual manner suggested in this chapter can help them to join us in the community of civic engagement on our campuses and in our communities, we must remind ourselves of, and repeatedly share with others, the reasons we're doing this work.

The headlines of newspapers or news websites on any given day provide evidence that we live in a world struggling to find common ground and in much need of empathy. There are no silver bullets, particularly in education, but civic engagement is an opportunity to create context for the content, with the goal of making a connection that will lead to more engaged, more empathetic faculty members and students. The task of working with faculty may be among the most fulfilling, transformative dimensions of your role as a CSLP; it is one of the many ways in which you "help education bring more light and life to the world" (Palmer, 1998, p. 7).

Acknowledgment

The authors wish to thank Bob Bringle and Barbara Jacoby for comments that significantly enhanced this chapter.

References

Abes, E. S., Jackson, G., & Jones, S. R. (2002). Factors that motivate and deter faculty use of service learning. *Michigan Journal of Community Service-Learning, 9,* 1.

Ash, S. L., & Clayton, P. H. (2004). The articulated learning: An approach to reflection and assessment. *Innovative Higher Education, 29*(2), 137–154.

Ash, S. L., Clayton, P. H., & Atkinson, M. P. (2005). Integrating reflection and assessment to improve and capture student learning. *Michigan Journal of Community Service Learning, 11*(2), 49–60.

Ash, S., Clayton, P., & Moses, M. (2009). *Learning through critical reflection: A tutorial for students in service-learning (instructor's version).* Raleigh, NC: Center for Excellence in Curricular Engagement, NC State University.

Astin, A. W., Vogelgesang, L. J., Ikeda, E. K., & Yee, J.A. (2000). *How service learning affects students.* Los Angeles, CA: UCLA Higher Education Research Institute.

Bringle, R. G., Hatcher, J. A., Jones, S., & Plater, W. A. (2006). Sustaining civic engagement: Faculty development, roles, and rewards. *Metropolitan Universities: An International Forum, 17*(1), 62–74.

Clayton, P. H. & Ash, S. L. (2004). Shifts in perspective: Capitalizing on the counter-normative nature of service-learning. *Michigan Journal of Community Service-Learning, 11*(1), 59–70.

Clayton, P. H. & Ash, S. L. (2005). Reflection as a key component in faculty development. *On the Horizon, 13*(3), 161–169.

Clayton, P. H., Ash, S. L., Bullard, L. G., Bullock, B. P., Day, M. G., Moore, A. C., O'Steen, W.L., Stallings, S.P. & Usry, R. H. (2005). Adapting a core service-learning model for wide-ranging implementation: An institutional case study. *Creative College Teaching, 2*(1), 10–26.

Clayton, P.H. & Moses, M.G. (2006). *Integrating service-learning: A resource guide.* Boston, MA: Jumpstart.

Eyler, J. S., & Giles, D. E. (1999). *Where's the learning in service-learning?* San Francisco: Jossey-Bass.

Eyler, J. S., Giles, D. E., & Schmiede, A. (1996). *A practitioner's guide to reflection in service-learning.* Nashville, TN: Vanderbilt University.

Eyler, J. S., Giles, D. E., Stenston, C. M., & Gray, C. J. (2001). At a Glance: *What we know about the effects of service-learning on college students, faculty, institutions, and communities, 1993–2000: Third Edition.* Nashville, TN: Vanderbilt University.

Hatcher, J. A., Bringle, R. G., & Muthiah, R. (2004). Designing effective reflection: What matters to service-learning? *Michigan Journal of Community Service Learning, 11*(2), 38–46.

Howard, J. (1998). Academic service learning: A counternormative pedagogy. In R. Rhoads & J. Howard (Eds.), *New directions for teaching and learning,* 73. San Francisco: Jossey-Bass, 21–29.

Palmer, P. (1998). *The courage to teach: Exploring the inner landscape of a teacher's life.* San Francisco: Jossey-Bass.

Ramaley, J. (2000). Embracing civic responsibility. *Campus Compact Reader, 1*(2), 1–5.

Saltmarsh, J. (2005). The civic promise of service-learning. *Liberal Education, 91*(2), 50–55.

Whitney, B.C, McClure, J.D., Respet, A. & Clayton, P.H. (2007). Service-learning as a shared developmental journey: Tapping the potential of the pedagogy. In L. McIlrath, & I. MacLabhrainn (Eds.). *Higher education and civic engagement: International perspectives.* Burlington, VT: Ashgate, 185–196.

Wiggins, G., & McTighe, J. (1998). *Understanding by design.* Alexandria, VA: Association for Supervision and Curriculum Development.

Zlotkowski, E., Longo, N.V., & Williams, J.R. (Eds.). (2006). *Students as colleagues: Expanding the circle of service-learning leadership.* Providence, RI: Campus Compact.

Additional Resources

Battistoni, R. (2002). *Civic engagement across the curriculum: A resource book for service-learning faculty in all disciplines.* Providence, RI: Campus Compact.

Campus Compact syllabi collection (available at www.compact.org/category/syllabi). More than 300 syllabi, sortable by discipline.

Howard, J. *Michigan Journal for Community Service Learning Course Design Workbook.* Fall 2001.

McTighe, W., Wiggins, G., & McTighe, J. (1998). *Understanding by design.* Alexandria, VA: Association for Supervision and Curriculum Development. (An excellent overview of cutting-edge thinking on course design in general, not specific to service-learning.)

Michigan Journal of Community Service Learning. University of Michigan, OCSL Press.

National Service-Learning Clearinghouse: http://www.servicelearning.org.

Service-Learning in the Disciplines Series, E. Zlotkowski (Ed.) (formerly AAHE, now published by Stylus Publishing: Sterling, VA). Multivolume set. Each volume is a collection of articles by practitioners within a discipline on their implementation of service-learning. See http://styluspub.com.

WORKSHEET

WORKSHEET 6-1: Reflection on Your Context

I. YOUR INSTITUTIONAL CONTEXT

A. *What?* Describe your institution.

• How many students? How many faculty?

_____

• Is its culture more focused on research, on teaching, or on service? What types of work primarily drive faculty tenure processes?

_____

_____

_____

_____

• Is it rural? Urban? Suburban?

_____

• Does it have a strong public mission? How connected to the community is it, and in what ways?

_____

_____

_____

_____

• What are the primary issues facing the local community surrounding the campus?

_____

_____

_____

_____

(continued)

- Who are the students it serves? Traditional? Nontraditional? First generation? Commuter?

  _____

- What range of majors does it offer students?

  _____

  _____

  _____

B. *So what?* Examine the institutional context in terms of implications for your work with faculty.

- How do you believe your work is different on this campus than it would be on another campus? In what ways is it the same, regardless of institution?

  _____

  _____

  _____

  _____

- In what ways is the culture of your institution conducive to service-learning? In what ways is it not?

  _____

  _____

  _____

  _____

- To what extent are civic engagement in general and service-learning in particular understood by students, by faculty, by staff, by administrators, and by the community?

  _____

  _____

  _____

  _____

(continued)

WORKSHEET

- What are the primary challenges your faculty face in teaching with service-learning, conducting community-based research, and so on as a function of the specifics of your institution?

  _____

  _____

  _____

  _____

- What primary challenges do you face in working with faculty, as a function of the specifics of your institution?

  _____

  _____

  _____

  _____

C. _Now what?_ What questions or concerns do you especially need to bring to your reading of this chapter?

  _____

  _____

  _____

  _____

II. YOUR PROGRAMMATIC CONTEXT

A. _What?_ Describe your community service-learning program.

- What are the highlights of the program's history?

  _____

  _____

  _____

  _____

(continued)

- Where is it housed?

  _____

- How many staff people does it have? What are your and their backgrounds?

  _____

  _____

  _____

  _____

- Is the program well funded, or limited in resources?

  _____

- What are the program's short- and long-term goals?

  _____

  _____

  _____

  _____

- How many faculty members does your program currently work with? What are their disciplines? How experienced are they with community service-learning? In what particular ways do they work in this area: Do they teach with service-learning? Advise civically oriented student groups? Collaborate on research projects with community members?

  _____

  _____

  _____

  _____

- What mechanisms are there to train and support faculty in undertaking this work?

  _____

  _____

(continued)

_____

_____

• How does your program define "faculty development" (e.g., primarily in terms of teaching with service-learning or more broadly)?

_____

_____

_____

_____

B. *So what?* Examine the programmatic context in terms of implications for your work with faculty.

• Is your program housed in a unit that is well respected by faculty? How do you know? What might need to be done to enhance their connection to your program?

_____

_____

_____

_____

• Which goals might faculty development help advance? Are the faculty development mechanisms in place structured adequately to advance these goals?

_____

_____

_____

_____

• What resources (funding, personnel, materials, mentors, and so on) are available specifically for faculty development and support? What additional resources might be needed?

_____

_____

(continued)

_____

_____

- How close is the program to achieving its goals in terms of numbers of faculty, courses, or projects, if there is such a goal? In terms of quality of implementation (e.g., of service-learning courses)? How do you know?

_____

_____

_____

_____

- Where are the untapped pockets of potentially involved faculty? Does your program adequately reach out to them? How might it reach out more, and more effectively?

_____

_____

_____

_____

- Is the program focused on working with inexperienced or experienced faculty, or both? Does it provide adequate support to faculty at all levels of experience?

_____

_____

_____

_____

C. *Now what?* What questions or concerns do you therefore especially need to bring to your reading of this chapter?

_____

_____

_____

_____

WORKSHEET

WORKSHEET 6-2: Reflection on Faculty Involvement

Write a paragraph each on how three of your faculty members came to service-learning. If you are not familiar enough with their stories to do this, go talk to them and then come back to this reflection.

A. *What?*

• In considering these stories and your community service-learning program, what are the primary ways in which faculty members become involved? Which of the approaches of self-selection, training the converted, or selling it apply to your program? What additional approaches might you employ?

_____

_____

_____

_____

• How do you make your program visible to faculty members? What role, if any, is played by experienced faculty in your efforts to connect with faculty new to this work?

_____

_____

_____

_____

B. *So what?*

Examine Billy's story (pages 97–98) and those of your faculty in terms of why faculty come to civic engagement and service-learning.

• In what ways does this discussion address the questions or concerns you noted in earlier reflections?

_____

_____

_____

_____

(continued)

- Is your program adequately visible to faculty on your campus? What are some additional ways to make your program visible?

_____

_____

_____

_____

_____

- What do people "see" when they hear the name of your program? A logo? A person? An idea? Something else?

_____

_____

_____

_____

- Does your program adequately represent the teaching, research, and service products of service-learning to faculty members? What are some additional or alternative ways to do so that might be more effective?

_____

_____

_____

_____

- Does your service-learning program adequately connect with the culture of your campus, particularly with faculty members' contexts? What are some additional ways to learn about and connect with faculty members' contexts?

_____

_____

_____

_____

(continued)

WORKSHEET

C. *Now what?*

- What are the most important take-away messages from Billy's story, from those of your faculty, and from this discussion of how and why faculty come to service-learning? Why are they especially important for you, in your context?

  _____

  _____

  _____

  _____

- What actions, if any, does your examination of these stories and this discussion lead you to consider taking?

  _____

  _____

  _____

  _____

- What additional questions or concerns do you now see the need to bring to your reading of this chapter or book and/or to your work with faculty?

  _____

  _____

  _____

  _____

WORKSHEET 6-3: Reflection on Process Design

Designing an approach to service-learning faculty development and support begins with many of the same questions as does designing the integration of service-learning into a course (or, for that matter, designing any learning experience):

- Who are my students (in this case, faculty)? What experience, skills, knowledge, abilities, interests, and so on do they bring? What do they not bring?

_____

_____

_____

_____

- Who am I? What experience, skills, knowledge, abilities, interests, and so on do I bring? What do I not bring?

_____

_____

_____

_____

- What are the learning objectives? Who is to have a voice in determining the objectives?

_____

_____

_____

_____

- What would success mean in this effort?

_____

_____

_____

_____

(continued)

W O R K S H E E T

- What resources are available?

_____

_____

_____

_____

- What challenges, obstacles, or constraints do we face in this effort?

_____

_____

_____

_____

- What is needed in terms of capacity building among all participants in order for this effort to succeed?

_____

_____

_____

_____

WORKSHEET 6-4: Reflection on Faculty Development

A. *What?*

- Describe an opportunity you have (or had, or would like to have) to offer faculty development, particularly in service-learning.

_____

_____

_____

_____

_____

- What are the primary drivers in your design of faculty development? Time? Financial cost? Your own skills? The objectives of the particular participant group? Other?

_____

_____

_____

_____

_____

B. *So what?*

- In what ways does this discussion of possible approaches to faculty development speak to the questions or concerns you noted in earlier reflections?

_____

_____

_____

_____

_____

(continued)

WORKSHEET

• In light of your responses in Worksheet 6-3, which of the 15 possible approaches listed in the box "A Continuum of Approaches to Faculty Development" (page 101) are most appropriate? What other approaches may be appropriate?

_____

_____

_____

_____

_____

• How might you include the suggested best practices in the design of this faculty development opportunity? What other best practices are you thinking of and how might you include them in your design?

_____

_____

_____

_____

_____

C. *Now what?*

• What are the most important take-away messages from Billy's story (pages 99–100) and the discussion of approaches to working with faculty? Why are they especially important for you and your faculty, in your context?

_____

_____

_____

_____

_____

(continued)

- What actions, if any, does your examination of Billy's story and this discussion of approaches to working with faculty lead you to consider taking?

  _____

  _____

  _____

  _____

  _____

- What additional questions or concerns do you now see the need to bring to your reading of this chapter, book, and/or to your work with faculty?

  _____

  _____

  _____

  _____

  _____

WORKSHEET

WORKSHEET 6-5: Reflection on Program Design and Implementation

Write a paragraph each describing three service-learning courses on your campus.

A. *What?*

• How do the instructors of these courses orient their students to the service-learning process?

_____

_____

_____

_____

• In what specific ways do they use reflection to connect course content to the service-learning experience? To promote civic learning? What other objectives do they have for their use of reflection?

_____

_____

_____

_____

• In what specific ways do they interact with community partners? In what ways do they bring community and student voices into the design and delivery of their courses?

_____

_____

_____

_____

B. *So what?*

• In what ways does this discussion of introductory principles address the questions or concerns you noted in earlier reflections?

_____

_____

(continued)

_____

_____

- To what extent does your program's definition of service-learning help to convey the assumptions underlying these introductory principles? How might it be modified to do so more effectively?

  _____

  _____

  _____

  _____

- Do you believe these courses adequately integrate (versus add on) service-learning? What are the signs of strong or weak integration that support your judgment? What might be done to enhance the level and quality of integration?

  _____

  _____

  _____

  _____

- On a scale of 1–10, with 1 being "very little" and 10 being "extremely," how counter-normative do you believe the students in these classes find service-learning to be? What signs of this perception on their part support your judgment? What might your faculty do differently, if anything, to help their students adapt to and take full advantage of the counter-normative nature of service-learning?

  _____

  _____

  _____

  _____

(continued)

WORKSHEET

C. *Now what?*

- What are the most important take-away messages from Patti's story and the discussion of introductory principles? Why are they especially important for you, in your context?

  _____

  _____

  _____

  _____

- What actions, if any, does your examination of Patti's story (pages 104–105) and the discussion of introductory principles lead you to consider taking?

  _____

  _____

  _____

  _____

- What additional questions or concerns do you now see the need to bring to your reading of this chapter or book and/or to your work with faculty?

  _____

  _____

  _____

  _____

WORKSHEET 6-6: Reflection on Program Enhancement

A. *What?*

- What are some ways in which faculty members on your campus are invited to enhance their involvement with civic engagement to best meet their professional and personal interests?

  _____

  _____

  _____

  _____

- What are some ways in which a faculty member's engagement with your community service-learning program might be used by her or him in other contexts (like Billy's use of reflection session process in the mountains [page 108])?

  _____

  _____

  _____

  _____

- In what ways do the policies regarding faculty roles and rewards on your campus support or hinder your faculty in developing long-term relationships with your program and in approaching the work as scholarship?

  _____

  _____

  _____

  _____

B. *So what?*

- In what ways does this discussion of helping faculty refine their work over time speak to the questions or concerns you noted in earlier reflections?

  _____

  _____

(continued)

WORKSHEET

_____

_____

• Does your program adequately support faculty in moving beyond service-learning as a teaching and learning strategy? To what extent do you believe it should do so, given your institutional context, the mission and size of your program, and the interests of your faculty? How might your program grow in this area, and what resources and support would doing so require?

_____

_____

_____

_____

C. *Now what?*

• What are the most important take-away messages from this discussion of helping faculty refine their work over time? Why are they especially important for you and your faculty, in your context?

_____

_____

_____

_____

• What actions, if any, does your examination of helping faculty refine their work over time lead you to consider taking?

_____

_____

_____

_____

(continued)

- What additional questions or concerns do you now see the need to bring to your reading of this chapter or book and/or to your work with faculty?

_____

_____

_____

_____

WORKSHEET

WORKSHEET 6-7: Reflection on Lessons Learned

Review your previous six reflections.

A. *What?*

• What three to five key issues seem to run through the reflections?

_____

_____

_____

_____

B. *So what?*

• What three to five important learning points have you achieved through the reflections on this chapter and on the implications for your work with faculty?

_____

_____

_____

_____

C. *Now what?*

• What three to five concrete actions do you want to take to your work with faculty as a result of this learning?

_____

_____

_____

_____

(continued)

- What three to five questions persist through your reading of this chapter that you should bring to your reading of this book and/or to your work with faculty?

_____

_____

_____

_____

WORKSHEET

CHAPTER SEVEN

Developing Your Strategy for Working with Students

Lacretia Johnson Flash and Carrie Williams Howe

S TUDENTS ARE THE REASON FOR OUR WORK. Our relationships with students often provide us with the greatest satisfaction and sometimes the greatest challenges. Because of the varying contexts in which we work and our different skills and experiences, no single approach will work in all situations or meet all needs for cultivating positive, powerful working relationships with students.

As we each strive to be our best as community service-learning professionals (CSLPs), many of us put great energy into building our knowledge of effective practices and social issues, the latest trends in programming, and service-related research. We also build skills for managing budgets, engaging in strategic-planning processes, managing staff, writing grants, and planning programs. These essential skills help us to function as competent professionals. For many of us, these skills were not acquired through formal training yet are critical for working effectively with students.

This chapter addresses questions such as: How do I create a strong working relationship with students in the context of my practice? What are the different ways in which I will come in contact with students? What are the joys and frustrations of working with students? How do I maintain a healthy balance in my life if I have intense, frequent contact with students? How do I stay connected to student voices, concerns, and energy if I am removed from direct student contact?

This chapter was inspired by the spirit of the poet Rainer Maria Rilke, who encouraged his protégé to place deep value on raising questions. Reflection and reciprocity are key components of service-learning. We explore these principles as we strive to cultivate functional, rewarding, meaningful, and reciprocal working relationships with students.

What Are the Contexts in Which We Work with Students?

Each of us knows that students are at the heart of our efforts; however, in day-to-day work, we have widely varying levels of interaction with them. Our positions range from those of us who work intensively and daily with students to those of us for whom student interaction is occasional or even rare. Our work falls into categories based on the amount of time we spend with students (and therefore the level of access we offer them) and the intensity of our relationships with them. Figure 7-1 shows where the positions might fall based on these two axes.

FIGURE 7-1: CSLP Position Continuum Related to Frequency/Intensity of Student Interaction

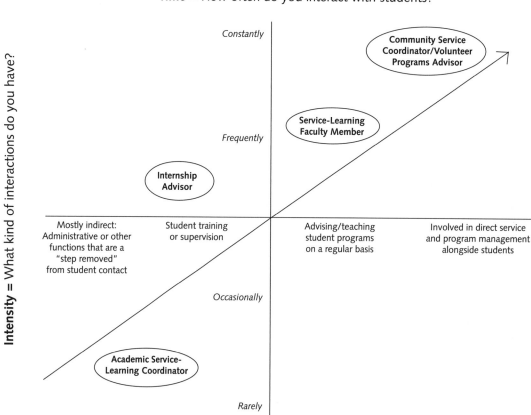

Our own job descriptions can be seen at two very distinct points on this continuum. One of us, an academic service-learning coordinator, supports faculty in creating service-learning courses, but in her original job description she rarely interacted with the students in those courses. The other author, a former community-service programs advisor, has a position that calls for interaction with students almost hourly and is highly involved in the programs that students coordinate.

See where you think your current or desired position falls on this spectrum. We have provided a few examples based on positions we have observed. Use the reflection questions in Worksheet 7-1 ("What is the Context in Which You Work with Students?") beginning on page 155 to facilitate your thinking on these topics.

The varying levels of interaction with students present a spectrum of professional opportunities that can meet the interests and preferences of CSLPs in meaningful ways. Remember, however, that none of these jobs is static. As professionals, we can help to "create" our jobs. Within our work, we can move widely along the spectrum within a range of programmatic responsibilities.

Can You Change Your Level of Student Interaction?

Though it is difficult to move permanently from one end of the spectrum to the other, moving a short distance along it or shifting daily is certainly possible. CSLPs whose main responsibility is training faculty to create academic service-learning experiences can integrate student leadership into their programming. For example, one author of this chapter created a service-learning teaching assistant program to involve students more in the work of her office. Alternatively, those whose role is to advise student groups and who feel that they are overwhelmed by student contact could regulate the amount of the time they make available to students. For example, by creating student-led positions that can perform some of the roles you may be trying to fill (e.g., advisor, communications coordinator, record keeper), you can enable students to assist their peers while learning leadership and other professional skills. Wanting a lower level of student contact is not something to feel guilty about. Some of us function better in roles that are not highly student-centered, but we still provide valuable services and programs. And those of us who function well in positions of high student contact also need to know our limits. We serve all students better when we are not overwhelmed or exhausted.

One useful strategy is to map all the services on your campus to see where other programs and services are meeting student needs and interests. At the University of Vermont, we created a map of community engagement activities, offices, and programs The map gives staff a better idea of where they can refer students for other opportunities and has alleviated our feeling that we need to be all things to all people. With student interaction, we now know that there are many opportunities in different offices, so we feel more comfortable focusing on our own specialties.

In addition to mapping service and civic engagement activities, it also helps to map career services, counseling services, academic support, and so on. This helps us to realize that we cannot always meet students' needs and that we may not, in fact, be the right person to do so. Referring them to another office might make the most sense. (See Worksheet 7-2 on page 159 for a mapping exercise.)

What Is Our Role in Working with Students?

As practitioners, we play multiple roles in our work with students. On some days, the role is task-oriented and clear: a student may need help navigating through a particular policy or institutional procedure, and thus we function in the role of administrator. On other days, our role is more relationship- or process-oriented: a student with whom we work closely may be struggling to clarify the direction of his or her life and career aspirations. In this case, we may function more as a mentor or counselor.

Resource: Students as Colleagues

In 2006, Campus Compact published *Students as Colleagues: Expanding the Circle of Service-Learning Leadership*. In this publication, editors Edward Zlotkowski, Nicholas Longo, and James Williams argue that the time has come to focus on student leadership in the academic service-learning movement. They offer three compelling rationales for this imperative. Students, they argue, can serve as enablers: "Carefully selected, well-trained undergraduates can play decisive roles in making academic-community collaborations powerful, successful experiences"(p. 4). In addition, involving students as leaders in service-learning reflects the democratic principles inherent in the movement, empowering students to be active change agents and to hold their institutions responsible for their public missions. Lastly, they argue, the current generation has come of age alongside the growth of service-learning; as such, they are in a unique position to offer leadership.

This publication goes on to profile numerous institutions and models in which students have served not just as advisees and campus organization leaders, but as staff, teaching assistants, scholars, committee members, etc. Concurrent with publication of this resource have been several national and regional conversations and events exploring opportunities for involving students as leaders in service-learning. The chapter authors highly suggest review of this publication and involvement in these ongoing conversations as you consider how to involve students meaningfully in your programs.

Each of our roles has particular functions, purposes, joys, and challenges. As you think about your various roles in working with students, you may want to consider the following:

- How do you balance your different roles? Do some roles come easily, while others are more challenging and take more energy for you to do effectively?

- How do you continue to build your skills in working with students and your capacity to serve students? What are your sources of professional and personal support?

- In what situations is it appropriate to take on certain roles (e.g., supervisor, mentor, friend) with a student? In what situations would assuming certain roles be inappropriate or a conflict of interest?

- What do you want your role(s) to be with students (right now and as your career evolves)? How will you get there (e.g., take on new or different work projects, change jobs, seek professional development)?

Table 7-1 on pages 151–154 presents some of the common roles in which practitioners interact with students. The roles and corresponding functions are presented within distinct categories, but in reality, they overlap. A table cannot begin to capture the many dimensions and nuances of how we connect with students. As you review the table, do so critically, paying particular attention to the ways in which your experiences connect to and diverge from the outline.

Questions for Advisor Meetings

Questions to ask your advisee at the initial meeting:

1. What do you need from an advisor?

2. How did you come to be involved with this issue and this service program?

3. As a leader or coordinator of this program, what do you do weekly in both the service project and behind the scenes to ensure that the project happens?

4. What are the strengths of your program? What do you do to maintain them?

5. What are the challenges or weaknesses of the program? How do you plan to work through these challenges?

6. What are your goals for your program this semester/term and year (e.g., number of volunteers, number of projects, etc.)?

7. How connected do you feel to the service agency you work with? With other service groups on campus and in the community? What would help you to feel more connected?

8. What are your next steps? What's on your to-do list?

9. How ready do you feel to take the next step? What resources and support do you need?

Questions and topics for structuring regular advising meetings:

1. What program, project, or organizational updates do you have (what's happened, what's coming up, highlights)?

2. Follow-up from last meeting (report on tasks completed or questions answered from last meeting).

3. What are your current or anticipated program challenges, concerns, and tasks?

4. What resources and support do you need to assist you with your tasks, challenges, and concerns?

5. What reflections, insights, thoughts, and new ideas do you have about service, your program, your leadership, and the social issues addressed by your program?

6. What actions do we need to take by our next meeting?

The table shows seven of the common roles of CSLPs, ranging from strictly professional to more personal and from heavily task-oriented to more relationship-oriented. For some students, you will interact in only one role. With others, you may find that you interact in multiple ways and that your relationships will continue to evolve, even after the students have graduated. (Because many CSLPs advise students, we provide some guidance for advisor meetings in the box "Questions for Advisor Meetings," above.)

What Are the Best Practices for Working with Students?

This section offers some best practices to help you support your students, no matter what your official role is. We propose that our goals as advisors are to empower students, ensure quality in our programs and courses, understand student needs, develop students as leaders, and be happy and sane while we do all this!

Further, we believe that our mission is both to *challenge* students and to *support* them as they develop as leaders, citizens, and community members. We asked ourselves, "What are the best practices for working with students in service programs?" In searching for the answer, we collected information using five approaches: (1) we distributed a survey and conducted a focus group with students in a co-curricular service program; (2) we observed and conversed with students involved in academic service-learning; (3) we surveyed CSLPs and conducted a focus group with them; (4) we reviewed relevant published materials; and (5) we reflected on our experiences.

In addition to focusing on the role of advisors in working with student groups in general, we narrowed our focus to a more specific question: *What is unique about working with students in the context of service and service-learning programs?* We wanted to know if there are important roles and responsibilities that come with our work in this context. To answer these questions, we asked friends, colleagues, and students to reflect on their own experiences as advisors and advisees, teachers and learners, and leaders and collaborators. What follows is a compilation of the results from our informal research, with a sprinkling of our own ideas. Each list is presented separately to highlight the voices of those who offered suggestions. Worksheet 7-3 on page 161 provides an opportunity for you to reflect on these lists of best practices and to apply them to your work setting.

What Students in Co-curricular Service Want from Advisors

We asked 15 students in a community service program about their relationships with advisors. We started with short, confidential questions: "Think about an advisor/supervisor/teacher you have had in a service situation—What has worked in that relationship? What would you want to change about that relationship?" We then asked students to fill out a brief questionnaire (Likert Scale questions on the prompt: "How important is it to you that your advisor…"). Using those as a starting point to get students thinking, we facilitated a conversation about what they wished advisors would do for them. After ten minutes of conversation, we worked together to generate ideas for a Top Ten List entitled "A Great Advisor Would…." Students were then asked to write one final thought on the back of their survey and turn it in.

The survey results suggest that in order to be the most effective advisor to students in co-curricular service, you should:

1. *Communicate.* Be in touch with students regularly to demonstrate your investment in their program or project; proactively check in with them. Communication is essential for meeting expectations and delivering successful service, especially when a community partner is depending on students.

2. *Be accessible.* Ensure that students can contact you, sometimes at unexpected times. As they venture off campus and work with complex projects and partners, students need to feel that backup is available. Nevertheless, they recognize and expect certain limitations.

3. *Demonstrate active interest.* Show students that you are invested in their programs by asking questions, attending events and meetings, and keeping up to date with their work. Create a balance between active investment and general oversight so that they feel valued but not micromanaged.

4. *Follow through.* If you say you will do something, call someone, or be somewhere, you must follow through. Make a mental note of students' challenges or successes and follow up with them.

5. *Encourage and facilitate reflection.* Students want their advisors to help them reflect on their experiences. Sometimes they get so caught up in the actual tasks of the project or program that they don't always take the time to think about what they are learning or what the experience means to them. They want you to be aware of the big picture and occasionally remind them of it by asking:

   a. Why are we doing service?

   b. What are we getting out of it? What are we learning?

   c. How can we look at our service from a variety of perspectives?

   d. How can we better organize our thoughts and feelings about the service we are doing?

   e. What is the big picture? What are the themes, issues, and ideas that surround what we are doing?

6. *Share your experience and your contacts.* You are a professional in this field, and students want to learn from you. Develop relationships with the community that can help them connect, and open your networks to students. Share your experience and involvement in service personally and professionally.

7. *Collaborate.* Be a collaborator, not a supervisor. Support students, but make sure that they take on leadership, create programs, and complete projects on their own.

8. *Encourage.* Service situations often call for a high level of motivation. Help students see the effect of their work, even in the face of challenges. Have a positive attitude.

9. *Be honest.* Students want their advisors to be honest with them and to trust them; they want to be able to trust their advisors in turn.

What Students in Academic Service-Learning Want from Advisors and Faculty

On October 28, 2005, Vermont Campus Compact hosted a daylong workshop called "Listening to Our Students," in which faculty, staff, and students discussed service-learning and its benefits, rewards, and practices (focusing heavily on academic service-learning). After a morning of conversation and questioning in small, rotating groups, the facilitator asked the students to share the "one thing you want us [faculty members and staff] to take from this conversation." The following is a summary of their responses:

1. *Acknowledge the shared risk.* Everyone embarking on service-learning shares certain risks (e.g., a project going in a different direction than planned, disagreements between partners, perceived disappointment with the end product). Discuss these risks openly and accept shared responsibility among all partners.

2. *Express shared responsibility and ownership.* Help students feel personally invested in the project. Build knowledge through a collaborative process in which everyone is responsible for contributing.

3. *Ensure clear communication.* Make sure that students, community partners, and others involved communicate frequently.

4. *Accept fluidity.* Be flexible and respond to students' needs for adjustment if a project takes a different direction. Make sure the service-learning project is clearly integrated into the course; students will see connections without you having to tell them.

5. *Be a role model.* Be equally invested in the work. As one student said, "If you're not walking the walk, how are we supposed to?"

6. *Establish loose deadlines.* Set up a flexible plan. As one student commented, "Accept the messiness."

7. *Find community partners who are also equally invested.* Discuss what the investment will mean in terms of time, energy, and planning. And make sure that the partners are able to commit.

8. *Challenge students.* Don't settle for on-the-surface reflection. Ask students to dig deeper by asking challenging questions.

9. *Show students your passion and enthusiasm.* It's contagious!

10. *Celebrate!* Give students a way to demonstrate learning or share progress with others.

Suggestions from Community Service-Learning Professionals

At a November 2005 Vermont Campus Compact meeting with representatives of service-related programs from campuses around the state, we conducted a survey and focus group of practitioners. Using the same prompting survey and a variation on the questions asked of students in co-curricular service (see above), we asked them to develop their own Top Ten List focusing on the question, "What are my best practices in developing positive relationships with students?" Their responses are summarized below:

1. *Be authentic.* Develop your whole self and be engaged with the world around you (not just in your work life). Let students see who you are, what you believe in, and what matters to you.

2. *Create an authentic relationship with your students.* Listen to students and be truly present when you are with them. Invest time and energy in creating strong relationships. Get to know students and what really matters to them.

3. *Empower students to act.* Guide and empower students to be full participants in creating powerful service and learning experiences. Know what they truly need from you and what they are capable of doing themselves.

4. *Help students reflect.* Help them see themselves clearly, including their strengths, accomplishments, and growth. Insist that students take the time to reflect on their experiences, particularly in areas of discomfort and their stereotypes, so that they are learning, not just doing.

5. *Provide students with resources.* Help students accomplish their tasks and goals by sharing helpful tools, resources, templates, and systems. This saves them from reinventing something that has already been created.

6. *Give students space to grow and create.* Allow students to go through the process of creating, even if they make some mistakes. When they have creative and innovative ideas, help them think through the details.

7. *Forgive mistakes; don't hold grudges.* Mistakes happen. When students make mistakes, help them separate themselves from their mistakes so that they do not internalize them. Learn what needs to be learned, forgive, and move on.

8. *Celebrate students.* Recognize the achievements, learning, contributions, and growth of your students in formal and informal ways. Offer ample praise.

9. *Help students make connections.* Be a bridge builder by helping to connect students to each other, campus communities, resources, the communities beyond campus, and sources of information relevant to their work and interests. Help students see the larger context surrounding the social issues they are concerned about, so that they begin to see complexities and interconnections in the world. Help them to see how their actions affect how the institution is viewed from the outside.

10. *Make your health and life balance a priority.* Take time to replenish yourself. If you are burnt out and exhausted, you cannot give fully to your students. Model healthy behavior and balance in your life, encouraging students to seek similar balance.

What's the most important thing we learned from our research? *Students need from us what we need from them!* In short, as much as we want them to be invested, accountable, honest, and reflective, they want us to encourage those practices and model them. All participants in the focus groups and discussions believe that creating a sound community in their group, their class, and their program between advisors, professors, and students helps them to fulfill their mission. Share the preceding best practices with your community partners. They are key facilitators of the learning process and therefore play an important role in advising and collaborating with students. (The following resources may be helpful in developing your own list of best practices for working with students: Kuh, Kinzie, Schuh, Whitt, & Associates, 2005; Dunkel & Schuh, 1998.)

Where Are Our Boundaries in Working with Students?

As we engage in our practice as CSLPs, we must know where our professional and personal boundaries lie. Our work is often filled with subtlety and nuance, rather than absolutes and clear distinctions. In this section, we present questions for your reflection on two dimensions of the boundaries through which you may need to navigate: personal relationship boundaries and legal and institutional boundaries.

Personal Relationship Boundaries

As we discussed earlier, we may develop close connections to students. We then begin to cross the lines between administrator or advisor and friend or colleague. How do we navigate between these two roles in ways that are fulfilling and rich, but also appropriate and ethical? Each of us is called on to think carefully and critically about developing our own guidelines. Here are some questions to ask yourself about personal boundaries in your work with students:

- How much access do you want to give students (e.g., workday by appointment, "drop in," evening meetings, weekends, informal time, sharing meals)?

- Are there times during your workweek when you need to work without interruptions?

- Are there occasions when 24-hour access is necessary (e.g., during an intensive week-long international service trip)?

- What times are off limits to students (e.g., your vacation)?

- How much personal information do you want to share with students or have them share with you (e.g., life experiences, political opinions, beliefs)?

- How can you ward off burnout by striking a balance between high-intensity times (e.g., working a 60-hour week to finalize the logistics of an intensive week-long service trip) and self-care (e.g., working fewer hours or taking a week off during a slower time in the school year)?

- Under what circumstances would you invite a student to your home (e.g., end-of-year celebration dinner)?

- How do you maintain balance among the tasks that you *have* to do, those you are *asked* to do, and those that you *want* to do?

- What do you need to do to have a balanced and healthy life?

Legal and Institutional Boundaries

Our students and we must function within a set of institutional constraints and legal parameters. Mistakes are a natural part of learning—for them and for us—and cannot or should not be entirely avoided. As practitioners, we need to consider how to promote the healthy development and experimentation in our students and ourselves, while also being thoughtful about how to navigate through the sometimes murky, uncertain waters of liability, risk, policy, and legal issues.

Next we offer some questions to consider as you think about the legal, institutional, and safety issues of boundaries to explore in your work. Since specific institutional policies and types of service projects vary greatly, we provide questions for reflection rather than answers.

SAFETY, LIABILITY, AND RISK

- What are your campus policies and procedures for field trips, transportation, liability waivers, and certifications?

- What areas of potential risk should you, as the practitioner, be mindful of as you implement service programs or work with students to implement their service projects and programs?

- What training and information needs for those involved ensure the safest service experience possible?

- What emergency protocols and back-up procedures need to be developed if a project does not go as planned?

- Under what circumstances would you postpone or cancel a project (e.g., bad weather, travel advisories, unresolved logistical issues)?

- In working with a particular site or population, what background checks, if any, need to be done, and by whom (e.g., your program or the community agency)?

- How can you work with students to help them develop good judgment and maintain composure when a project goes awry?

INSTITUTIONAL, LEGAL, AND OTHER ISSUES

- Does your institution have constraints and other parameters (e.g., policies, procedures) of which you should be mindful? How do these constraints and parameters translate to or influence the service programs and projects on which you work with students?

- With regard to student activism and protests, what laws and other parameters govern the boundaries of what is permissible and what is not? How can you support students' desire and right to express their thoughts and opinions?

- What are the expectations and norms for consumption of alcohol and use of other substances? What are the procedures if a violation occurs?

- What do you do if your personal views and values conflict with those of your institution or the expectations of your professional role? How far will you go to stand in solidarity with your students and voice your personal convictions and perspectives on a social or institutional issue?

- What mistakes would be catastrophic to a student, a program, your institution, or a partnership? How can you help your students avoid mistakes of this magnitude?

As you think about the boundaries in working with students in the context of service-learning, recognize that you are functioning as an educator, not a legal expert. On all college campuses, many sources of expertise can help you recognize and clarify your boundaries. Common sources of support and information include the risk management office, institutional legal counsel, legal issues workshops at conferences and trainings, supervisors, and colleagues. Boundaries ensure that we can safely and comfortably enjoy continued success in our programs. Viewed as assurances of success rather than consequences or red tape, boundaries are an essential tool for improving our work with students.

Conclusion

Ballet dancers always strive for perfection and constantly work to achieve the perfect line of their bodies as they move with expressiveness, musicality, and dynamism (Ellison, 2003). Dance is both an art and a craft, as is our work with students. As with the ballet dancer, success in our work is not achievable without hard work and reflection on our strengths and weaknesses. Imagining the mirrors that surround a dance studio, we have tried in this chapter to hold a mirror up to ourselves—to reflect on the context of our practice and to sort out what we believe about our work with students.

What have we learned? We have derived two conclusions from our reflections:

- *Our jobs are never boring.* The more we work with students, the more we must adapt, adjust, and renew. We must develop new skills, seek feedback on our practices, and be open to new experiences. Students are, more often than not, full of energy, idealism, and passion. They have usually chosen to be involved in our programs and courses; that is a gift in itself. Each year brings a new group of students who enrich our professional and personal lives.

- *Renewal is not possible without reflection.* We must ask ourselves the questions that determine what types of jobs and programs we want to be involved in and what kind of professionals we want to be. When working with students, we must ask ourselves: How can

I be the best advisor, teacher, and colleague I can possibly be? How can I further students' development through the right mixture of challenge and support, allowing them to grow into citizens who will make the world a better place? Reflection is arguably the most important element of service-learning, one that we must encourage not only in others but also in ourselves.

This chapter has offered opportunities to examine our relationships with students through questions, reflection, and advice from the field. As you continue your valuable work, we encourage you to constantly consider and reconsider your role as you work with students, to envision new possibilities, and to deal with existing realities.

Acknowledgments

The authors would like to thank the following friends and colleagues who contributed to our research: the student leaders of the University of Vermont's "Volunteers in Action" group; the Vermont Campus Compact staff, especially Cheryl Whitney Lower and Amy Gibans McGlashan; student attendees at "Learning from Our Students," a daylong Vermont Campus Compact workshop; faculty workshop facilitators Richard Schramm (University of Vermont) and John Isham (Middlebury College); and members of the Vermont Campus Compact Network Group.

References

Cuyjet, M. J. (1996). Program development and group advising. In S. R. Komives, D. B. Woodard, Jr., & Associates (Eds.), *Student services: A handbook for the profession* (3rd ed.) (pp. 397–414). San Francisco: Jossey-Bass.

Dunkel, N. W., & Schuh, S. H. (1998). *Advising student groups and organizations.* San Francisco: Jossey-Bass.

Ellison, N. (2003). *The ballet book: Learning and appreciating the secrets of dance.* New York: Universe Publishing.

Kuh, G.D., Kinzie, J., Schuh, J.H., Whitt, F.J., & Associates. (2005). *Student success in college: Creating conditions that matter.* San Francisco: Jossey-Bass.

Zlotkowski, E., Longo, N., & Williams, J. (Eds.). (2006). *Students as colleagues: Expanding the circle of service-learning leadership.* Providence, RI: Campus Compact.

Additional Resources

Brady, S. M. (1999). Students at the center of education: A collaborative effort. *Liberal Education, 85*(1), 14–21.

Campbell, S., & Niedergang, M. (1996). *Youth issues, youth voices: A guide for engaging youth and adults in public dialogue and problem solving.* Pomfret, CT: Study Circles Resource Center.

Carter, K. A., & McClellan, G. S. (2000). An overview of relevant theories and models for student affairs practice. In M. J. Barr, M. K. Desler, & Associates (Eds.), *The handbook of student affairs administration* (2nd ed.) (pp. 231–248). San Francisco: Jossey-Bass.

Chesler, M.A., Kellman-Fritz, J., & Knife-Gould, A. (2003). Training peer facilitators for community service learning leadership. *Michigan Journal of Community Service Learning, 9*(2), 59–76.

Evans, N. J., Forney, D. S., & Guido-DiBrito, F. (1998). *Student development in college: Theory, research, and practice.* San Francisco: Jossey-Bass.

Eyler, J. & Giles, Jr., D. E. (1996). *A practitioner's guide to reflection in service-learning: Student voices and reflections.* Scotts Valley, CA: National Service-Learning Clearinghouse.

Fielding, M. (2004). "New wave" student voice and the renewal of civic society. *London Review of Education, 2*(2), 197–217.

Fisher, I., & Huff Wilson, S. (2003). Partnerships with students. In B. Jacoby (Ed.), *Building partnerships for service-learning* (pp. 85–105). San Francisco: Jossey-Bass.

Justinianno, J., & Scherer, C. (2001). *Youth voice: A guide for engaging youth in leadership and decision-making in service-learning programs.* Washington, DC: Points of Light Foundation.

King, P. M., & Kitchener, K. S. (1994). *Developing reflective judgment: Understanding and promoting intellectual growth and critical thinking in adolescents and adults.* San Francisco: Jossey-Bass.

McEwen, M. K. (1996). The nature and uses of theory. In S. R. Komives, D. B. Woodard, Jr., & Associates (Eds.), *Student services: A handbook for the profession* (3rd ed.) (pp. 147–163). San Francisco: Jossey-Bass.

TABLE 7-1: Typical Roles in CSLPs' Work with Students

PRACTIONER ROLE	STUDENT ROLE	PURPOSE	FUNCTIONS OF CSLP	FUNCTIONS OF STUDENT	ISSUES FOR CSLP TO CONSIDER
Advisor	Advisee Student group leader	Advisor and advisee work together to execute a student-run program or project and to maintain or improve the functioning of a student organization	Assists students in maintaining their organization or program Stimulates the student group to develop programs that enrich the campus community and promote development Provides continuity between changing leadership and transmits organizational history	Has in-depth knowledge of and commitment to student organization Is able to identify issues and concerns related to organization and communicate these to advisor	How much time and energy do you have to adequately support student leaders? What strategies can you use to maximize your impact and efficiency in this role? How can you empower rather than overpower students?
Supervisor	Student employee	Supervisor works with student to meet departmental and program goals, which are typically determined by departmental staff or leadership	Provides guidance, resources, instructions, parameters, and feedback to student employee Helps student develop career skills and content knowledge	Performs project-related tasks Asks for clarification when needed Offers student perspective on projects as appropriate	What is your preferred management style? What training, resources, and supervision do you need to provide to ensure success? What supervision and management skills do you need to develop?

(continued)

TABLE 7-1: Typical Roles in CSLPs' Work with Students (cont.)

PRACTIONER ROLE	STUDENT ROLE	PURPOSE	FUNCTIONS OF CSLP	FUNCTIONS OF STUDENT	ISSUES FOR CSLP TO CONSIDER
Administrator	Student leader Student with an idea	Administrator works with student to help him or her navigate through institutional policies, procedures, and practices	Serves as sounding board for new ideas or approaches that student has Interprets institutional or departmental policy for student Serves as contact and mediator between student and other entities (on-campus and off-campus)	Has an idea or program he or she would like to pursue Is willing to articulate ideas to administrator Is willing to hear feedback and suggestions Asks for clarification of policies and procedures that are unclear	How can you help student think through the steps necessary to implement a project? How can you share institutional boundaries and constraints without suppressing ideas generated by students?
Mentor	Mentee	Mentorship provides opportunity for a one-on-one learning relationship between established professional and less experienced person	Is willing to share knowledge, experiences, and professional philosophy Functions as guide and role model for professional practice Helps student clarify personal and career values and goals	Is open to learning and growing Possesses knowledge of own values, goals, and skills (or is willing to explore them) Is able to communicate needs and aspirations to mentor	How much time and energy do you have to build a fruitful relationship with mentee? What can you offer mentee? What do you hope to gain as mentor?

(continued)

PRACTIONER ROLE	STUDENT ROLE	PURPOSE	FUNCTIONS OF CSLP	FUNCTIONS OF STUDENT	ISSUES FOR CSLP TO CONSIDER
Teacher and learner	Learner and teacher	Knowledge between teacher and learner is created and shared together	Serves as content or information resource, willing to share knowledge and experience	Serves as content or information resource, willing to share knowledge and experience with practitioner	On what issues and areas do you have substantial knowledge? In what areas would you like to grow and learn?
			Poses questions to help students access their own wisdom	Is open to learning from the wisdom and insights of practitioner	How open are you to learning from your students? What factors may hinder you from doing so?
			Helps students see problems from multiple angles, and within cultural and historical contexts	Shares his or her perspective as student (can be valuable to practitioner who may be removed from student experience)	What are you interested in learning more about?
			Is open to learning from wisdom and insights of students		What steps can you take to ensure that you are a lifelong learner?
Colleague	Colleague	Colleagues have complementary and relevant knowledge, experience, and resources in which they can collectively make powerful contributions to a project or program	Promotes open communication in sharing ideas, assigning tasks, and providing feedback	Promotes open communication in sharing ideas, assigning tasks, and providing feedback	Are you comfortable sharing decision-making power with students?
			Has relevant knowledge, experience, or resources, and/or willingness to learn new approaches to enhance project outcomes	Has relevant knowledge, experience, or resources, and/or willingness to learn new approaches to enhance project outcomes	How can you help to create a mutually rewarding professional relationship?
			Is willing to listen to insights of student	Is willing to share ideas freely (not intimidated by experience of practitioner)	What potential projects may be ripe opportunities for forming a collegial relationship with students?

(continued)

TABLE 7-1: Typical Roles in CSLPs' Work with Students (cont.)

PRACTIONER ROLE	STUDENT ROLE	PURPOSE	FUNCTIONS OF CSLP	FUNCTIONS OF STUDENT	ISSUES FOR CSLP TO CONSIDER
Friend	Friend	In friendship, there is voluntary and reciprocal caring or connection that goes beyond tasks that need to be performed or content that needs to be mastered in order to execute a project	Shares common interests Expresses caring Is willing to have honest communication about boundaries and comfort zones Is aware of power dynamics in relationship and willing to work through them	Shares common interests Expresses caring Is willing to have honest communication about boundaries and comfort zones Is aware of power dynamics in relationship and willing to work through them	Are there any ethical issues or conflicts that could be raised in forming friendship with student (e.g., supervisory role or instructor role)? What does friendship involve (e.g., attending the student's graduation)? How will you manage tensions that may develop?

Source: Some of the information in this chart is adapted from Cuyjet (1996) and Dunkel & Schuh (1998).

WORKSHEET 7-1: What Is the Context in Which You Work with Students?

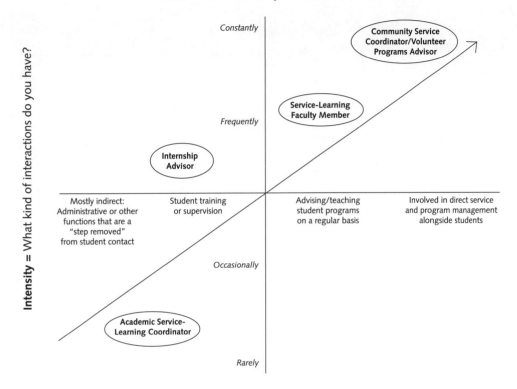

Where does your job description appear on the above continuum? Where would you like it to be? How can you change it? The following ranges in a job description are aspects you can consider:

1. Duration or time for student access:

   a. One-time (service days, information fairs or sessions, presentations)

   b. Short-term (trainings, specific project with a definite end date)

   c. Semester or yearlong (ongoing and more complex projects)

   d. Several years during a student's college career (as student progresses in his or her leadership capacity, experiences with service, and knowledge of an issue)

NOTES

_____

_____

_____

_____

_____

_____

_____

_____

_____

(continued)

WORKSHEET

e. During college years and beyond (mentoring that extends after graduation, ongoing career development, collegial relationships with students)

2. Level of access (which may heavily affect duration or time):

   a. Daytime business hours (Monday–Friday)

   b. Evenings and weekends (occasional to frequent)

   c. By appointment

   d. Spontaneous drop-ins

   e. Formal meetings

   f. Informal gatherings (e.g., hosting a group of student leaders in your home for a special meal or celebration on completion of a project)

3. Intensity and dimension of relationships with students:

   a. Work relationship centered on finite, discrete administrative tasks or functions. (e.g., practitioner answers a question about a policy or procedure, or provides one-time funding for a project).

   b. Work with student leaders to create or manage a program, work with volunteer membership, or manage an organization. Issues such as crisis or change management may intensify the level of contact practitioners have in working with students versus working with students to maintain a stable or well-established program.

   c. Work with student leaders to plan service projects that involve travel (domestic and international) or trips that involve higher levels of risk and special safety considerations.

NOTES

_____

_____

_____

_____

_____

_____

_____

_____

_____

_____

_____

_____

_____

_____

_____

_____

_____

_____

_____

(continued)

Practitioner Reflection: Interactions with Students

- What are your goals for student interaction at this point in your career? Why?

  _____

  _____

  _____

  _____

- How much contact do you want with students?

  _____

  _____

- What do you bring to this relationship?

  _____

  _____

  _____

  _____

- What do you have to gain from this relationship?

  _____

  _____

  _____

  _____

- What are the personal joys you have experienced or do you anticipate experiencing in working with students?

  _____

  _____

  _____

  _____

(continued)

WORKSHEET

W O R K S H E E T

- What frustrations or challenges have you experienced or do you anticipate experiencing in your work with students?

  _____

  _____

  _____

  _____

- How have your goals evolved as you develop professionally?

  _____

  _____

  _____

  _____

- What have been highlights, "aha" moments, and critical incidents in your work with students?

  _____

  _____

  _____

  _____

- How have you made sense out of your "aha" moments?

  _____

  _____

  _____

  _____

Worksheet 7-2: Mapping Exercise

What other faculty, staff, or offices on your campuses work in similar or related roles? You aren't the only one who fulfills the role of student advisor, student supervisor, and so on. Ask yourself where your position fits in the larger context of the institution. In what other places do students interact with staff? How should your position balance with and/or complement these other positions? Can you map out these offices (through language or a visual diagram)?

Use the following prompts to think about where you fit with students:

1. What other service-related offices and programs exist on campus?

   a. Curricular

   _____

   b. Co-curricular

   _____

   c. Residence-based

   _____

   d. Orientation

   _____

   e. Alumni programs

   _____

   f. Personal counseling

   _____

   g. Other

   _____

2. Where do students find the following?

   a. Career counseling or professional development

   _____

   b. Personal counseling

   _____

(continued)

WORKSHEET

c. Health advice

_____

d. Coaching

_____

e. Other

_____

3. How can you get to know these other offices, better refer your students to them, and help others see that your office or program fits in context with them?

_____

_____

_____

_____

WORKSHEET 7-3: Reflection: What Are Your Best Practices?

Think about your initial response to the lists of best practices in working with students on pages 142–145. Consider the following:

- Which best practices do you feel are the most salient in your situation? Place a star next to those practices. Write some examples here.

  _____

  _____

  _____

  _____

- Which best practices are your strengths? Place a plus sign (+) next to those practices. Jot down a few examples.

  _____

  _____

  _____

  _____

- Which best practices would you consider to be your weaknesses? Place a minus sign (–) next to those practices. Jot down why you think these are weaknesses.

  _____

  _____

  _____

  _____

- Now, pick two strengths and two weaknesses to pay close attention to over the next few weeks.

  o   Are you demonstrating the strengths in a variety of situations? List a few.

  _____

  _____

  _____

  _____

(continued)

WORKSHEET

o   Are your weaknesses detrimental? How?

_____

_____

_____

_____

o   What are you doing to improve on your weaknesses? Is it making a difference?

_____

_____

_____

_____

Try this reflection exercise a few times, thinking each time about how your practices change or don't change. You'll begin to get a picture of what your best practices might be and which can become your best practices over time.

CHAPTER EIGHT

How to Develop Campus-Community Partnerships

Susan Robb Jones and Rev. Ann Palmerton

DEVELOPING CAMPUS-COMMUNITY PARTNERSHIPS, although often presented in the literature as formulaic and based on principles of good practice, is much more than craft. We do not dispute the importance of principles of good practice; they are necessary guideposts in the work of partnership development. We have found, however, that much in the partnering process closely resembles ministry and poetry and conveys the essence of the common commitment when campus and community come together. We try here to capture this essence by telling the story of a particular partnership because, as Witherell and Noddings (1991) note:

> Stories can join worlds of thought and feeling, and they give special voice to the feminine side of human experience—to the power of emotion, intuition, and relationships in human lives. They frequently reveal dilemmas of human caring and conflict, illuminating with the rich, vibrant language of feeling the various landscapes in which we meet the other morally. Through the poignant grip of story and metaphor we meet ourselves and the other in our mutual quest for goodness and meaning. (p. 4)

We explore a partnership between a church and a public research university and what it means to "meet the other morally" in the context of developing campus-community partnerships. This is the craft, ministry, and poetry of partnership development.

We examine the After School Academic Partnership (ASAP) program in the context of what is known about developing and sustaining campus-community partnerships. ASAP is sponsored by Broad Street Presbyterian Church; Ann Palmerton supervises the program in one of her roles as an associate pastor at the church. From the beginning, the program partnered with an undergraduate service-learning class—Leadership in Community Service—and a graduate program—Higher Education and Student Affairs—at Ohio State University (OSU), where Susan Jones, a church

Teaching children of this age, when it's done right, is more than craft; it's also partly ministry and partly poetry.

—Kozol, 2000, p. 277

member, was on the faculty. Since its inception in 2000, the partnership has undergone shifts in staffing, resources, and commitments, which has exposed important issues integral to effective service-learning, such as relationship building, sustainability, and vulnerabilities.

The Context for Our Story

Broad Street Presbyterian Church is a predominantly white congregation located in an African-American neighborhood called the Near East Side in Columbus, Ohio. Poverty and its attendant issues, including substandard housing, unemployment, and lack of opportunity, have eroded this community over several generations. Reflecting the segregated nature of Columbus, the public schools around the church have a majority of African-American students. Founded in 1887, Broad Street Presbyterian Church has actively participated in the neighborhood for many decades, resolving not to move to the suburbs during the racial tensions and "white flight" of the 1960s and 1970s, and more recently advocating for children through its social outreach programs. In addition to ASAP, the church, in partnership with a nearby African-American Presbyterian Church congregation, has offered a neighborhood food pantry for the past 38 years and a summer camp of academic enrichment for kids, which ended recently after 26 years in operation. A full-time licensed child-care center, housed in the church, serves a mix of infants and toddlers from families whose childcare funding sources are both privately paid and publicly funded.

When the ASAP program began, it represented the church's most recent attempt to listen to the needs of Near East Side and to respond tangibly as a good neighbor. The church discerned a need for one-on-one after-school tutoring at area schools. ASAP's original goals and purpose focused on providing academically based tutoring to children in the neighborhood surrounding the church. In partnership with the church and the neighborhood, its tutors would come from the church's congregation and from neighboring congregations and community groups. Because many church members felt more comfortable *inside* the church building, ASAP was adapted to facilitate their wishes. The program was designed to take place in the church building, with parents and guardians responsible for providing transportation for their students.

After much publicity in the local schools and conversations with area educators, parents and caregivers finally came one evening to register their children for the first session of ASAP. We had wondered if anyone would come through the church doors, particularly since outside transportation was necessary. Much to our amazement, families kept coming throughout the evening. We soon realized that we had far more children registered than we had tutors! We also found that generating a regular commitment from church members was more difficult than we had anticipated. This dilemma meant we had to look outside the church for reliable individuals willing to tutor. Susan, who was involved in OSU's service-learning initiatives at the time, laid the groundwork for students enrolled in service-learning classes to serve as tutors. Thus the seeds for a partnership were planted.

Principles and Frameworks of Partnership Development

Community service and service-learning programs cannot exist without partnerships with community organizations, agencies, and programs (Jones, 2003). Yet, this integral relationship is perhaps the least understood, least studied, and most complex dimension of cultivating and sustaining efficacious programs (Stoecker & Tryon, 2009). Partnership development requires that community service-learning professionals (CSLPs) work collaboratively in all phases of the relationship. They must develop a clear sense of purpose that meets both campus and community needs and interests, pay attention to power dynamics, capitalize on community assets rather than deficiencies, communicate and assess, and focus on logistics so as not to burden community organizations (Jones, 2003; Kretzman & McKnight, 1993; Maurrasse, 2001; Seifer & Maurana, 2000; Torres, 2000).

Although a focus on the mechanics of partnership development might be tempting, partnerships require us to look inward and explore the assumptions, stereotypes, expectations, and values we carry into the community. Without reflection, a professional may unwittingly replicate the inequalities such partnerships are designed to eradicate. As Saltmarsh (1998) explained, without attention to partnership relationships, "the best of community service-learning will not be about community, the service provided will be directed toward the students, and the learning fostered will ultimately tend to perpetuate the social system that produces the inequality, impoverishment, and injustice students witness" (p. 22). More recently, Stoecker and Tryon (2009), based upon interviews with the "unheard voices" of staff members from small to medium-sized nongovernmental organizations, demonstrated the unintended consequences of well-intentioned service-learning for many community organizations: That is, despite much "institutional hype" (p. 2) about the positive outcomes of service-learning, the more consistent reality is that community organizations experience service-learning very differently than what is typically defined by higher education, and the way in which many colleges and universities implement their service-learning programs places a burden on the community organizations with whom they claim to partner.

What does it mean to *really* meet community organizations' needs, a hallmark of effective campus-community partnerships? Take a moment to reflect on your own assumptions, stereotypes, expectations, and values using Worksheet 8-1 beginning on page 177.

We do not provide a full description of the principles and theories of partnership development described in the service-learning literature, although CSLPs should become familiar with them and locate their own goals for partnership within a particular framework. We do, however, allude to highlights from the literature as a guide for analyzing our story and for drawing implications for partnership development.

Principles of good practice in partnership development are found in two oft-cited documents: Campus Compact's *Benchmarks for Campus/Community Partnerships* (Torres, 2000) and the Community-Campus Partnerships for Health (CCPH) publication "Developing and Sustaining Community/Campus Partnerships," which outlines nine principles of partnership (Seifer & Maurana, 2000). Both documents clearly identify criteria on which to build and sustain partnerships between campuses and communities. They emphasize such principles and practices as mutuality in all decision-making, collaboration, ongoing communication, regular evaluation and assessment, and relationship building anchored in trust, respect, and balance of power.

After a review of these statements of principles and taking into consideration the contextual and cultural influences on partnership development, Jones (2003) identified characteristics of effective partnerships when translating principles into practice. These included sufficient time to cultivate and sustain partnerships, a close fit between community goals and activities and university learning outcomes, attention to power dynamics and differentials, ongoing communication, acknowledgment that expertise resides in both university and community settings, and continual assessment and evaluation of all phases of the partnership, of all participants affected by the partnership, and of the partnership itself.

Enos and Morton (2003) offer another useful framework for thinking about campus-community partnerships. Their theory of partnership development, which is relationship-based, distinguishes between *transactional* and *transformational* relationships. Applied to partnership development, this conceptualization addresses differences in goals and purposes, scope of commitment, and boundaries. Transactional partnerships are limited in scope, short-term in commitment, and ask little of partners in terms of long-term change. In essence, when a CSLP anchors community relationships in a transactional approach, the focus is simply on finding volunteer sites for college students.

Transformational partnerships, in contrast, require that, as a result of the relationship, both partners change through an ongoing commitment to a goal larger than each. Because partnerships are anchored in reciprocal relationships, the focus is less on the transaction or exchange of services and more on the common goal that all partners are working to achieve. What grows from transformational partnerships is a deepening commitment to the partnership itself and to the issues associated with the partnership (e.g., literacy, poverty, academic achievement, HIV/AIDS, hunger). Although careful not to pass judgment on a preferred model, we believe that in the context of service-learning, all partnerships should have transformation as a goal. We recognize that working toward this goal requires time and effort, but not to engage in a relational process that makes claims on all parties in a partnership seems to us to be at odds with the essence of an authentic partnership and the goals of service-learning.

Most recently, Stoecker and Tryon (2009) identified seven issues that emerged through interviews with community organizations. These themes represent important elements to be considered for the development of effective partnerships: (1) goals and motivations of community organizations for service-learning; (2) finding and selecting service-learners; (3) structuring service-learning; (4) managing service-learners and service-learning projects; (5) diversity and service-learning; (6) relationship and communication with the higher education institutions; and (7) indicators of success (p. 14). Tending to these issues provides a good place to start when developing campus-community partnerships.

Getting Started

Implicit in the principles of partnership development is the focus on relationship building and intentionally designed relationships that support the mission and purposes of the community organization and the learning objectives of the program or course. For the CSLP, this means that not all partnerships are appropriate and that students should not be left to fend for themselves in identifying community sites. Figuring out which sites are appropriate for service-learning partnerships is an important first step. Several considerations may guide the CSLP in making decisions about appropriate sites and getting started on cultivating partnerships.

Knowledge about the Community

CSLPs should be familiar with each community site so that they can assist in the orientation and ongoing supervision of students, respond to their questions, and troubleshoot. They should also learn about the larger context in which the community organization functions; this requires time and energy to become acquainted with the mission, activities, and individuals of each site, the social issues, and the socio-cultural context. This critical step lays the foundation of trust and respect on which authentic and productive partnerships are built.

Assets and Limits

CSLPs should discern the assets, capacities, and potential limitations that each partner brings to the relationship. They should focus mainly on capacities rather than deficiencies. Focusing solely on assets, however, puts partners and the partnership at risk of surprises and lack of preparation. For example, in our partnership between ASAP and Ohio State University, staffing changes were always a potential liability, both in the teaching staff of the service-learning course and in the director position of ASAP. Partnerships are often designed and initiated as if all aspects will remain static, which is rarely the case. Resource limitations, lack of time for sustaining the partnership, and weak infrastructures are common limitations that may have an impact on a partnership but are important to acknowledge as partnerships are cultivated.

Nature of Service and Reflection

When exploring potential community sites, CSLPs should consider the nature of the work in which students will be engaged. Here again, the emphasis in the service-learning literature is on the importance of meaningful work that is closely aligned with desired learning outcomes. We do not dispute this goal but suggest that coming up with meaningful work may place a burden on community organization staff, whose primary work may be less meaningful or even menial. Such an emphasis on meaningful work also privileges campus-based definitions of what constitutes such work. For example, many community organizations, often leanly staffed and resourced, must tend to routine activities for their survival. These activities may not always seem to students and campus staff as the work that produces transformative learning. Nevertheless, the work must be done and is the most helpful way in which service-learners can participate. It is important to help students understand that the work they are doing—whether tutoring a child or preparing refreshments—is related to the goals of the community organization.

In our case, we found that students who serve as tutors were discouraged or even critical if their ASAP student didn't show up. We encouraged the tutors to take initiative and get involved with another activity of the program, or we tried to help them understand what not showing up might really mean. The ASAP program director brought considerable strength to these unplanned, teachable moments.

Direct service with people in the community setting is most influential in promoting the learning outcomes sought from service-learning, although direct service may not always be transformative. Direct service links students to course content and the mission of a community organization. It also connects students to the real-life situations and dilemmas experienced by those served by the community organization. When students begin to personalize complex social issues, their learning takes on a more meaningful, purposeful nature (Jones & Abes, 2003). This learning can prompt further critical thinking and continued commitment, which ultimately benefits community organizations if volunteers continue their service after meeting their course requirements. For the CSLP, this means that although not all the important work of community organizations involves direct service, students must have some substantive opportunities to engage in direct service in order to achieve positive outcomes.

Relationships between Community Staff and Students

The importance of translating students' experiences into learning and meaningful work also suggests an integral relationship between the community organization staff and students. What OSU students learned had much to do with the time that the ASAP directors spent with them, helping them to understand what they saw and experienced. The ASAP directors clearly understood what we were hoping to accomplish with the service-learning class. One OSU student commented: "The relationship I formed with Dr. James [ASAP director] is wonderful in the sense where I can look up to her to be a mentor . . . She wanted me to develop a strong character when it came to community service." Another student stated: "I have been extremely impressed by Joe's [ASAP director] dedication and concern for the ASAP program. He really believes this program is important. I have been trying to pay attention to how he runs things for personal future planning of my own programs like ASAP."

We also witnessed teaching relationships forming between tutors from the church and tutors from the OSU service-learning classes—an unintended outcome. Informal mentoring relationships clearly emerged, although more serendipitously, as generations worked side by side and interacted with each other. The tutors from the church, near the age of the OSU students' grandparents, were keenly interested in the students. The students saw them giving their uncompensated time for the larger purpose of breaking the cycles of poverty, educational inequality, and lack of opportunity. Students observed faith in action and often commented about the tutors volunteering because "they wanted to, rather than having to" (which is presumably how the students saw their own participation). The nearly seamless learning environment was an anchor of the partnership and was built on the relationship of the ASAP program directors with OSU faculty and students. CSLPs should seek out those community sites with the potential for this kind of relationship between community members and campus staff. These relationships take time to cultivate and sustain but are essential to partnership development.

Infrastructure of Support

When starting campus-community partnerships, CSLPs must ensure that they have an infrastructure to deliver on promises to their community partners. CSLPs may not view themselves as rich in resources, but in terms of time, staff, and funding, their resources generally exceed those available to community organizations. As a result, community organizations committed to a partnership come to depend on their campus partners for real, tangible services and results. In our case, during the evolution of ASAP, the program was sometimes entirely dependent on OSU service-learning students for tutors. The success of the program was riding on OSU's ability to deliver well-oriented, culturally sensitive, knowledgeable tutors who always showed up when they were scheduled. OSU faculty and students also got more deeply embedded in the whole operation of the ASAP program, rather than simply providing students with a placement site for their service-learning requirements, which meant that campus faculty and staff needed to be responsive beyond the immediate needs of the ASAP program. This is a critical factor in sustaining authentic partnerships.

Using Worksheet 8-2, beginning on page 180, reflect on how to start a partnership.

Sustaining Partnerships

Sustaining a partnership is challenging, but it distinguishes a relationship-driven partnership from a placement site. Torres, Sinton, and White (2000) identified three factors integral to sustaining partnerships: people and relationships, evaluations, and institutional commitment. They also listed seven elements of highly sustainable programs: (1) clarity of mission or vision; (2) community demand for and strength of programs, services, or activities; (3) organizational leadership; (4) appropriateness of organizational structures; (5) strength of human resources (internal and external); (6) strength of financial resources (internal and external); and (7) willingness to assess, improve, and change (p. 23). These elements are integral to success in sustaining campus-community partnerships but are dynamic and thus affect a partnership in different ways. Some challenges in sustaining partnerships are contained in the ASAP/OSU partnership story.

Mutual Respect and Trust

From the beginning of the development of the campus-community partnership, the Broad Street Presbyterian Church was open to a formalized relationship with the university. Ann's job description as an associate pastor at the church included community networking, and Susan's interest in community-based approaches to teaching and learning in her role as an OSU faculty member provided a natural link for us to work together to develop an infrastructure for the ASAP program. Our respect for each other, commitment to the vision and goals of ASAP, and confidence in creating a service-learning partnership were contagious within both contexts. We believe that this somewhat obvious point—following such natural links as a foundation for sustaining partnerships—often goes undeveloped in the service-learning literature. In essence, we were committed to sustaining the partnership because it also sustained us. As Lawrence-Lightfoot (1999) commented in her research on respect, "Respectful relationships also have a way of sustaining and replicating themselves" (p. 10).

A respectful relationship between individuals, then, extends to a respectful partnership. For us, this meant that as we worked to develop and sustain the partnership, it was important that the university know several things about the church as an organization. As might be expected, the church valued reciprocity with its community partners and anticipated the formation of workable, engaging relationships. For the CSLP, the expectation was that campus faculty and staff spend time at the site, get to know the ins and outs of the community site, and foster relationships with their partners. In addition, just as the university is a complex institution, so is the church! Both partners entered strange new worlds of acronyms, hierarchies, and networks, each with its own learning curve. For the partnership to develop and flourish, each partner needed to commit to becoming more knowledgeable about the other, and to "meet the other morally" and respectfully.

In the case of ASAP, those from the church were aware that interacting with faculty and students from outside this specific faith community could lead to more active reflection on, and even mutual sharing of, the life stories and experiences of those within it. The church was clear from the beginning that the purpose of tutoring was not religious in nature, yet we were aware that volunteers from the congregation saw their commitment to tutoring as an extension of their life of faith. This dynamic was part of the fabric of the partnership. It is important that CSLPs understand and respect the social, economic, cultural, and religious aspects of any partnership, especially when the CSLP is an outsider in a community setting. A respectful partnership cannot exist without understanding and appreciation.

Layers in Partnerships

We discovered that partnerships exist in multiple places and at many layers, which influences the efficacy of the partnership and the ability to sustain it. In the case of ASAP, numerous stakeholders were involved: church staff and congregation members; OSU faculty, students, other tutors; ASAP children, parents, and caregivers; school teachers and principals; and ASAP advisory board members. Even the head of church maintenance took an active interest in the program. Each partner brought assumptions and expectations about the partnership and the goals for participation. A CSLP must tune in to all the multiple layers of a partnership because all are integral to sustaining it (see the box, "ASAP Partners' Perspectives," on the following page).

CSLPs should not just work with the staff member responsible for a particular program. Sustaining partnerships requires much more depth of engagement with all aspects of a community organization. Without paying attention to the layers in any partnership, the CSLP may be responding to one set of interests that may be at odds with another. Navigating tensions can be challenging, but anticipating them is essential when focusing on sustaining relationships with any community organization.

Life of the Community Organization

Related to the depth of engagement is the breadth of involvement in a partnership. A partnership of a transactional nature would most likely involve campus faculty, staff, and students coming to the community site for a specific purpose and role—in our case, to provide tutoring for the children of ASAP. Activities of this kind can be sustained, but they do not promote much growth in a relationship or lead to a transformational partnership. As the quotes in the box attest, the initial involvement of OSU faculty and staff in the ASAP program grew from a focus on setting up the program and developing the partnership to an active involvement in all aspects of the program.

After being invited to join the advisory board, an OSU instructor wrote: "I continue to attend meetings and keep the lines of communication open because I am not seen as just the 'teacher of the service-learning course,' but rather as a 'true partner' or 'honorary church member' dedicated to the same worthy cause." This growing involvement in the life of the ASAP program

---

ASAP Partners' Perspectives

Growing up in a suburb and attending private school did not give me much exposure to inner-city public school children. Any preconceived notion about these children going into the program [ASAP] was completely washed away by the end. Some of the things these kids knew fascinated me.
—*OSU student and ASAP tutor*

I have been a tutor in the ASAP program for three years. I am a graduate chemical engineer and have spent my career in the field of plastic development. Education has been and continues to be very important to me. This last year at ASAP was extremely fulfilling and fun. I spent the beginning of the school year establishing a relationship with the students and enjoyed the year. Both students made the honor roll several times during the year. The work with the students is rewarding. I have a feeling of making a difference in their lives.
—*Church member and ASAP tutor*

During this school year, I had a student who was drastically behind. She had a very bad attitude, was failing to turn in most assignments, and didn't seem to care about school. The tutoring she received through ASAP truly benefited her. She began completing and turning in assignments more regularly. This boosted her confidence, and she began participating in school more. Her negative attitude was subsiding and being replaced by a positive attitude and self-confidence of an engaged learner. I

believe that ASAP was instrumental in making this turnaround happen.
—*Columbus Public School fourth grade teacher*

As a retired elementary school principal, I believe students who participate in ASAP benefit in two ways. The program provides one-on-one tutoring that benefits the student socially and contributes to the building of the student's relationship and citizenship skills. ASAP's hallmark is student academic involvement. The tutors realize that time on task is a major factor in student academic growth. The program director is in constant communication with students' principals and teachers. As a lifelong learner and educator, I believe the ASAP program is an effective and efficient learning opportunity for both students and tutors.
—*ASAP advisory board member*

My work with the ASAP program was unique to me. The first year that I helped out with the program, I spent most of my time meeting the director and the other members of the board and learning about all the details of the tutoring program. The second year, I felt much more like a part of the organization because I was invited to sit on the board and became a tutor myself. I was a lot more invested in the program because of my role with the tutors from OSU and having a hand in shaping the program in a more direct way.
—*OSU service-learning class instructor*

---

was not purely an organizational or administrative move on the part of the church. Indeed, the more involved campus faculty, staff, and students became in all aspects of the program, the greater their investment in its success, which in turn benefited the individuals involved, the program, and the partnership. We believe this full immersion in the life of the community organization is a natural outgrowth of a transformational campus-community partnership.

Assessment and Evaluation

As all the literature on campus-community partnerships suggests, assessment and evaluation are integral to sustaining partnerships. From our experience, we believe that both need to occur continuously throughout the life of the partnership, in multiple settings, both formally and informally, and with all constituent groups. In our case, we asked OSU students to complete surveys about their experiences and the outcomes associated with their community service. We also conducted focus groups with tutors from the congregation and with the children's parents and caregivers. We invited their teachers and principals to provide written documentation of the outcomes of the ASAP program from their perspective. In addition to these typical assessment and evaluation strategies, we incorporated two other activities that yielded significant data.

First, because we find that college students typically focus on what they have *given* to their community site, we asked each OSU tutor to write a letter to the director of the ASAP program describing what they contributed and, more important, what they were *taking away* from the experience. This shift in point of reference from the student to the community organization provided important feedback to both the service-learning faculty and the ASAP program director. It was also gratifying to the ASAP staff to read about the influence of the program on the lives of college students—in terms of both their personal development and their learning outcomes.

Second, we held an annual end-of-year-celebration for all ASAP participants. The ASAP director presented certificates of completion to the children and tutors. Others, most notably the kids and their parents and caregivers, offered spontaneous testimonials about the powerful influence of the program on the lives of these children. These voices provided a source of program evaluation information; perhaps more important, they were energizing and motivating for all involved.

Embracing Vulnerabilities

Because partnerships are most often built around relationships between people, rather than organizations and institutions, they are always vulnerable to changes in personnel. Developing an infrastructure to support partnerships and assuring institutional commitment helps offset this vulnerability, but neither can completely buttress the partnership against such fragility because partnerships most typically are driven by people. In the ASAP-OSU partnership, after the initial implementation of the program, both the ASAP director and the OSU faculty member most involved in the development of the partnership moved on to different jobs in different states. Since then, six directors have run the ASAP program. In addition, it was difficult to ascertain whether OSU's commitment to the partnership remained the same as new individuals moved into oversight positions there. On the face of it, the partnership seemed to be vulnerable to these shifts and in danger of unraveling. This dilemma was exacerbated because the position of ASAP director was not full time, which made filling the position difficult. What we discovered, however, was that continuity of the program was not based upon who the director was but on the reputation of the program itself. In fact, one parent eloquently conveyed this at an end-of-the-year celebration. She said, "When I learned that Davida [former ASAP director] was leaving I was worried that the program couldn't possibly be the same, but then you found Kyle [most recent ASAP director]. He set my mind at ease. This year has been great for my children. Parents listen up; you can count on the Board to find a new director who will keep this program going for our children. So no matter who the director is, sign up for next year!" Such free, unsolicited advertising/testimony is priceless.

Reflect on how to sustain your partnerships using Worksheet 8-3, beginning on page 183.

Lessons Learned

We have compiled a list of what we have learned about developing and sustaining campus-community partnerships from the ASAP-OSU partnership and from our work together. We brainstormed together and offered individual perspectives on each item.

1) *Recognize the importance of flexibility.* By flexibility, we mean not only our own but also flexibility in expectations for the nature of the partnership. The community partner may find this easy because flux and change seem to be typical of the rhythm of community organizations. CSLPs, on the other hand, may be eager to get things set. In our experience, things are rarely set, and the work of a partnership is never done. We also discovered that the program we were setting out to create unfolded very differently from what we had expected. Surprises emerge in any partnership, so embracing them rather than resisting helps. Both the community and campus partners need flexibility in making adjustments and changes that affect the individuals and the partnership.

2) *Explore the tensions in dynamic locations.* CSLPs must respect the boundaries of the elements in the partnership, whether church, university, or other setting, and understand where these spaces intersect and overlap. The CSLP must be willing to "change places" (Clark & Young, 2005), encounter differing social practices within these spaces, and then become a skilled and respectful "border crosser" (Giroux, 1992), able to navigate the terrain of multiple life space. The CSLP must also work with students to respect these spaces, coming to understand what it means to provide community service in a particular setting (e.g., a church) and with children or others who are most often from different racial, ethnic, and social class backgrounds.

3) *Acknowledge the risks involved in partnering.* We tend to focus on the many benefits of partnerships. But there are also risks for all involved. It is best to discuss these at all stages of the partnering process. In our case, OSU's involvement in the program became so deep that the ASAP program was quite dependent on the partnership. This made ASAP particularly vulnerable to any shifts in staffing and enrollment patterns at OSU. In addition, from a faculty perspective, significant time is required to develop and sustain truly authentic, transformative partnerships. This commitment potentially puts the faculty member or CSLP at risk in evaluation for promotion and tenure or in annual reviews, particularly if the institutional commitment does not mirror that of the CSLP.

4) *There are no substitutes for firsthand knowledge.* Community partners should not have to take on the issues and challenges involved with students' presence on site. The CSLP should be on site frequently enough to tune in to the daily rhythm of the program's activities and work directly with students in order to avoid burdening the site itself. Although ultimately this responsibility is shared, the partnership will suffer if the burden becomes too great for the community partner. In one instance, an OSU student remarked that she did not know that "inner-city kids" who attended public schools ever went to college. The CSLP should work out any issues that arise with naïve, ill-informed students.

5) *Campus-community partnerships are cyclical and dynamic.* We have learned the importance of navigating the tension between developing partnerships that work because of the people and their relationships and not entirely depending on those people for success. One strategy is to develop partnerships that are deep enough that they don't depend on only a few individuals for success or sustainability. Developing commitment not only to the community program but also to the partnership at both the campus and community organization levels serves as a potential safeguard against the vulnerability from partnerships driven by individuals.

6) *Reframe "sustainability."* We have learned over the course of the nine years of the ASAP program that a program and partnership can be sustained even when in flux. In fact, although we may think of sustainability as everything staying the same, including continuity in staff and resources, we have seen the trust parents, the ASAP advisory board, children, and tutors have in the program even when it appears to be undergoing significant change. Despite changes in the director of ASAP and shifting connections with the university, the bonding and mentoring that takes place between students and tutors every day that ASAP is offered is enduring and clearly sustainable.

7) *Take time to celebrate.* In the midst of our busy lives and multiple responsibilities, it is important to step back and celebrate accomplishments. Celebrating both the partnership and all the partners is an important, affirming use of time that provides even greater energy and commitment. At ASAP, celebratory events enhance relationships among all partners, focus on achievement of desired outcomes, and lend a playful quality to the program's earnest weekly work. They serve as representations of everyone's value to the partnership.

Conclusion: "Meet the Other Morally"

Robert Coles (1993), in *The Call of Service*, probed the depths of real reciprocity in the context of community service. He recalled an undergraduate student in his class who offered this perspective:

> It is not just a matter, Julia reminded me, of an enlarged sensibility and awareness (one hopes and prays) being brought to the academic setting, but of a broadened mind and deepened heart (again, one hopes and prays) being brought back to the place where community service is being done. (p. 167)

CSLPs must look beyond the boundaries of traditional academic goals and outcomes when developing campus-community partnerships. Authentic, transformational partnerships cannot be sustained by campus-centered initiatives alone, but instead, as the quote from Coles suggests, by enabling the dynamic, reciprocal partnership process to unfold. This requires a commitment to relationship building with individuals as well as to the partnership itself. Principles of good practice and models of partnership development provide useful templates for getting started. CSLPs must be open to the ambiguities, complexities, and dynamic nature of campus-community partnerships, which is helped by the presence of respect, trust, patience, and flexibility. This is the craft, ministry, and poetry of partnerships.

References

Clark, C., & Young, M. (2005). Changing places: Theorizing space and power dynamics in service-learning. In D. Butin (Ed.), *Service-learning in higher education: Critical issues and directions* (pp. 71-87). New York: Palgrave Macmillan.

Coles, R. (1993). *The call of service.* Boston: Houghton Mifflin Company.

Enos, S., & Morton, K. (2003). Developing a theory and practice of campus-community partnerships. In B. Jacoby (Ed.), *Building partnerships for service-learning* (pp. 20–41). San Francisco: Jossey-Bass.

Giroux, H. A. (1992). *Border crossings: Cultural workers and the politics of education.* New York: Routledge.

Jones, S. R. (2003). Principles and profiles of exemplary partnerships with community agencies. In B. Jacoby (Ed.), *Building partnerships for service-learning* (pp. 151–173). San Francisco: Jossey-Bass.

Jones, S. R., & Abes, E. S. (2003). Developing student understanding of HIV/AIDS through community service-learning: A case study analysis. *Journal of College Student Development, 44,* 470–488.

Kozol, J. (2000). *Ordinary resurrections.* New York: Crown Publishers.

Kretzmann, J. P., & McKnight, J. L. (1993). *Building communities from the inside out: A path toward finding and mobilizing a community's assets.* Chicago, IL: Urban Affairs and Policy Research Neighborhood Innovations Network, Northwestern University.

Lawrence-Lightfoot, S. (1999). *Respect: An exploration.* Reading, MA: Perseus.

Maurrasse, D. (2001). *Beyond the campus: How colleges and universities form partnerships with their communities.* New York: Taylor & Francis.

Saltmarsh, J. (1998). Exploring the meanings of community/university partnerships. *National Society for Experiential Education Quarterly,* (Summer), 6–22.

Seifer, S. D., & Maurana, C. A. (2000). Developing and sustaining community-campus partnerships: Putting principles into action. *Partnership Perspectives,* 7–11.

Stoecker, R., & Tryon, E. A. (2009). *The unheard voices: Community organizations and service learning.* Philadelphia, PA: Temple University Press.

Torres, J. (2000). *Benchmarks for campus/community partnerships.* Providence, RI: Campus Compact.

Torres, J., Sinton, R., & White, A. (2000). *Establishing and sustaining an office of community service.* Providence, RI: Campus Compact.

Witherell, C., & Noddings, N. (1991). *Stories lives tell: Narrative and dialogue in education.* New York: Teachers College.

Additional Resources

Bringle, R. G., & Hatcher, J. A. (2002). Campus-community relationships: The terms of engagement. *Journal of Social Issues, 58*(3), 503–516.

Ferrari, J. R., & Worrall, L. (2000). Assessments by community agencies: How "the other side" sees service-learning. *Michigan Journal of Community Service Learning, 7,* 35–40.

Gelmon, S., Holland, B., Seifer, S., Shinnamon, A., & Connor, K. (1998). Community-university partnerships for mutual learning. *Michigan Journal of Community Service Learning, 5,* 97–107.

Gugerety, C. R., & Swezey, E. D. (1996). Developing campus-community relationships. In B. Jacoby (Ed.), *Service-learning in higher education: Concepts and practices.* San Francisco: Jossey-Bass.

Scheibel, J., Bowley, E. M., & Jones, S. (2005). *The promise of partnerships: Tapping into the college as a community asset.* Providence, RI: Campus Compact.

Vernon, A., & Ward, K. (1999). Campus and community partnerships: Assessing impacts and strengthening connections. *Michigan Journal of Community Service Learning, 6,* 30–37.

Ward, K., & Wolf-Wendel, L. (2000). Community-centered service learning: Moving from "doing for" to "doing with." *American Behavioral Scientist, 43*(5), 769–780.

WORKSHEET 8-1: Examining Your Assumptions, Stereotypes, Expectations, and Values

1. Why am I interested in this partnership?

    _____

    _____

    _____

    _____

2. What values and commitments do I have that are reflected in the goals and mission of this community organization?

    _____

    _____

    _____

    _____

3. What assumptions am I bringing to this potential partnership that might either contribute to or interfere with relationship development?

    _____

    _____

    _____

    _____

4. What stereotypes might I have of the population this partnership will serve?

    _____

    _____

    _____

    _____

(continued)

W O R K S H E E T

WORKSHEET

5. What prior experience do I have with the issues and concerns of this site?

_____

_____

_____

_____

6. What expectations do I have of a partnership with this organization?

_____

_____

_____

_____

7. How much time do I have to devote to partnership development?

_____

_____

_____

_____

8. What barriers might I encounter?

_____

_____

_____

_____

9. How might I overcome these barriers?

_____

_____

_____

_____

(continued)

10. What sources of support might I tap?

_____

_____

_____

_____

W O R K S H E E T

WORKSHEET

WORKSHEET 8-2: Getting Started

(to be completed by both campus and community partners)

1. What do we need to know about one another and our organizational settings to initiate a partnership?

   _____

   _____

   _____

   _____

2. What experience does the campus have in working with similar community organizations?

   _____

   _____

   _____

   _____

3. What experience does the community organization have working with college students and/or campus programs?

   _____

   _____

   _____

   _____

4. How would college students best be involved in the community organization? In what work would they be engaged?

   _____

   _____

   _____

   _____

(continued)

5. What issues or questions would involvement in this community organization potentially raise among students?

    _____

    _____

    _____

    _____

6. What strengths does each partner bring to the relationship?

    _____

    _____

    _____

    _____

7. What potential liabilities exist?

    _____

    _____

    _____

    _____

8. What resources are needed to initiate the partnership? From the campus? From the community organization?

    _____

    _____

    _____

    _____

(continued)

WORKSHEET

9. What roles and responsibilities will those involved from the campus and the community organization have?

    _____

    _____

    _____

    _____

10. What structures will we need to put in place to maximize the potential for success (e.g., regular meetings, evaluation, time on site, celebratory events)?

    _____

    _____

    _____

    _____

WORKSHEET 8-3: Sustaining Partnerships

1. How will we know if the partnership is working (e.g., meeting goals and expectations of all partners)?

    _____

    _____

    _____

    _____

2. What needs to be in place to move the partnership from a transactional to a transformational relationship?

    _____

    _____

    _____

    _____

3. What challenges might we encounter in sustaining a partnership?

    _____

    _____

    _____

    _____

4. How will we resolve conflict or challenges as they arise?

    _____

    _____

    _____

    _____

(continued)

WORKSHEET

5. What strategies can we develop that protect the partnership from vulnerabilities such as staffing changes and/or resource limitations?

    _____

    _____

    _____

    _____

6. What qualities would celebrations need to have to truly affirm and reflect the "poetry" of the partnership?

    _____

    _____

    _____

    _____

CHAPTER NINE

Leveraging Financial Support for Service-Learning: Relevance, Relationships, Results, Resources

Barbara Holland and Mark N. Langseth

LIKE OTHER RELATIVELY RECENT INNOVATIONS IN HIGHER EDUCATION, service-learning and civic engagement programs often depend on grant funding and can become vulnerable in a context of tight campus budgets. Many community service-learning professionals (CSLPs) are concerned that their current financial resources are inadequate to ensure high-quality programming, accommodate desired growth, or sustain campus-community partnerships.

Thus, two key questions emerge for CSLPs:

1. What financial resources are necessary to support high-quality, well-integrated service-learning efforts on your campus?

2. How can I ensure the long-term sustainability of these efforts?

If you are unsure exactly how to answer these questions, know first that you are not alone. Few CSLPs come to their jobs with extensive experience in leveraging financial resources. More and more CSLPs, however, are gaining the necessary skills.

> Far beyond simplistic notions of fundraising, leveraging financial support for service-learning is a complex process that involves demonstrating relevance, documenting results, and developing relationships with potential resource providers—all building on a well-crafted strategy for growing and sustaining your program. Success depends on your understanding of these processes. Learn to think strategically about why and how others can be motivated to partner with you and to provide new resources.

The purpose of this chapter is to provide information about the fundamentals of resource generation. We include a detailed discussion on internal and external allies, strategies, and resource providers; a series of reflection questions; and a list of information resources to help guide your ongoing work.

We use the terms *resource providers* or *prospects* rather than *donors* or *funders* to describe possible sources of financial support because the latter terms most often connote what we call "external" (off-campus) resource providers. One of our most important assertions is that "internal" (on-campus) resource providers should be a major focus of your efforts to leverage financial resources.

Generating resources is a complex process. In the "Fundamentals" section that follows, we explain: (1) factors that influence potential resource providers, (2) a basic framework for leveraging resources, and (3) two sample cases. In the subsequent section, we look at this complex process and the CSLP's relationship to it through four "Rs": relevance, relationships, results, and resources. You may find one particular "R" most appropriate, or you may pick and choose insights from each to form your own framework for approaching the resource-generation process. During challenging budgetary times, you should consider a plan that encompasses all of the four "Rs" in order to best position your service-learning and engagement agenda as core work essential to the success of your institution. Our goal is not to give you a simplistic, generic answer to the resource-generation puzzle. Rather, we wish to spark your own creative thinking about how you approach this complex process.

Fundamentals

Most of us fantasize about an ultra-rich benefactor swooping in to endow our program or dream about the campus administration finally realizing that our program is so critical that it deserves a bigger piece of the budget pie. Likewise, many of us are frustrated that those who hold the purse strings don't seem to understand the importance and complexity of our work or appreciate the power of service-learning in addressing larger campus, community, and societal challenges.

Each college or university has an annual budgeting process, and different potential sources of funding are discussed in that context. In development circles, flexible funds that can be used for any purpose the campus desires are deemed *unrestricted*. Wherever these unrestricted sources are, the advantage of pursuing and securing them is that your campus leadership has great discretion in how to use them. Institutional decision makers can allocate dollars from these sources to your program whenever they wish. You may also be able to seek base funding by attaching your activities to the budget requests for key strategic initiatives such as student recruitment or retention, or improving learning outcomes, among others. While funds are constantly being negotiated, each institution has a formal budget-request process. Take time to learn about the annual budgeting process at your institution, and be prepared to participate. Study the institution's strategic plan and budget guidelines so that, at the right time, you are able to prepare a written budget proposal with supporting narrative that links your resource request to your institution's budgetary context.

Factors Influencing Potential Resource Providers

Potential resource providers, both on and off campus, are extremely unlikely to fulfill these fantasies without very hard work on your part to capture their attention and interest, which precede their propensity to share money. First, you need to understand the most common factors that sway potential resource providers as they consider where to invest. Generally, the four most influential factors are:

1. *Synergy with their passions, interests, and concerns.* A major focus in professional fundraising is what is called *prospect research,* or the process of understanding the interests and capacity of a potential resource provider. Perhaps the best indicator of interest is past behavior. If an external prospect has invested substantial resources in a particular cause, he or she probably has a passion for that cause. Similarly, if your president or other internal resource providers wake up every day worried about a particular issue, their interest in supporting effective efforts to address that concern is likely. Connecting your cause to resource providers' passions, interests, or concerns must be a major focus of resource-generation efforts.

2. *Relationships with people they trust.* Another focus of prospect research is determining whom potential resource providers trust or who "has their ear." While causes are important, unless prospects trust the advocates and champions of the cause, they will be unlikely to give. Similarly, if a person they trust introduces them to a new rationale for a cause or operation, they will be more likely to respond. "It's all about relationships" may overstate the case, but relationships are, indeed, important.

3. *Clear goals, outcomes, and evidence.* Prospects must also understand the specific, tangible goals of your program and its outcomes. Usually, prospects are most interested in outcomes for the end users. In the case of service-learning, end users can be the students who benefit from enhanced learning and development, the community residents positively affected by your program, and various constituents on campus who benefit (e.g., faculty whose commitment to excellence in teaching is renewed by integrating service with learning in a course). In fact, the three-for-one (student-community-institutional) benefits reaped by service-learning programs can be an attractive feature for resource providers who want to maximize the impact of their investment. Collecting systematic data about student, community, and institutional outcomes builds a body of evidence that will enhance resource-provider confidence. (Strategic planning, assessment, and documentation strategies are covered elsewhere in this book and therefore are not discussed in great detail here. All three are critical to your resource-generation efforts.)

4. *Clear financial need.* Potential resource providers must also be able to see a clear financial need that relates directly to your current and future goals. Most want to help something get bigger or better and to know that their investment will also help ensure the long-term sustainability of the program. While some may simply support your program exactly as it is, most resource providers want to fund positive change and create a long-term legacy that arises directly from their investments.

Your role in these fundamental elements of leveraging resources is critical. Don't worry about addressing them alone, however. Faculty allies and allies in the administration, in the development or advancement office, and in the government relations office on your campus can be particularly helpful in leveraging resources. (We discuss partnerships with these potential allies later.)

Framework for Leveraging Resources

As they approach major fundraising campaigns, development or advancement professionals often see their work as falling into four categories: leadership, cases, prospects, and marketing. Even if you're not envisioning your resource-generation work as a major campaign, you can use these categories to scope out your overall approach to leveraging internal or external resources.

LEADERSHIP

Because leveraging resources is a complex process, ally with others who share your passion and who might help. If you want to cultivate allies who will act on your resource-generation goals, involve them early to determine your program and financial objectives and to help shape a resource-generation strategy. You want to select people—informally or formally—who:

- Are true believers in service, service-learning, and/or civic engagement programs;

- Understand how these programs can help advance other important student, community, or campus goals;

- Have relationships or influence with potential resource providers that you would like to reach; and

- Are willing to take action on behalf of your program(s).

You may choose to formalize their role on a committee or simply ask them to serve as an informal "kitchen cabinet" to set and achieve goals for resource development. A key role for this inner circle of allies is to connect you with other allies. For example, you will likely need the president and other members of the administration to support you, both by providing financial resources and by providing connections to outside donors. Your inner circle of allies should include people who can reach these influential campus leaders.

MAKING THE CASE

Making the case for your cause almost always involves three elements:

- Demonstrating an understanding of the larger campus and/or community context, including critical issues that many people care about;

- Making clear connections between your program and at least one of these critical issues; and

- Showing why your program in particular is well suited to address one or more of these critical issues.

Situate your program in the context of broader concerns in which your top prospects are keenly interested. An advantage of service-learning is that it can make an impact on a wide range of student, campus, and community challenges. One attendant risk, on the other hand, is that you might seem to be boasting that service-learning is a cure-all or "all things to all people."

While you might develop a core case statement and use that universally, you will likely need to make a slightly different case to different prospects, based on their interests. This doesn't mean distorting the truth; it simply reflects the fact that service-learning addresses many issues and therefore can be framed differently to help various audiences understand all aspects of its importance.

PROSPECTS

Factors that influence potential resource providers apply equally to internal and external prospects. One of the big decisions you need to make, based on the advice of your allies, is the extent to which you want to focus on cultivating internal versus external prospects. As with many new innovations on campus, service and service-learning programs often rely initially on at least some external funding from corporations, foundations, or government sources. The most successful programs eventually inspire enough stable, internal investment to maintain quality, accommodate growth, and ensure long-term sustainability. Ultimately, the goal is to inspire campus leaders to include a healthy investment in your programs in the annual operating budget. Yet, because even the most successful programs rely on periodic external funding to help augment their efforts, we discuss both internal and external prospects at length later.

MARKETING

Call it what you will—marketing, advertising, raising visibility, attracting attention, spreading the word—it is a critical part of leveraging resources. Any good marketing effort begins with an audience, in this case your most desired, highest-potential prospects. Once you have determined your best prospects, keep a laser focus on the messages and the message-delivery vehicles most likely to connect these prospects to your cause. If you have two or three major categories of prospects, you will likely need tailored marketing strategies for each category. Again, although the core of your case and message-delivery vehicles may be the same for all prospects, most successful marketing is tailored at least in part to the specific interests of the prospects you want to reach.

The messages and media used to market your program to students or other end-users may not be the same as those that will be most effective with prospective resource providers. You may use some of your marketing materials with prospects, but those will likely need to be supplemented with more tailored materials (such as letters or fact sheets) that appeal to a specific prospect's passions, interests, and concerns. A combination of evaluation-based evidence and heart-tugging stories tends to motivate potential resource providers more than just one or the other. Facts and anecdotes are both important and highly complementary.

See the boxes on pages 190 and 193 for examples of how CSLPs have used a range of strategies to build support.

Leveraging Strategies: The Four Rs

In this section, we offer a perspective for leveraging resources, using the four "Rs"—demonstrating *relevance,* developing *relationships,* documenting *results,* and determining the most appropriate potential *resource providers.*

Example #1: Using Influence and Alliances to Build Visibility

A regional, comprehensive university with 15,000 students located in a metropolitan area recently completed both a university-wide strategic planning process and a subsequent general education curriculum revision. As a result of previous cultivation of relationships with two highly influential faculty members—one from biology and one from sociology, both of whom integrate service-learning into a course—the campus's CSLP was actively engaged in both processes. She served as a formal member of the general education review team, along with her supportive biology professor.

For the past seven years, the service-learning program has been funded mostly from external sources—state, federal, and foundation grants. Two years ago, the CSLP successfully convinced the university to cover half her salary and benefit package through the student affairs budget. The vice president of student affairs (VPSA) agreed because the CSLP had been successful in raising external dollars and because of very positive campus-wide attitudes toward her and co-curricular and course-based service-learning.

Building on this progress, she hoped to secure 100% of her salary and benefit package and a $10,000 operating budget for service-learning from the campus's general operating budget. Because the service-learning program had strong co-curricular and curricular elements and because the campus strategic plan gave priority to integration of student and academic affairs, she decided to pursue joint funding from both student and academic affairs to reach this goal.

As both the strategic planning and general education revision processes unfolded over the previous two years, the CSLP and her two faculty allies had systematically worked behind the scenes to increase the vice president for academic affairs's (VPAA) understanding of, and interest in, service-learning. Previously, the VPAA had spoken positively about service-learning but had not requested any additional funds for service-learning in his annual budget. The CSLP and her faculty allies, one of whom had the ear of the VPAA, were able to convince him to attend two local and two national conferences on service-learning convened by the American Association of State Colleges and Universities and by the state Campus Compact office. Two of the four workshops were designed specifically for VPAAs and provosts who wanted to learn more about service-learning and its potential impact on students, communities, and—most important—larger campus issues such as diversity, town-gown relations, and improvement of teaching and learning.

During this same period, the CSLP and her faculty allies completed an intensive assessment process to study the impact of service-learning on students, community, and faculty teaching and learning. The assessment was partly funded by an external grant for service-learning and partly by an internal grant aimed at improving campus assessment. A description of the study's positive impact was included in a "Service-Learning Works" brochure, along with student testimonials and well-chosen photos of students in the community and in the classroom. This brochure was distributed widely on and off campus, to all members of the strategic planning and curriculum revision teams, university advancement leaders, and the university foundation's board of trustees. The faculty allies included personal notes to all, inviting the recipients to consider service-learning as they deliberated about priorities.

Ultimately, "community and civic engagement" emerged as one of six themes in the new university strategic plan. "Increased opportunities for students to combine experience with learning" became a priority in the guidelines for the new general education curriculum, including a major emphasis on international education and brief mention of service-learning. Building on this base, the CSLP and the two faculty allies formed an alliance with the director of international education on

(continued)

campus and produced a joint proposal that packaged international education and service-learning as highly complementary strategies to address the new strategic and curricular priorities. Concurrently, they completed a presentation to the university's foundation board at the request of the board chair, who liked the marketing brochure and wanted to ensure hat the board was aware of the university's efforts.

The university's development director and vice president for advancement were very impressed with the presentation, as was the board chair. Through a series of subsequent conversations in the advancement division and among the board, "challenge" funding for the CSLP salary and benefit package and $10,000 budget was secured for two years from a local foundation, on the condition that the university cover the costs in the third year and beyond. After successful presentations before the academic affairs leadership team and the student affairs leadership team, the VPSA and VPAA agreed to split these ongoing costs. The CSLP's goal was achieved.

Demonstrating Relevance

When we speak of relevance, we are suggesting the importance of considering the relevance of service-learning *from the perspective of prospective resource providers*. As a professional in the field, you understand firsthand the relevance of service-learning to a range of outcomes, from improving teaching and learning to developing the next generation of active citizens and addressing critical community issues. Prospective resource providers may not have the privilege of such firsthand understanding.

Consider the analogy of designing service-learning classes to ensure a focus on specific learning outcomes and/or types of students. One of the strengths of service-learning is that it can be shaped to fit different learning styles, life experiences, and paths to understanding. Many service-learning practitioners skillfully tailor the *learning* side of service-learning so that the learning objectives will most likely to be achieved. Yet it is easy to forget that potential resource providers have equally diverse backgrounds, including their ways of learning and their sense of institutional mission and priorities. Thus, we cannot expect them to respond to only one way of explaining service-learning and engagement.

Consider your personal perspective on service-learning as it relates to financial giving. Other chapters of this book have encouraged you to reflect deeply on your personal commitment to this work. Perhaps you are deeply committed to experiential education, to excellence in teaching and learning, to social justice, to developing students as active citizens, or to engaging your institution in learning activities that address a particular community issue. Whatever your passions, your decisions about giving your own time, effort, and resources are likely to follow your expectations. It is the same with prospective financial contributors to your program.

If you wish to persuade potential resource providers, you must discover and address *their* passions, perspectives, interests, and concerns. Another strength of service-learning is its ability to attract people from widely diverse political, moral, religious, and philosophical perspectives. In a world increasingly divided along all these lines, service-learning has the power to bridge differences. The opportunity to engage a diverse array of prospective supporters through diverse messages and media is an extension of this power.

Finally, you should situate your program within a larger context. Proactively address the benefits of service-learning with regard to *larger community or campus concerns that matter to prospective resource providers.* Placing your efforts in a specific context of importance to the prospect builds relevance and stimulates interest in your program. You can devise an appropriate strategy for approaching prospects only if you know the causes they are interested in advancing. Is their passion for social justice, promoting volunteerism, developing student skills for the future workforce, improving student learning or retention, or a specific community issue such as poverty, early education, economic development, homelessness, or the environment? To make service-learning relevant to potential resource providers, place the story of service-learning in the context of issues or goals of importance to them.

Developing Relationships

Our experience with community service and service-learning professionals over the past 20 years tells us that you are a highly principled group. For many of you, the idea of developing a relationship with someone simply because you seek to acquire resources from him or her might seem distasteful at best, unethical at worst. If this were the only outcome of your resource-generation efforts, we could not agree more. Fortunately, there is much more to it; strategies to generate resources are successful only in the context of an authentic relationship that is based on the articulation of shared goals and interests.

There are many other ways to view the process of developing relationships in a fundraising context. From our experience, the first step is identifying the common ground on which the relationship can be built.

The process of developing relationships and sharing the potential of service-learning is not just a means to an end but an end itself. Even if prospective resource providers choose not to support you financially, they will most likely appreciate knowing about your work and may offer non-financial support. Consider the process of building trust and relationships with internal and external prospects as a mission in and of itself.

As described above, focus on the importance of engaging your allies in the process of defining your goals and generating resources. Your allies on your leadership team are important in part because they bring their own networks of high-trust relationships to assist in resource generation. Assemble this group as you consider the essential element of relationships in your resource-generation plan. If you do not yet have such relationships to draw on, it is time to begin forging them. Wide participation in shaping your resource generation plan creates visibility, builds a wider base of support, and signals a high level of internal and external support.

Documenting Results

Assessment and documentation of service-learning impact and results is discussed in detail in Chapter 10, but here we want to emphasize the importance of evidence in developing and

---

Example #2: Using Evidence to Make the Case for Resources

A human services instructor at a 1,000-student community college was given a quarter-time release to serve for one year as coordinator of service-learning, funded by a small federal Learn and Serve America grant she received from her state Campus Compact office. The purpose of the grant was to provide in-service workshops for faculty, to survey the campus for service-learning activity and interest, and to evaluate the effectiveness of existing efforts, both co-curricular and course-based. The evaluation component also emphasized assessing service-learning's potential impact on student retention because retention had recently emerged as a top strategic priority for the college. The instructor worked closely on the grant proposal and implementation with the vice president for student affairs (VPSA), who was charged by the president with leading the process of developing an aggressive plan to increase student retention by 20% over the next three years.

As a result of the grant, five faculty were identified who were already effectively integrating service-learning into their courses, four additional faculty were recruited to pilot service-learning in one of their courses, and evidence was collected about service-learning's positive impact on student learning and retention. Specifically, the human services instructor/CSLP convinced the five current service-learning faculty and the institutional assessment officer to add two questions regarding retention and service-learning to the standard campus assessment in five of their courses. Over 90% of the students in these courses reported that service-learning had a positive impact on their likelihood of persisting through the end of the course. Even more important, over 90% of these same students reported that if more courses at the college contained well-designed service-learning components, they would be more likely to stay in college through graduation.

Due to these positive results, the VPSA agreed to increase the human service instructor's release to half-time, the vice president for academic affairs agreed to sustain annual in-service workshops through her budget, and the president asked the advancement office to make further expansion of service-learning a priority in the college's fundraising.

---

implementing a plan to leverage resources. Both quantitative and qualitative data are useful in the resource-generation process.

If numbers or statistics are the "hard wiring" that convinces potential supporters that your program works, then stories from students, community members, and faculty that tug at prospects' emotions or resonate with their goals are the electricity. Likewise, while informing prospects about numbers and stories on paper is important, there is no substitute for prospects hearing directly from participants themselves. Create opportunities for students and community partners who have been profoundly affected by your program to communicate directly with internal and external potential resource providers. Be strategic about which students and community representatives you place in front of which prospects. Opportunities for prospects to meet with participants include meals, trips to community sites, visits to prospects' offices, or recognition events. Hold a "Service-Learning Celebration Day" and invite internal administrators to host the program, with time for students and community partners to tell their stories. Regardless of the setting, make sure students and community representatives are well prepared to deliver messages that prospects will find compelling. If a prospect is focused on improving student learning or retention, then that should be the focus; if the prospect is interested in benefits to the community and the image of your institution, then take that focus. The advantage of having presentations as a team is that it allows you to ensure that multiple objectives are raised.

You should also populate your website with an array of community partnership project descriptions that align with major institutional and community goals and concerns. Just as you would prepare to deliver a tailored message to a specific prospect, you must prepare students and community representatives to deliver focused messages on the key topic, always being mindful of the prospect's interests and perspectives. Finally, showing that your attention to evaluation of results has allowed you to improve the efficiency and impact of programmatic operations can be especially persuasive.

Identifying Potential Resource Providers

In this section, we focus separately on internal versus external sources of financial support because *specific* strategies for each can be quite different. What remains the same are the general approaches outlined above.

INTERNAL SOURCES, STRATEGIES, AND ALLIES

The ultimate goal for your resource-generation efforts is to weave adequate funding for your program(s) into your institution's annual operating budget to create a sustained base of support. Sources of general operating funds, all of which can be tapped, include student tuition and fees, legislatively driven base funding (for state institutions), annual giving, and endowments. You should understand all these sources and the expenses they commonly cover.

Tuition and fees

The most flexible source of core operating support for colleges and universities is tuition and fees. As states cut base funding for core operating support of public colleges and universities, institutions rely more heavily on tuition revenue to balance budgets, leading to some combination of tuition increases or enrollment growth. Private colleges and universities have always relied intensely on tuition income to support their operations. Wherever you work, tuition is likely to be the major source of funding you receive from the general operating budget.

Most campus leaders view tuition and fee income as a core source of support for the academic operations on campus—courses, internships, and other academically based programs. Why is this important? If your program is strongly tied to course-based service-learning, you have a much better case to make for tuition-based operating support. If your program is largely co-curricular in nature, administrators will be less likely to view tuition as an appropriate place from which to support service-learning.

Although tuition is most often tied to academic affairs, student fees are often a major source of support for student affairs activities. If your program's current and future focus is co-curricular, student fees may be an option for generating funding for your program. Generally, student government leaders heavily influence or determine fee allocation. In a number of institutions, student governments help fund service-learning through student fees. In either case, your chances of getting support from tuition or fees will be influenced by the degree to which the program is viewed as integral to the teaching, learning, and development of students, so a focus on relevance, relationships, and results still applies!

State legislative support

Due to decreasing state appropriations to postsecondary education, almost all public colleges and universities now draw less than half of their total revenue for general operating support from this source. Though the total percentage of such dollars is shrinking, the investment of these funds is very much at the discretion of campus leaders. Before deciding whether these dollars are a good source for your program, analyze how quickly their availability is shrinking. If state dollars are decreasing rapidly, you do not want to vie for them as a source for your program, both because there is likely intense competition for them and because you do not want to hitch your program to a source likely to continue to decline. As public funding decreases, these funds are most likely to be used for activities viewed as core business, so it is strategic to align service-learning and engagement with other successful initiatives.

On the positive side, some state legislatures have appropriated dollars specifically for service-learning or similar outreach and engagement programs, usually through a statewide program aimed at expanding service-learning and civic engagement. (We cover these sources in more detail later in the "External Resources" section under "Government," starting on page 200.) We cite these programs here partly because evidence of state support for service-learning suggests that legislators would support allocation of campus general operating funds for these purposes as well. A key strategy would be to link your institution's service-learning program to high-priority state goals such as workforce preparation, job generation, increasing educational attainment and lifelong learning, increasing literacy, etc.

Usually, tuition and state appropriations are melded into one "pot" of general operating revenue on campus. Still, you should understand the original sources of each of these fund categories as you consider how you might make the case that your program deserves funding from one or both sources.

Annual giving

Most institutions seek general support from their friends, including alumni, parents, community members, and campus employees, for some kind of annual fund. Your campus might call it another name, but this fund is most often coordinated by the development or alumni office. The annual fund often contributes to scholarships or special projects. One way to find out what the annual fund supports on your campus is to commit a gift—no matter how large or small—to the fund. Then, meet with the annual fund coordinator to find out where your gift will go. You might be able to discern this without making a gift, but you will be able to discover even more if you are asking as a donor who wants to understand the options for designating your gift.

Some campuses have created designated annual fund categories for service and civic engagement programs. At Macalester College, for example, the development office wanted to raise the percentage of giving by recent graduates. A successful strategy for inspiring them was to let them designate their gift to the service-learning program. Most of the gifts were made by students directly affected by the program. In the case of Macalester, both the service-learning office and the development office were able to meet their goals by working together to generate the gifts. You should consider approaching your annual fund coordinator about a similar partnership. Students whose lives have been changed by your program ought to be among your important prospects.

In keeping with economic changes, however, annual giving levels fluctuate. Although the annual fund may support your program one year, you may not be able to rely on the same level of support every year.

Endowments

Endowment gifts from major external donors are used for many purposes, both restricted and unrestricted. These are large sums of money (often in the millions or even billions for the wealthier institutions) that are invested to generate interest and revenue each year. A portion of the interest or investment revenue is allocated to the purposes defined by the donor or donors, or in the case of unrestricted endowments, by the presidents and/or other campus administrators. The corpus, or principal, of the endowment remains intact and thus provides a reasonably stable base (depending on investment success) from which to draw such funds year after year, which makes endowments much prized.

The number of endowed centers for service-learning across the nation, at both public and private institutions, has grown steadily. Endowment gifts can be in the range of several thousand to several million dollars, and most bear the name of the primary donor. Once an endowment fund is established, other resource providers can be invited to build the fund in order to support additional program strategies. For example, a center may be named for the primary donor, but others may provide additional gifts to the endowment to support student service-learning scholarships or particular partnerships or whatever other service purpose the donor designates. These program elements can also bear the names of donors.

At public institutions, these endowments are typically managed by the college or university foundation. An institution's foundation is a separate, but highly connected, nonprofit organization whose mission is to provide support for the campus, governed by its own board of directors. Foundations provide a vehicle for donors to make tax-deductible contributions to public universities. Usually, the campus foundation and the development or advancement office work very closely together. At private colleges and universities, the advancement or development division often manages endowment dispersals, and there is no separate foundation. In both cases, a finance committee or committee of investment advisors generally provides counsel on how to maximize the short- and long-term return on investment from the endowment.

Service-learning programs, with their "right here, right now" ability to make a difference in communities and on campus, provide a unique opportunity for potential investors, regardless of whether their primary interest lies in the community or on the campus. Often they are interested in strategies that involve the college or university in community issues they already support. Donors to service-learning also often want to inspire the next generation of active community members and philanthropists.

(Endowments are a growing source of general operating support for service-learning programs. National and Michigan Campus Compact have published *The Service and Service-Learning Center Guide to Endowed Funding* [2003], which includes dozens of examples of such programs throughout the United States.)

ORGANIZATIONAL STRUCTURES AND STRATEGIES

Where you and your program are positioned on the institution's organizational chart and how you are perceived internally have great impact on your ability to generate resources. Begin by understanding the goals and expectations of your program. How do others describe the current and future role of your program? Whether you are located in academic affairs, student affairs, or elsewhere, know and understand the broader priorities and goals of the larger unit. Also be aware of the alignment between your program and that of others in your unit and the alignment between your program and larger institutional priorities. As we mentioned earlier, *always look for ways to demonstrate how your program can contribute to larger goals within your organizational unit or the institution.*

In some cases, you may decide that your program's focus and potential may not align with your formal place in the organization. For example, resource providers may be confused if you are charged with developing more service-learning courses and greater faculty involvement, while your position is attached to the career center housed within student affairs. You don't necessarily need to work for a change in organizational location; however, you might consider doing so, at least by working to create alliances across other organizational units on campus.

Getting involved in organizational politics can be risky, but sustainable access to resources may depend on your ability to negotiate the waters of internal organizational and political challenges. Creating a process for describing your goals, roles, and impact can help objectify the discussion. As mentioned earlier, you should document your program goals, benefits, and achievements; develop a strategic plan involving leaders from other program units across the campus to build alliances; develop a cadre of internal advisors who have links to higher-level decision makers; and volunteer to participate in unit or campus strategic planning discussions. You want to be seen as a valued, accessible asset to other related programs and activities, regardless of your formal location.

A good way to frame discussions and alliances is to focus on the alignment between the key goals and challenges of your unit and your institution. Service-learning has been shown to have positive impact on a variety of student, faculty, and organizational outcomes. Think about the larger unit where your program resides, as well as other units and influential campus leaders. What are their big goals and challenges? Through conversations and documents, you can provide information and examples about service-learning's contributions to the successful achievement of institutional goals, such student learning outcomes; recruitment, including increased enrollment from the immediate region and from underserved populations; retention or timely progress toward graduation; innovative teaching and learning environments; town-gown relations or other dimensions of campus image; and opportunities for fundraising or grant acquisition.

Familiarity with the campus strategic plan and current curricular issues is essential. Is general education about to be reformed, or has a new design been launched recently? What core learning outcomes or attributes are sought for graduates of your institution? You can demonstrate how service-learning aligns with those strategies and goals, many of which have both academic and student affairs dimensions.

Any of the ideas in the "Be Creative" box to the right will be enhanced if you improve your awareness of institutional goals, needs, and conditions. The institutional research (IR) office has interesting data on many dimensions of the institution, especially about student and faculty characteristics. The IR staff members maintain a portfolio of survey instruments and regularly collect data that might help you as you craft your internal case and strategy. They know the institution's key issues and

---

Be Creative: Connecting Service-Learning to Campus Challenges

- Get to know members of curriculum or teaching/learning committees, special working groups, and/or task forces related to strategic initiatives.

- Share examples of service-learning's impact on achieving learning goals with deans or department chairs.

- Share information about service-learning's recruitment value with admissions staff; volunteer to participate in recruitment events.

- Get involved in new-student orientation; propose a service-learning component.

- Work with student affairs to strengthen or launch a student leadership development program with a service-learning dimension.

- Create a celebration event that recognizes current students, faculty, and partners involved in service-learning; invite key campus leaders to participate.

---

often have comparative data on similar institutions. Educating IR staff about the potential impact and benefits of service-learning will help them recognize useful data for promoting your program. IR and student assessment staff can often share such data with others. They may be willing to add a few questions to existing surveys to help you gather more relevant data about your program's impact (see the community college case study presented in the box "Example #2," on page 193). They are also a good source of information about forthcoming major initiatives such as strategic planning, accreditation visits, or enrollment planning. In some cases, IR staff may be willing to advise you and help design a comprehensive assessment plan for your program so you can enhance your own body of evidence.

Perhaps most important is building an alliance with the offices and individuals on your campus who work on institutional advancement or development. Typically, these include public or media relations, alumni affairs, fundraising or development, and, in some cases, government or community relations. Remember that you are an asset to these units. You have information and success stories that they need. Institutional advancement or development (and government relations) units are in the business of "friend-raising and fundraising" for your college or university, which involves working on positive media coverage, keeping alumni actively involved, and inspiring individuals, corporations, foundations, and government sources to invest finan-

---

Tips for Building Partnerships with Institutional Advancement and Development

1. Begin by looking at the advancement or development organization and its annual report to become familiar with its goals and strategies.

2. Meet with media-relations staff to explore ways to make your program and partnerships more visible internally and externally.

3. Discuss with alumni affairs staff any ideas you have for involving alumni in community service projects, recognizing alumni who have become community partners and leaders, or inspiring alumni donations. They can also tell alumni about service-learning activities; many are proud of their alma mater for making a difference in communities.

4. Meet with development or government-relations staff to explore how service-learning aligns with current fundraising priorities and prospects. You can provide examples of positive campus action through student and faculty involvement in particular communities or issues of interest.

5. Work with development staff to create a "case statement" for service-learning as a funding priority, and build a list of appropriate funding prospects.

6. Share your strategic plans and evidence of the effects of service-learning to form a partnership with development team members that could encourage their direct involvement in fundraising, including the possibility of an endowment fund for service-learning.

7. Remember that fundraising is based on relationships and takes time to bear financial fruit. Fundraising calls for patience and persistence; you always want to follow the lead of your development team, the members of which are experts in timing and strategy.

---

cially in the institution. They need positive, compelling stories about the impact of the institution on its students and on society. As a CSLP, you have good stories to tell and carefully collected evidence to support those stories. You can approach institutional advancement and government-relations staff with the confidence that you are seeking a mutually beneficial relationship. (See the box above for more advice.)

EXTERNAL SOURCES, STRATEGIES, AND ALLIES

As we mentioned earlier, external sources of financial support are generally not sustainable over the long term. Such sources, however, are often important to campus service programs in three ways:

1. External sources are quite often necessary to launch a service-learning program on campus. In tight budget climates, it is common for a new program to be launched with external sources (often called "soft funding").

2. External sources commonly sustain a program in the short term. Many service-learning programs depend on external funding for their first three to five years or sometimes

longer, as they concurrently work to build the internal support necessary to transition, at least partly, into the campus budget.

3. Even programs that receive their core funding from internal sources often rely on external sources to help fuel innovation or growth in their program's scope or impact.

External sources can be divided into government, corporations and foundations, professional associations, and individuals (non-alumni). Awareness of and investment in service-learning programs has risen significantly among all four groups over the past two decades, largely because of the belief that service-learning helps produce job-ready graduates and better citizens, and that it addresses important community issues. The box on this page offers other benefits of service-learning as a resource-generating strategy.

Government
The most common government sources are federal and state funding, but local and county governments are also possible sources. At the federal level, the Learn and Serve America program of the U.S. Corporation for National and Community Service (CNCS) provides millions of dollars each year to support K-12 and postsecondary service-learning

> ### Service-Learning as a Valuable Resource-Generating Strategy
>
> 1. Service-learning can attract new donors who do not currently give to higher education but who give generously to community causes.
>
> 2. Wealthy donors who currently give only small amounts to the institution may give more in order to support particular service-learning activities in areas of interest to them.
>
> 3. Stories of service-learning can activate alumni who are not yet donors, if service-learning was meaningful to them during college. Stories can inspire alumni to do more community service themselves, which reflects well on the institution and can increase their philanthropic spirit.
>
> 4. Service-learning generates goodwill. Positive attention focused on the college or university can lead to greater political and corporate support.

programs. Learn and Serve America Higher Education funds are distributed directly to campuses and to state consortia, which then make competitive sub-grants to campuses in their states. Historically, state Campus Compacts have been the most common recipients of state consortia funding.

CNCS, founded in the early 1990s, has evolved into the federal government's largest hub of citizen service funding, including the national AmeriCorps and VISTA volunteer programs, and the national Senior Corps program, which aims to mobilize older Americans to serve their communities. In addition to tens of millions of dollars distributed to campuses via Learn and Serve America, CNCS human resources—in the form of full- or part-time AmeriCorps or VISTA volunteers—have also been secured by many campuses to assist with service-learning program development and implementation. Many state Campus Compact offices administer VISTA programs.

Another major federal supporter of campus partnerships is the Community Outreach Partnership Center (COPC) program, a program of the Office of University Partnerships at the

U.S. Department of Housing and Urban Development. This program targets community development-oriented partnerships between campuses and their surrounding communities. Though these partnerships most often emphasize institutional engagement on specific community issues (e.g., economic development, job training, educational improvement, youth development, neighborhood improvement, public safety), many also involve service-learning because the grant requires student involvement in the partnership. COPC grants are awarded annually through a rigorous, competitive, peer-reviewed process. The availability of funds for new grants is uncertain from year to year because the program depends on annual appropriations from Congress. (Information on the Office of University Partnerships is offered in the resources section at the end of this chapter. Note that in 2009 an effort was launched to increase COPC funds.)

More and more state legislatures are taking an interest in service-learning, as reflected by their investment of state dollars in postsecondary service-learning. For example, the Minnesota state legislature has appropriated an average of $200,000 per biennium since 1989 for a postsecondary service-learning grant program. Public and private campuses can apply for small grants to create or expand service-learning through this program. In California, the state legislature has allocated millions to the California State University System to support expansion of service-learning statewide. The Kentucky state legislature provides base funding to its regional public universities to support a specified agenda of public service and outreach programs, some of which include service-learning. (Contact Campus Compact for more information about which states have similar programs.)

Other government funding is available at both the federal and state levels, depending on the specific topic or issue. Often, faculty members involved in service-learning activities are aware of government agencies that may offer support in their particular discipline or topic of interest. In general, funds may be available through competitive grant programs (you can monitor opportunities on www.grants.gov, which also has advice on preparing successful proposals) or through earmarks or other special appropriations made specifically to your institution for a particular purpose. You may also find that some of your community partners are eligible for certain kinds of support and may be willing to collaborate with you in seeking those funds; you should return the favor by being alert to opportunities to include partners as co-applicants. In either case, collaborative fundraising activity requires detailed written agreements about responsibilities, roles, and the distribution and uses of funds.

Whether seeking a competitive grant or a special fund, begin by talking with your supervisor, your advancement or development office, the office for research, and the government-relations office. The solicitation of state, federal, county, or local government support can be politically complex and sensitive, and you will need the expert guidance and leadership of those appointed to these tasks for your institution. Pursuing governmental support on your own without their approval and assistance is perilous and unwise.

Consider exploring local or county government support by visiting your city and county websites and by meeting with local and county public officials. (Portland State University, for example, has received county support for its service-learning efforts.) Again, consult with your

Corporate and Foundation Sources: A Primer

Most large corporations give in two different ways:

1. *Sponsorships* are typically targeted at events or other high-profile projects that have significant marketing value for the corporation. Sponsorship dollars usually come from corporate marketing budgets. In some corporations, representatives from community relations or the corporate foundation are also involved in making sponsorship decisions. As always, consult your advancement or development office for help in determining how sponsorships are handled at a particular corporate prospect.

2. *Corporate foundations* are separate nonprofit organizations that distribute a percentage of corporate pretax profits from previous years to charitable causes. Corporate foundations provide a vehicle for corporations to support charitable causes, while also allowing for corporate tax deductions and corporate control over how the funds are used.

Following are descriptions of two other common types of philanthropic organizations:

1. *Private foundations* are typically created by wealthy individuals or families who want to leave a lasting legacy to their communities. These foundations usually have a sizable endowment (millions or even billions of dollars for the largest) from which at least five percent of earnings are donated each year.

2. *Community foundations* operate in much the same way on the grant side (donations made from endowment investment income), but their revenue sources are not from one individual or family; rather, many wealthy individuals and families pool their donations into a community foundation, which then handles most, if not all, aspects of the investment and grant-making processes. These foundations often carry the name of their local community, such as The Saint Paul Foundation in Minnesota or The Oregon Community Foundation in Portland.

government-relations office on campus before personally contacting local and county officials, as it can help determine whether such sources might be worth exploring.

Corporations and foundations
On most campuses, the advancement or development office knows of all corporate and foundation sources in your area. Moreover, the office is likely charged with coordinating approaches to these sources in order to avoid competing proposals being submitted to the same funding source. Most advancement or development offices take this coordination role quite seriously. You want to work closely with your advancement or development office in determining possible sources and the timing of conversations and proposals. Corporations and foundations generally do not look kindly on uncoordinated proposals or on random conversations with their representatives about potential funding.

Most corporations and foundations focus much of their giving on communities near their headquarters. Typically, only medium-sized and large corporations and foundations make several annual gifts of $10,000 or more. Only the largest corporations and foundations are usually able even to consider gifts of $100,000 or more. You should carefully consider their corre-

How to Gain Support and Attention

- Demonstrate that you know how the fundraising and government-relations processes work and are familiar with the current funding priorities of the institution.

- Share stories about program outcomes and impact.

- Have solid data about your program's performance.

- Develop a few specific, creative ideas that might be fundable, preferably in partnership with community members, students, and/or faculty members.

- Do some basic research on possible resource providers or programs, without making your own contacts.

- Demonstrate your ability to write aspects of proposals and to manage external funds.

- Always work closely with your advancement, development, or government-relations office throughout the entire resource-generation process.

sponding budgets and patterns of giving as you assess which corporations or foundations might be promising prospects. Again, we recommend strongly that you work with key development or advancement staff and to identify your best possible sources. (See the boxes on this and the prior page for information on corporate and foundation funding sources and on gaining support among these and other resource providers.)

Doing some research on possible prospects before you meet with advancement or development officers can help them see you as a serious partner in fundraising. Look for foundations that align with your project idea, have a history of funding academic institutions, and serve your community or region. Learn about the application process and calendar, and put together some basic proposal ideas before approaching the development staff for assistance.

Professional associations

Professional associations that either focus specifically on service-learning or have special initiatives related to service-learning often provide financial support to service-learning through competitive grant processes. Campus Compact, both at the state and national levels, is perhaps the largest, most consistent provider of such support. The American Association of Community Colleges supports community colleges. Many other associations, such as the Council for the Advancement of Private Higher Education and the American Association of State Colleges and Universities, have created special service or civic learning initiatives that support campuses either financially or with other services to help advance service-learning. Faculty in specific disciplines may know of special service-learning initiatives in their disciplinary associations, and other allies on campus might also be aware of opportunities via their professional associations. Due to the rapid growth in service-learning over the past 20 years, more and more associations have developed service-learning initiatives, so consider them as possible financial supporters for establishing, growing, or sustaining your program.

Individuals (non-alumni)

Though individual alumni might be motivated to give because of loyalty to their alma mater, non-alumni must be motivated to give on the basis of your cause and their trust in your operation to advance it. Typically, these people are wealthy members of the community who feel a special bond with a particular community issue or educational agenda and believe that your institution is committed to it. They may have a special interest in children, the environment, or another community concern. Or they may be deep believers in alternative approaches to education, such as service-learning. Or they may be concerned about nurturing the next generation of active citizens and philanthropists. Regardless, they must come to believe that your program is important for advancing their priorities. The advancement or development staff know which wealthy individuals are interested in which causes, and they are charged with coordinating approaches to them. Work closely with your advancement office as you consider pursuing individual donors.

Wherever you seek external support, be sure to consider the donor's financial and program reporting requirements. Sometimes these can be a burden or require expertise not easily available to you. Part of successful fundraising is being prepared to be a successful gift manager. Your reputation as a gift recipient will be shaped not only by the quality of your program but also by your ability to adhere to reporting requirements and meet deadlines. You should also consider how your resource provider wants to be recognized and involved in the program so there are no surprises or complications in the relationship.

Conclusion

As the field continues to evolve, so too will the CSLP's role. Increasingly, your ability to generate financial resources to grow and sustain programs is important to that role. Because there are so many ways to approach the complex process of resource generation, we have presented multiple strategies through which you should view this process. We have also encouraged you throughout this chapter to see the important links between resource-generation and processes outlined in other chapters of this book, including clarity about program goals, effective design of programs, assessment and documentation of results, and knowledge about how higher education works, both in general and on your campus. (See Worksheet 9-1 on page 207 for ways to reflect on generating resources.) Developing an internal network of allies that will help you connect to institutional priorities is essential to this approach.

We have addressed some of the personal concerns you may have about engaging in the process of fundraising and related engagement in campus politics. We hope we have convinced you that engaging in these processes is essential to increasing resources for service-learning. Finally, we hope our discussions of external and internal sources will help you grow and sustain your program. Your work aims to benefit students, communities, institutions, and society at large via service-learning, and you have many opportunities to enhance support.

Reference
National and Michigan Campus Compact. (2003). *The service and service-learning center guide to endowed funding.* Providence, RI: Campus Compact.

Additional Resources

Publications

Crews, R. J. (2002). *Higher education service-learning sourcebook.* Westport, CT: Oryx Press.

Ferguson, J. (1995). *Education grantseeker's guide to foundation and corporate funding.* 2nd ed. Alexandria, VA: Capitol Publications.

The Foundation Center. (2003). *The foundation center's guide to grantseeking on the web.* New York: Author.

The Foundation Center. (2004). *Grants for higher education.* New York: Author.

Henson, K. (2004). *Grant writing in higher education: A step-by-step guide.* Boston: Allyn & Bacon.

Langseth, M., & McVeety, C. (2007). Engagement as core leadership position and advancement strategy: Lesson from an engaged institution. *International Journal of Educational Advancement 7*(2), 117–130.

Langseth, M., & Plater, W. (2004). *Public work and the academy: An academic administrator's guide to civic engagement and service-learning.* Bolton, MA: Anker Publishing.

New, C. C., & Quick, J. (2003). *How to Write a Grant.* Hoboken, NJ: John Wiley & Sons Publishing.

Associations

Association for Fundraising Professionals (http://www.afpnet.org). The professional association for fundraising in the broader nonprofit sector.

Campus Compact (http://www.compact.org). A coalition of more than 1,100 presidents committed to advancing the civic purposes of higher education, and the nation's largest organization of higher education leaders devoted to advancing service-learning.

Council for the Advancement and Support of Education (http://www.case.org). The professional association for advancement or development professionals in education. Your institution's advancement staff are probably members of this organization. The website is a good source of information about development tools and strategies.

Council on Foundations (http://www.cof.org). A national association of grant-makers with public information. The website includes information about state associations of grant-makers. Most state associations publish annual directories of foundations, their priorities, grants, etc.

Online Resources

SERVICE-LEARNING AND FUNDING

National Service-Learning Clearinghouse (http://www.servicelearning.org). The Clearinghouse is supported by the Learn and Serve America program of the Corporation for National and Community Service. It maintains an active list of current funding opportunities as well as advice on preparing funding proposals and requests.

See NSLC Fact Sheets about Funding Resources at:
http://servicelearning.org/instant_info/fact_sheets/he_facts/index.php

FOUNDATION FUNDING

Foundations.org (http://www.foundations.org). A listing of major foundations.

Foundation Center (http://foundationcenter.org). A good place to search for funders and to learn more about fundraising in general.

FEDERAL FUNDING

Federal grants (http://www.grants.gov)

Learn and Serve Higher Education grants (http://www.learnandserve.gov/about/programs/higher_education.asp)

Office of University Partnerships Foundations Database (http://www.oup.org/funding/upcfoundation/PubSearch.asp). A directory of foundations that have invested in community-campus partnerships.

U.S. Department of Education: Grants & Contracts (http://www.ed.gov/fund/landing.jhtml?src=ln)

NEWS SOURCES

The Chronicle of Philanthropy (http://philanthropy.com/). The most prominent national periodical in the field of philanthropy.

The Chronicle of Higher Education (http://chronicle.com). The most prominent national periodical in the field of higher education, including frequent articles and information regarding fundraising and grant opportunities.

WORKSHEET 9-1: Reflection Questions on Leveraging Resources to Support Service-Learning

1. How do I feel about getting involved in fundraising?

   _____

   _____

   _____

   _____

2. What are key goals/challenges articulated by the leaders of my institution? How might service-learning connect to those issues?

   _____

   _____

   _____

   _____

3. Who are my current institutional allies? How can I structure formal or informal opportunities for these allies to act on my behalf?

   _____

   _____

   _____

   _____

4. What are my goals for fundraising?

   _____

   _____

   _____

   _____

(continued)

WORKSHEET

WORKSHEET

a. What is the baseline funding necessary to sustain my position and the core functions of this office?

_____

_____

_____

_____

b. Can I articulate specific program goals and priorities? To what degree do those require permanent versus temporary/transitional funding?

_____

_____

_____

_____

c. Which ideas might be most likely to attract internal funding? Which would attract external funding?

_____

_____

_____

_____

d. Where do funds come from today? What is the timeline for current grant/gift-funded programs?

_____

_____

_____

_____

(continued)

5. What are the key community issues our service-learning students are addressing?

   a. Who in our community or region also cares about and supports work on these issues?

   b. Which faculty members are doing research that might attract government funding for research on these issues?

6. What are my five best stories of service-learning impact on students and/or on community partners that I can share with institutional advancement staff?

(continued)

W O R K S H E E T

7. How can I most effectively involve students or partners in documenting and sharing their personal stories of service-learning?

    _____

    _____

    _____

    _____

8. What other documented evidence of positive service-learning impact do I have?

    _____

    _____

    _____

    _____

CHAPTER TEN

Developing Your Assessment Plan: A Key Component of Reflective Practice

Julie A. Hatcher and Robert G. Bringle

NEW HABITS ARE HARD TO DEVELOP. Armed with both the best intentions and familiar excuses, we find it challenging to begin a new regimen even when we know it is good for us. New professional habits too are hard to develop, requiring a commitment of time, energy, and resources. We develop, practice, and refine new habits as we become reflective practitioners (Schon, 1995). This chapter encourages you to use your experience and to leverage the involvement of others in order to improve your work through systematic assessment and evaluation. We provide a rationale for the value of assessment, define common terminology, describe some principles of good practice, and advise you on developing an assessment plan for your work.

With increased expectations in higher education for documented evidence of student learning, assessment is fundamental to good practice. Yet, for many community service-learning professionals (CSLPs), assessment is an unpopular or unfamiliar activity. Perhaps a perceived lack of expertise brings forth a justified sense of anxiety over terms such as *accreditation, coefficient alpha, learning outcomes, program evaluation,* and *rubrics.* The demands of day-to-day program implementation and operations leave little room for the added responsibilities of assessment.

CSLPs, however, should value assessment as a way to demonstrate outcomes of their work to both internal and external stakeholders. Assessment can yield new knowledge, and this new knowledge can generate new action to advance the public purposes of higher education. Assessment is a critical tool to advance understanding and garner support for their important work.

Many CSLPs are highly reflective about their work. Just as reflection is a fundamental component of service-learning (Ash & Clayton, 2004; Ash, Clayton, & Atkinson, 2005; Bringle & Hatcher, 2000; Eyler & Giles, 1999; Hatcher & Bringle, 1997; Hatcher, Bringle, & Muthiah, 2002), we are convinced that *reflective* practice (Schön, 1995) is a key dimension of *effective* practice as a CSLP. Schon's work on reflective practice honors the importance of traditional professional preparation that can inform practice but acknowledges the ambiguity that results from facing novel, unfamiliar circumstances. A propensity towards reflective practice allows a professional to grow through challenges. By using reflection and observation, you are showing confidence that you have designed an effective service experience, supported the development of undergraduates through an alternative spring break service trip, or provided valuable resources to community agencies. We contend, however, that part of a CSLP's professional responsibility is to capture this information so that others can also take confidence in the value of such programs.

Assessment is "generating and using information about performance that is fed back into the system from which it comes to improve that system" (Cambridge, 1999, p. 176). Thus, assessment activities are one type of reflection that can advance the work of civic engagement in higher education and, at the same time, enhance your professional development. Done appropriately, assessment, program evaluation, and research allow you and others to learn from your work by systematically collecting information about your programs.

As you more diligently assess your programs, you and others, such as campus administrators and potential funders, will better understand their impact and quality. Additional support and resources are, in turn, more likely to come your way. The information can promote increased confidence about program initiatives and can represent the work to others through publicity, websites, presentations at professional meetings, newsletters, annual reports, and professional publications. In addition, the information can be used to defend your programs to campus administrators when budget issues arise. External funders value the results of initiatives they have supported. Including assessment results in grant applications can establish your rationale for new programs. Furthermore, the knowledge base developed from systematic assessment can be used to design effective programs that target particular outcomes. In summary, assessment improves professional practice.

Types of Assessment Activities

We have not yet differentiated the terms *assessment, evaluation,* and *research.* All three refer to systematically gathering information and processing it to reach conclusions. There is some variation in how these terms are used. For example, to some, *research* is an inclusive term referring to any form of gathering information; to others, it is a narrow term that refers to particular procedures, which is our position (Bringle & Hatcher, 2000). Furthermore, these terms have different meanings in different disciplinary contexts. Some use the term *assessment* as a general umbrella for all the other terms; we also take this approach. In academic settings, however, assessment can relate more specifically to assessing students' academic learning, often for the sake of assigning a grade in a class. In the following section, we differentiate these and other related terms:

- *Reflection:* oriented toward the self-assessment of persons who are engaged in an experience.

- *Program evaluation—process evaluation:* produces information about *how* a class, course, or program was implemented.

- *Program evaluation—outcome evaluation:* produces information about *what* outcomes occurred as a result of a class, course, or program.

- *Correlational studies:* produce information about *what* relationship exists between aspects of a class, course, or program.

- *Research, including experimental studies:* produces information about *why* a specific outcome occurred. (Bringle & Hatcher, 2000)

Reflection

Reflection involves gathering and processing information for new action. Dewey (1916) provided a basis for reflective practice that became the foundation for Kolb's (1984) experiential learning theory and for Schon's (1995) view of the reflective practitioner. As a cognitive activity, reflection can be both retrospective, by looking back on past experience, and prospective, by making new meaning from past experience to influence future action (Hatcher & Bringle, 1997). Well-designed reflection links experience to learning, is guided, occurs regularly, involves feedback to enhance the learning, and helps clarify values (Bringle & Hatcher, 1999).

Reflection is often seen as a student activity, ensuring that students involved in community service can process and learn from their service experience. Yet it is also a useful assessment tool for CSLPs and others associated with a program, including participants and community partners. Reflection can also be used to assess the degree of institutionalization of service-learning on a campus. Strategic planning is often a reflective exercise in which current programs are assessed—where they should be in three to five years, and what strategies will achieve those goals. The value of structured reflection is at least self-referential (i.e., new insights are gained by those engaged in the activity), but in addition, others can learn from the results of the reflection such as a case study (Yin, 1989).

Program Evaluation

Program evaluation is the "use of social research procedures to systematically investigate the effectiveness of social intervention programs" (Rossi & Freeman, 1985, p. 19). This is the most common type of assessment strategy used in grant-funded programs. Funders want to know to what extent their investment in a program yielded the promised results. In addition, program evaluation is increasingly expected to demonstrate campus accountability toward student learning goals. Accrediting associations in higher education expect clear documentation and evidence of student learning outcomes. CSLP professionals can gather evidence in various domains (e.g., civic responsibility, leadership, respect for diversity, commitment to social justice) if these outcomes are part of program design and evaluation.

Typically, program evaluation has two components: *process evaluation* and *outcome evaluation* (Cronbach, 1982; National Science Foundation, 1993). The purpose of *process evaluation* is to monitor the program's implementation and show the consistency of the implementation and its fidelity to the program design. Key questions in process evaluation include:

- Do the activities and strategies match those described in the plan? If they do not match, are the changes in the activities justified and described?

- Were the activities conducted according to the proposed timeline? By the appropriate personnel?

- Are the actual costs of project implementation in line with initial budget expectations?

- Are the participants moving toward the anticipated goals of the project?

- Which activities or strategies help the participants move toward the goals?

- What barriers were encountered? How and to what extent were they overcome? (Frechtling & Westat, 1997)

The purpose of *outcome evaluation* is to provide information about the program's impact on participants and whether it produced the intended results, including student learning outcomes. Key questions for outcome evaluation are:

- Did the program meet its overall goals?

- Was the program equally effective for all participants?

- What components of the program were the most effective?

- What significant unintended impacts did the program have?

- Is the program replicable and transportable? (Frechtling & Westat, 1997)

Correlational Studies

Correlational studies examine the information collected to identify the relationships between two or more variables and the degree to which a change in *x* is associated with a change in *y*. This can be accomplished informally (e.g., respondents in focus groups who were involved in community service voiced a greater sense of social responsibility) or by statistically evaluating relationships with quantitative data. Correlational research may be part of program evaluation or may be conducted as independent research. For example, are levels of involvement in community service in high school correlated to interest in service-learning among entering college students? Exploring patterns between and among different areas of interest can inform program planning and evaluation, although correlational research is typically limited to explaining why two variables are related.

Research

Research, including experimental studies, is directed at understanding why a program produced a particular result. Research is based upon data, and there are a variety of methods used to gather and analyze data, including qualitative, quantitative, or a mixed-methods approach.

Regardless of the approach, Furco (Gelmon, Furco, Holland, & Bringle, 2005) notes that good research (1) provides a theoretical frame (see Bringle, 2003); (2) uses scientific design (e.g., experimental method, analysis of covariance to control for preexisting differences) to control for extraneous explanations and allow for causal inferences (see Bringle & Hatcher, 2000); (3) uses measurement techniques that have demonstrable validity and reliability (see Bringle, Phillips, & Hudson, 2004); (4) uses appropriate statistical procedures for analysis; and (5) generalizes beyond the idiosyncratic case so others can learn from the results (see Bringle & Hatcher, 2000). Whereas program evaluation yields useful information about a particular program and its outcomes, research contributes to a knowledge base that informs others about future program design and practice by evaluating the usefulness and scope of a theory that is the basis for the program or intervention.

Principles of Good Practice in Assessment

Like good reflection, good assessment should:

- Link the abstract and the concrete;

- Be structured;

- Occur regularly;

- Provide feedback for learning; and,

- Explore and clarify values. (Bringle & Hatcher, 1999; Hatcher & Bringle, 1997; Hatcher, Bringle, & Muthiah, 2002)

We recommend that assessment activities conform to these principles of good practice identified for reflection. The following section briefly discusses each characteristic of good practice, identifies implications for assessment, and presents questions to consider when designing assessment strategies.

Link Abstract to Concrete

All community service-learning experiences, whether curricular or co-curricular, should be purposively designed to meet specific outcomes for the participants. Well-designed activities involve a rationale that could be phrased, "If these participants (e.g., students, community members, faculty) engage in these activities, then these outcomes are expected to occur." The rationale for the design of these community-based experiences represents an abstract conceptualization for why you believe certain activities are designed in particular ways. Basing this rationale on preexisting theory (e.g., student development theory, community partnership theory, faculty development theory) increases your ability to conduct theory-based research on your programs (see Bringle, 2003).

As CSLPs, you have an implicit understanding of why you design service-learning experiences in a particular way. As reflective practitioners gathering evidence about your work, you need to be able to express your rationale clearly to others. Funders expect clear, persuasive statements in grant proposals that explain the rationale for the connection between proposed activities and expected outcomes. Thus, key questions to consider with this principle are:

- What theory provides the framework for program design?

- What am I trying to accomplish in this program? What are the key learning outcomes for students?

- Why do I think these proposed activities will accomplish these goals? Why are alternative approaches inferior?

- What evidence will lead others and me to conclude that these assumptions are correct and that this program is successful?

Structure Information

The reflection process operates informally all the time. CSLPs collect information about their work through observation, discussions with participants, "hall talk" with colleagues, and feedback from key individuals. Reflecting on information in a more structured way, such as in an annual report, increases the likelihood that it will be used in subsequent decisions about continuing, improving, or eliminating a program.

Key questions to consider with this principle are:

- How can I collect information about the quality of my programs in structured, systematic ways (e.g., surveys, focus groups, archival data)?

- How will I identify the sample of respondents (e.g., representative sample, known-group sample) that aligns with my assessment goals?

- What procedures will give me confidence that the information is meaningful (e.g., existing surveys to measure student achievement or to compare programs to national benchmarks)?

- What procedures will give others confidence in my conclusions from the information I gather (e.g., how can I control for alternative explanations for the outcomes)?

Assess Regularly

Although most practitioners informally collect information during the planning, implementation, and conclusion of a program, good assessment warrants using systematic methods throughout each phase. Developing evidence across programs demonstrates your seriousness about monitoring and improving programs. During the planning phase, develop a grid to identify participant outcomes and the activities designed to reach these outcomes. You can use this grid to ensure that activities align with desired outcomes. In the implementation phase, the grid may come into play as situations call for changes in planned activities. At the conclusion of the program, the grid becomes a basis for assessing the degree to which the participants achieved outcomes in relation to activities. Activities can then be modified as necessary. Key questions to consider with this principle include:

- What are my assessment tasks that I routinely follow each year?

- How can I systematically gather convincing evidence that the program was well designed? That its implementation was consistent with its design? That it produced the immediate and long-term outcomes intended?

- What information is best collected at the beginning, midpoint, and end of the year?

- What information do I need to routinely track in order to be prepared for campus requests for information about a program in a timely manner?

- What is the easiest and most meaningful information to gather?

- How can I create a process for faculty to routinely ask students to complete an end-of-course survey in a service-learning class?

Provide Feedback for Learning

Assessment is most valuable when it improves decision making about program planning and implementation. The design of procedures to gather information systematically should be guided by what information will be useful to you and others (e.g., accrediting agencies, campus administrators, potential and current donors or funders) for making subsequent decisions about program design, expansion, or termination (Patton, 1990). Thus, even though data are useful from a historical perspective (e.g., "What happened in this program?"), the most important information has implications for future practice and program improvement (e.g., "In what ways can the service-learning scholarship program be improved next year?").

One misunderstanding often associated with assessment is that it is done for its own sake: data are gathered because others expect you to do it, and data collection is an end in itself. Another prevalent misunderstanding is that the purpose of gathering information is to answer all questions related to a program or to document all outcomes. In reality, systematic gathering of information may need to be limited to that which provides useful information to you and others who are concerned with your work. Key questions to consider with this principle include:

- Who will use this information?

- How have I included principal stakeholders in identifying key questions?

- Given what I already know about the success of my program, what additional data would help me better understand what is occurring?

- What information would help those to whom I report become stronger advocates for my program?

- What information would a potential funder want to know?

- What information would be useful, not simply interesting?

Explore and Clarify Values

Although the issue of values may seem out of place in a discussion of assessment, program evaluation (and research) values enter into what you are attempting to accomplish through your programs and how participants react to their experiences. Your work can never be free of values. CSLPs do, for example, want students to challenge and discard their inaccurate stereotypes of marginalized populations. Values should be acknowledged in the assessment process and may even become the focus of the feedback obtained through systematically gathering information.

Values also enter into assessment in the ways CSLPs gather information. Civic engagement, co-curricular volunteering, and service-learning are imbued with the values that these activities should be participatory and democratic, and should reflect the integrity of and a respect for all parties involved. Similarly, the ways assessment activities are conducted should reflect similar values. The tenets of participatory action research are excellent guides for designing research with these values in mind (e.g., Strand, Marullo, Cutforth, Stoecker, & Donohue, 2003). These include: (1) collaboration between the campus and community; (2) democratization of knowledge that acknowledges different ways of knowing and different types of knowledge; (3) social change through actions (based on the research) that promote social justice; (4) focus on the adequacy of the process as well as the outcomes; (5) peer review by multiple stakeholders, including academic; (6) outcomes for multiple stakeholders; and (7) dissemination to multiple stakeholders.

Key questions to consider with this principle include:

- What values are implicit and explicit in how you design your programs and their expected outcomes, as well as in the information that will be gathered?

- What campus values should you keep in mind when designing assessment questions and strategies?

- What values are shared by others (e.g., participants, recipients, community-based organizations), and how do they differ?

- What key values underlie your programs?

- How can the assessment of these programs reflect the same values?

A Strategy for Assessment

Too often, CSLPs do not address assessment until a program is over. We strongly recommend developing an assessment plan during program design, rather than during or after implementation. Early on, decisions must be made about whom to include in developing a plan. Will you, an external consultant, or a staff member conduct the evaluation? Do other units on campus have the expertise or interest? Which stakeholders should you involve in developing the plan (e.g., staff, participants, those receiving the report, community members)? How much time is there for assessment planning and implementation, including data analysis? How should the process be structured? There are a number of sample worksheets and templates for planning an evaluation available through the University of Wisconsin-Extension (see Taylor-Powell, Steele, & Douglah, 1996).

Development of the evaluation plan must align with your available resources (e.g., money, staff time, expertise). The process should identify and prioritize questions in order to provide the necessary information to the most important questions. In the case of funded grants, the funder will have certain expectations written into the grant guidelines. Consider what else you can include in an evaluation to provide additional useful information. Finally, collaborate with others, including faculty and graduate students doing theses and dissertations, on research projects that target teaching and learning. Bringle (2003) notes, "Service-learning [and co-curricular service] provides a powerful test bed that is both convenient and appropriate for evaluating hypotheses from theories about human behavior and increasing civic involvement among students" (p. 17).

Collaborate

When planning to conduct an assessment, program evaluation, or research project, you will have opportunities to collaborate with others who have valuable expertise and common interests in the information gathered. Community members and staff at nonprofit and government agencies may have unanswered questions about issues, clients, programs, or the best ways to involve students and faculty in community-based work. Faculty members may also have an interest in conducting research on topics that align with your work (e.g., academic achievement, attitudes toward diversity or social justice, character development, leadership, retention) or your program in the community (e.g., environmental issues, youth violence, teen pregnancy).

Furthermore, collaborating with CSLPs on other campuses and through organizations such as the national or state Campus Compact offices enables larger studies that might be impossible on a single campus. Collaboration can contribute special areas of expertise (e.g., methodology, statistics, content); distribute the workload; add resources (e.g., research grants, other institutional funds); provide larger and more heterogeneous samples; broaden the scope of questions; and contribute to the richness of the work. During the past decade, we have found that collaboration greatly increases our productivity in program evaluation and research, develops allies and colleagues who support our work, and advances scholarly contributions to the field of service-learning and civic engagement.

Meet Campus and Institutional Goals

Because of external demands, colleges and universities increasingly want to document the outcomes of various community engagement activities. For example, regional accrediting associations require institutions to include such information in self-studies for the reaccreditation process (e.g., quality enhancement plans, North Central Accreditation Criterion 5: Engagement and Service). The Carnegie Foundation for the Advancement of Teaching has an elective classification for "Community Engagement" that gives national recognition to campuses that designate resources to support, implement, recognize, and evaluate community engagement activities.

Documenting the impact of community service programs is important for your campus in order to gain national recognition. Because of these increasing needs for information about civic engagement, there are professional staff who focus on assessment, program evaluation, and institutional research and who can be collaborators on assessment of civically oriented programs. For example, a number of campuses have institutional research offices that annually survey students (prospective, entering, continuing, or graduate), faculty, and alumni. Participation in surveys such as the National Survey of Student Engagement can give you valuable benchmark data over time. Individual faculty members, departments, and centers (e.g., those devoted to teaching and learning, diversity, or leadership) may be interested in student outcomes and collaborate with you on research to identify the student-learning outcomes for service and service-learning.

Ask the Right Questions

Because all forms of assessment require a considerable investment of time and resources by staff and participants, focusing and narrowing the questions are critical. For example, assessment questions may come directly from a civic engagement program or may result from collaboration with others to determine how the programs are related to other campus initiatives (e.g., first-year success seminars, general education outcomes, diversity, retention). Asking questions about the needs and assets of constituencies (e.g., students, staff, community, executive leadership, or government officials) should occur before program design. An assessment of needs and assets can tell you where to strategically focus new program initiatives.

Process evaluation and outcome evaluation each entail different questions. Process evaluation questions address the design of the program itself, whereas outcome evaluation examines the results and outcomes of a program. What questions do you have about your programs (relationship between program and outcomes)? These can be broad (does the program promote civic growth of students?) or narrower (do service-learning students understand the organizational structure of the community agency in which they serve?). The questions can be descriptive (numbers and characteristics of participants, or what they did), comparative (different groups of students, or using benchmarks or standards), correlational (studying the association between variables), or causal (determining why something occurred).

Generally, there are more questions than one assessment project can address. The process of determining which questions to include should take into account the reason for the assessment and the information that will be most useful and accessible. Purposes of assessment include program expansion or redesign, budget justification, grant proposals, or requests for institutional funding. Questions used in the assessment should be shaped by the targeted audiences for the assessment results, the types of evidence most persuasive to those audiences, and their priorities.

Ensure Institutional Compliance

In all cases, assessment must conform to ethical practices for research involving human participants. Research that might be presented in a public forum, such as reports, a presentation at a conference, or a scholarly publication, must have the approval of your campus's institutional review board (IRB). Research is defined in federal regulations (Code of Federal Regulations, 2005, Title 45, Part 46) as a "systematic investigation, including research development, testing and evaluation, designed to develop or contribute to generalizable knowledge." All investigators in designing and conducting research must review an online tutorial and pass a short test to confirm their knowledge of compliance issues. Contact the IRB office on your campus about issues related to institutional management of research that involves human participants, including observational and archival studies. There are additional considerations if you are assessing a program's impact on youth under 18 years old, such as those involved in an America Reads tutoring program. We advise that you work with a faculty member skilled in navigating the IRB process on your campus and allot adequate time to complete this required step.

Consider Types and Sources of Evidence

As you clarify the focus of the assessment strategy, you need to consider the types of evidence to collect, by what methods, from whom, and by whom. As the questions guiding the plan develop, you need to specify the information that will answer those questions. Are you interested in opinions and attitudes (how someone feels), beliefs (what someone thinks), facts (what someone has learned), behavioral intentions (a student's plans after graduation), or behaviors (student's observations or self-reports)? Bennett and Rockwell (1995) provide a hierarchy of evidence to consider when designing an assessment strategy:

1. *Resources:* staff and volunteer time devoted to a project; salaries; resources used (equipment, travel).

2. *Activities:* events, methods used; subject matter taught; publicity, promotional activities.

3. *Participation:* number of people reached; characteristics or diversity of people; frequency and intensity of contact or participation.

4. *Reactions:* degree of interest in activities; feelings toward the program; positive or negative interest in type of activity; acceptance of activity leaders or structure of event; and attraction to methods used.

5. *Learning:* knowledge (awareness, understanding, mental abilities); opinion (outlooks, perspectives, viewpoints); skills (verbal or physical abilities); aspirations (ambitions, hopes).

6. *Actions:* patterns of behavior and procedures, such as decisions taken, recommendations adopted, practices implemented, actions taken, technologies used, policies enacted.

7. *Impact:* social, economic, environmental conditions intended as outcomes or benefits of programs; public and private benefits.

Within this hierarchy, the outcomes are stronger and more convincing at the higher levels (actions or impact), but they are also more time-consuming and expensive to collect. The assessment plan should consider the most useful types of evidence, including the possibility of including more than one type of measure. In addition to monitoring participation, for example, you can ask participants how satisfied they were with their experience and how their behavioral intentions are different as a result.

While developing a plan for assessment, you need to identify types and sources of information (e.g., evaluation forms, journals, institutional data, log sheets, participants, syllabi). The information can come from students, peers, staff at a community agency, community residents, supervisors, or instructors. Experts, such as other CSLPs and key partners, including community leaders, may also supply critical information on the program's quality or results of the experience. The information might come from observations (Lofland & Lofland, 1995), from archival sources (log sheets, student journals, minutes of meetings; see Denzin & Lincoln, 1994), or from broader indicators such as long-term impact (vandalism in schools), social indicators (high school graduation rates), and institutional measures (retention rates of college freshmen in service-learning classes). When multiple types and sources of information converge, there is added confidence in the conclusions about the impact of program activities (Greene, Caracelli, & Graham, 1989; Kidder & Fine, 1987).

Methods for gathering information are usually qualitative (Denzin & Lincoln, 1994; Marshall & Rossman, 1995; Patton, 1990) or quantitative (Bringle, Phillips, & Hudson, 2004; Kidder & Fine, 1987). Qualitative methods capture the different kinds of experiences that occur; quantitative methods provide numerical summaries of experiences. There are great differences between these two categories. Qualitative research involves an interpretive approach; researchers attempt to make sense of, or interpret, phenomena in terms of the meanings people bring to them. Data collection strategies include case studies, interviews, observations, review of historical documents, and group interactions (Denzin & Lincoln, 1994).

In contrast, quantitative methods focus their attention on precision (accuracy of measurement or survey instrument) and control (of extraneous variables) through prescriptive procedures (experimental designs or statistics) to test theories assumed to have broad applicability (Bringle & Hatcher, 2000). Table 10-1 at the end of this chapter summarizes various methods for collecting information, with their advantages and challenges. As the table indicates, the selection of a method is closely connected to the nature of the question.

Analyze Information
After gathering information for program evaluation or research, you need to determine how best to organize it—by observation setting, by theme or variables, by research questions, or by

program objective. The procedures for organizing and reducing data to a form that can be summarized and used are different for qualitative and quantitative data. For qualitative information, use an explicit procedure to organize it around common themes or categories and then identify patterns (Patton, 1990). The nature of the qualitative information and the research questions may require a template or rubric—either designed before data collection or after—that you or others use to organize and summarize the findings (see Lofland & Lofland, 1995; Miles & Huberman, 1994; Wolcott, 1994). Quantitative information needs to be numerically summarized (average ratings or frequencies) and possibly more extensively analyzed using inferential statistics (see Fink, 1995; Fitz-Gibbon & Morris, 1987).

Because there are many ways to analyze information, neither qualitative nor quantitative analyses are simple or straightforward, especially to those inexperienced with particular methods. Often, it is necessary to try different strategies for data analysis before you can identify the approach that yields the most meaningful results and insights. Some analyses might be appropriate for certain purposes or audiences. Consulting or contracting with an expert in statistics and data analysis may be worthwhile.

The analyses need to be put into perspective according to their relevance to the questions that were the focus of your assessment plan. The perspective for interpretation might be one of the following: the expected results (program goals); a standard or benchmark; a comparison within the set of data (first-year versus upper-division students); comparisons over time (achievement of learning outcomes or changes in attitudes); results from past research (in the research literature or at your institution); and implications for future programming (strengths, weaknesses, or recommendations). Interpretation of results should be appropriate for the confidence inherent in the selected methods and should acknowledge limitations, as appropriate. While analyzing and interpreting both qualitative and quantitative data, be careful to avoid common pitfalls (see the box "Common Pitfalls in Data Analysis and Interpretation," on page 224).

Tailor Reports to Others

The value of assessment, program evaluation, and research lies in systematically generating information about the quality of your programs. Therefore, you should tailor reports on the results of your assessment to particular audiences and purposes. If you are conducting a program evaluation, you should probably prepare more than one document to report the findings and conclusions (e.g., executive summary, detailed research report, short paragraphs for a newsletter, manuscript for journal publication, PowerPoint presentation). Each document should contain the necessary details for the intended audience, with graphic and tabular representations of the findings, as appropriate. The conclusions and recommendations should distinguish between robust data and more speculative data. Promises of confidentiality should always be honored.

We find that most readers are interested in quantitative data supported by qualitative narrative statements from participants. For example, each year, at the Center for Service and Learning, we track the number of America Reads tutors, the free hours of tutoring provided to children in the local community, the improvement in reading achievement of elementary students, and

---

Common Pitfalls in Data Analysis and Interpretation

- You assume that the program is the only cause of positive changes documented. Several factors, some of which are unrelated to project activities, may be responsible for changes in participants or in a community. It is usually impossible to isolate impact; the evaluation report should at least acknowledge other factors that may have contributed to change.

- You forget that the same evaluation method may give different results when used by different people, or that respondents may tell the evaluator what they believe he or she wants to hear. For example, two interviewers may ask the same questions but receive different answers because one was friendlier or more patient than the other. Real problems or difficulties may be ignored or hidden because people want the project to succeed or appear to be succeeding.

- You choose the wrong groups to compare, or compare groups that are different in too many ways. For example, gender, age, race, economic status, and many other factors can all have an impact on project outcomes. If comparisons between groups are important, try to compare those with similar characteristics except for the variable you are studying.

- You claim that the results of a small-scale evaluation also apply to a wide group or geographic area. For example, it is misleading to evaluate participants' responses to a particular intervention in one city and then claim that the results apply to the whole country. While this may well be the case, an evaluation report should reflect only the data analyzed (Kellogg Foundation, 2005).

---

retention and graduation rates for tutors. We share this quantitative data in campus annual reports, newsletters, and subsequent grant reports and proposals. We also gather qualitative data in the form of quotes from various participants (e.g., college student tutors, community site supervisors, elementary students) through open-ended surveys and interviews. We use these quotes (with permission) to supplement the quantitative data. Together, the information paints a picture of the success of the America Reads tutoring program.

Conclusion

In conclusion, we return to the CSLP as reflective practitioner. Although Kolb's (1984) experiential learning theory has been applied widely to service-learning pedagogy in designing interventions to increase student learning, it is not typically used for planning activities that enhance the learning of other constituencies. Kolb's model, however, applies directly to our work as CSLPs in that it encourages us to become reflective practitioners (Schon, 1991).

Conducting assessments that include program evaluations and research is not easy. It might even be perceived as risky if the evidence collected uncovers negative consequences or if anticipated program outcomes are not found. Unexpected, negative, or null results, although discouraging, can provide a basis for subsequent program redesign and improvement. Nevertheless, most consumers of assessment reports appreciate both the effort made and the usefulness of the results, even if the reported results were unanticipated. Assessment communicates a level of integrity and stewardship in committing to monitor program implementation and impact, which is respected in both the higher education and funding communities.

You may not have all the skills that the complete assessment process requires. Yet, in many cases, 90% of what you need is a systematic approach, clear thinking, and common sense. Fortunately, campuses have many persons with technical skills. You should seek help with the technical aspects of assessment, such as sampling, experimental design, measurement, survey construction, statistical analysis, and conducting focus groups. Your ability to seek input demonstrates your attention to this aspect of your professional work and development.

An important way in which you can grow as a professional is by dedicating time and resources to evaluate and research programs for which you have direct responsibility. Through collaboration with other professionals, you are well positioned to advance civic engagement by giving others concrete evidence of the quality of your work. You will need to develop some new skills, manage new responsibilities, and form new working relationships with others on campus. New habits are not easy, but they can reap rewards for you as a professional and generate recognition for your institution.

References

Ash, S. L., & Clayton, P. H. (2004). The articulated learning: An approach to reflection and assessment. *Innovative Higher Education, 29,* 137–154.

Ash, S. L., Clayton, P. H., & Atkinson, M. P. (2005). Integrating reflection and assessment to improve and capture student learning. *Michigan Journal of Community Service learning, 11(2),* 49–59.

Bennett, C. F., & Rockwell, S. K. (1995). *Targeting outcomes of programs (TOP): An integrated approach to planning and evaluation.* Lincoln, NE: Cooperative Extension, University of Nebraska.

Bringle, R. G. (2003). Enhancing theory-based research on service-learning. In S. H. Billig & J. Eyler (Eds.), *Deconstructing service-learning: Research exploring context, participation, and impacts* (pp. 3–21). Greenwich, CT: Information Age.

Bringle, R. G., & Hatcher, J. A. (1999). Reflection in service learning: Making meaning of experience. *Educational Horizons, 77(4),* 179–185.

Bringle, R. G., & Hatcher, J. A. (2000). Meaningful measurement of theory-based service-learning outcomes: Making the case with quantitative research. *Michigan Journal of Community Service Learning: Strategic Directions for Service-Learning Research,* 68–75.

Bringle, R. G., Phillips, M., & Hudson, M. (2004). *The measure of service learning: Research scales to assess student experiences.* Washington, DC: American Psychological Association.

Cambridge, B. L. (1999). Effective assessment: A signal of quality citizenship. In R. G. Bringle, R. Games, & E. A. Malloy (Eds.), *Colleges and universities as citizens* (pp. 173–192). Needham Heights, MA: Allyn and Bacon.

Code of Federal Regulations. (2005). Title 45-Public welfare. Department of Health and Human Services. Part 46. Protection of human subjects. Retrieved September 14, 2009, from http://www.hhs.gov/ohrp/humansubjects/guidance/45cfr46.htm#46.

Cronbach, L. (1982). *Designing evaluations of educational and social programs.* San Francisco: Jossey-Bass.

Denzin, N. K., & Lincoln, Y. S. (Eds.). (1994). *Handbook of qualitative research.* Thousand Oaks, CA: Sage.

Dewey, J. (1916). *Democracy and education.* New York: Macmillan Company.

Eyler, J. S., & Giles, D. E. (1999). *Where's the learning in service-learning?* San Francisco: Jossey-Bass.

Fink, A. (1995). *How to analyze survey data: The survey kit.* Newbury Park, CA: Sage.

Fitz-Gibbon, C. T., & Morris, L. L. (1987). *How to analyze data. Series: Program Evaluation Kit* (2nd ed.). Newbury Park, CA: Sage.

Frechtling, J., & Westat, L. S. (1997). *User-friendly handbook for mixed-method evaluations.* Retrieved September 14, 2009, from http://www.nsf.gov/pubs/1997/nsf97153/start.htm.

Gelmon, S., Furco, A., Holland, B., & Bringle, R. G. (2005). *Beyond anecdote: Challenges in bringing rigor to service-learning research.* Panel presented at the 5th Annual International K-H Service-Learning Conference, East Lansing, MI.

Greene, J. C., Caracelli, V. J., & Graham, W. F. (1989). Toward a conceptual framework for mixed-method evaluation designs. *Educational Evaluation and Policy Analysis, 11,* 255–274.

Hatcher, J. A., & Bringle, R. G. (1997). Reflections: Bridging the gap between service and learning. *Journal of College Teaching, 45,* 153–158.

Hatcher, J. A., Bringle, R. G., & Muthiah, R. (2002). Institutional strategies to involve freshmen in service. In E. Zlotkowski (Ed.), *Service learning and the first year experience* (pp. 79–90). Columbia, SC: National Resource Center for the First-Year Experience and Students in Transition.

Kellogg Foundation. (2005). *Evaluation toolkit.* Retrieved September 14, 2009, from http://www.wkkf.org/default.aspx?tabid=75&CID=281&NID=61&LanguageID=0.

Kidder, L., & Fine, M. (1987). Qualitative and quantitative methods: When stories converge. In M. M. Mark & L. Shotland (Eds.), *New directions for program evaluation* (pp. 57–75). San Francisco: Jossey-Bass.

Kolb, D. A. (1984). *Experiential learning: Experience as the source of learning and development.* Englewood Cliffs, NJ: Prentice-Hall.

Lofland, J., & Lofland, L. H. (1995). *Analyzing social settings: A guide to qualitative observation and analysis.* Belmont, CA: Wadsworth.

Marshall, C., & Rossman, G. B. (1995). *Designing qualitative research* (2nd ed.). Thousand Oaks, CA: Sage.

McNamara, C. (1999). *Basic guide to program evaluation.* Retrieved September 14, 2009, from http://www.managementhelp.org/evaluatn/fnl_eval.htm#anchor1585345.

Miles, M. B., & Huberman, A. M. (1994). *Qualitative data analysis* (2nd ed). Newbury Park, CA: Sage.

National Science Foundation. (1993). *User-friendly handbook for project evaluation: Science, mathematics, engineering and technology education,* NSF 93–152. Arlington, VA: Author.

Patton, M. Q. (1990). *Qualitative evaluation and research methods* (2nd ed.). Newbury Park, CA: Sage.

Rossi, P. H., & Freeman, H. E. (1985). *Evaluation: A systematic approach* (3rd ed.). Newbury Park, CA: Sage.

Schön, D. A. (1991). *The reflective turn: Case studies in and on educational practice.* New York, NY: Teachers Press, Columbia University.

Schön, D. A. (1995). *The reflective practitioner: How professionals think in action.* New York: Basic Books.

Strand, K., Marullo, S., Cutforth, N., Stoecker, R., & Donohue, P. (2003). *Community-based research and higher education: Principles and practices.* San Francisco: Jossey-Bass.

Taylor-Powell, E., Steele, S., & Douglah, M. (1996). *Planning a program evaluation.* Retrieved September 14, 2009, from http://learningstore.uwex.edu/Planning-a-Program-Evaluation--P1033C238.aspx.

Wolcott, H. F. (1994). *Transforming qualitative data: Description, analysis and interpretation.* Thousand Oaks, CA: Sage.

Yin, R. K. (1989). *Case study research: Design and method.* Newbury Park, CA: Sage.

TABLE 10-1: Methods for Collecting Information

METHOD	OVERALL PURPOSE	ADVANTAGES	CHALLENGES
Questionnaires, surveys, check-lists	To quickly and easily get information from people in a nonthreaten-ing way	Can complete anonymously Inexpensive to administer Easy to compare and analyze Can administer to many people Can get lots of data Many sample questionnaires already exist	Might not get careful feedback Wording can bias client's responses Are impersonal In surveys, may need sampling expert Doesn't get full story
Interviews	To fully under-stand some-one's impres-sions or expe-riences, or learn more about answers to question-naires	Can get full range and depth of information Develops relationship with client Can be flexible with client	Can take much time Can be hard to analyze and compare Can be costly Can bias client's responses
Documentation review	To learn how program oper-ates, without interrupting it, by reviewing applications, finances, memos, min-utes, etc.	Can get comprehensive and historical information Doesn't interrupt program or client's routine in program Information already exists Few biases about information	Often takes much time Information may be incomplete Need to be quite clear about what you're looking for Not flexible means to get data; data restricted to what already exists
Observation	To gather accurate infor-mation about program, par-ticularly about processes	View operations of a pro-gram as they are actually occurring Can adapt to events as they occur	Can be difficult to interpret seen behaviors Can be complex to categorize observations Can influence behaviors of program participants Can be expensive

(continued)

TABLE 10-1: Methods for Collecting Information (cont.)

METHOD	OVERALL PURPOSE	ADVANTAGES	CHALLENGES
Focus groups	Explore topic in depth through group discussion, (e.g., about reactions to experience or suggestion, understanding common complaints, etc.); useful in evaluation and marketing	Can quickly and reliably get common impressions Can be efficient way to get range and depth of information in short time Can convey key information about programs	Can be hard to analyze responses Need good facilitator for safety and closure Difficult to schedule 6–8 people together
Case studies	To fully understand or depict client's experiences in program, and conduct comprehensive examination through cross-comparison of cases	Fully depicts client's experience in program input, process, and results Powerful ways to portray program to outsiders	Usually quite time consuming to collect, organize, and describe Represents depth of information, rather than breadth

Source: McNamara (1999). Used by permission.

CHAPTER ELEVEN

Situating Service-Learning in the Context of Civic Engagement

Julie E. Owen and Wendy Wagner

NOTING THAT ADDRESSING THE COMPLEX SOCIAL ISSUES of today's rapidly changing world will require citizens who are knowledgeable, capable, and motivated to engage in democratic processes, many are calling for civic engagement to be emphasized as an important learning outcome of higher education (American College Personnel Association & National Association of Student Personnel Administrators, 2004; Campus Compact, 1999; Colby, Ehrlich, Beaumont & Stephens, 2003; Jacoby, 2009; National Leadership Council for Liberal Education and America's Promise, 2007). While involvement in volunteering is increasing (Kiesa et al., 2007) and many students take part in direct service in their communities through service-learning programs, recent research reveals that these experiences are not leading students to engage in other forms of civic engagement (Hollander & Hartley, 2003; Keeter, Zukin, Andolina, & Jenkins, 2002). For example, it is not uncommon for student volunteers to feel passionate about their environmental clean-up and recycling programs and yet be unaware of the effect of current government regulations on the environment or their government representatives' stand on environmental issues. Many students volunteer to serve food to the homeless people in their communities without ever joining with other like-minded people to address the issue of homelessness through collective action.

It cannot be assumed that community service experiences will automatically result in the knowledge, skills, or motivations needed for civic engagement. Studies have shown that recent increases in volunteerism have not led to increased knowledge of civic or political processes or interest in civic issues (Colby, Ehrlich, Beaumont, & Stephens, 2003; Jacoby, 2009; Lopez, Levine, Both, Kiesa, Kirby & Marcelo, 2006). College students today have complex attitudes toward institutions such as government and the media. They want authentic opportunities to discuss social issues and solutions but mistrust political spin and the highly polarized political party system (Kiesa, et al., 2007). In general, they do want to be actively involved in improving their local, national and global communities (Kiesa, et al., 2007), but intentional educational practices are needed to help them become knowledgeable and responsible citizens.

This chapter explores the links between the work of community service-learning professionals (CSLPs) and broader civic engagement efforts. It describes the various forms of civic engagement and the knowledge, skills, and attitudes (here called *habits*) necessary to be effective. In addition to focusing on the engagement of individual students, this chapter explores how colleges and universities can be civically engaged. At many institutions, service-learning has served as a catalyst for campus-community partnerships, community-based research, and public scholarship. Conversely, CSLPs have found that by joining campus-wide civic engagement efforts, they gain institutional support for service-learning.

To understand how one's service-learning program will fit into the framework of civic engagement, it is helpful for practitioners to first clarify how they are defining civic engagement. Some define civic engagement by differentiating it from processes of political engagement, putting voting and signing petitions in the latter category and community volunteering or the work of non-governmental organizations in the former. They would describe both as aimed at benefiting the common good. Others have come to believe that the line between political and apolitical acts is too blurred, so they include any kind of activity aimed at improving one's communities into the single category of civic engagement (Barber, 1998a; Colby, Beaumont, Ehrlich, & Corngold, 2007; Long, 2002). See the "Definitions" box on the following page for descriptions of other commonly used terms related to service-learning.

Another question for educators to consider is whether civic engagement is the learning outcome itself, or if it is the process by which students learn other outcomes, such as critical thinking or appreciation of diversity: "Is it a program, a pedagogy, or a philosophy? Can it be all of these?" (Jacoby, 2009, p. 6). Educators might also consider defining civic engagement by asking the question asked by Colby et al. (2007): "What do democracies need from their citizens?" (p. 26). These researchers suggest that students need the knowledge, skills, and motivation to be "reasonably well-informed, capable, engaged and public-spirited citizens" (p. 26). It would be a worthwhile exercise for educators to consider this question for themselves.

Despite a variety of issues and considerations, civic engagement clearly involves a broad array of activities, all intended to make the community a better place for everyone. A study of civic engagement programs in higher education (Lawry, Laurison, & Van Antwerpen, 2006) found that nearly all of these programs defined civic engagement in terms of feelings of responsibility to common or community interests that reach beyond purely individual interests.

While recognizing the multitude of definitions for civic engagement, this chapter will use the definition offered by the Pew Partnership for Civic Change: "The will and capacity to solve public problems" (Ferraiolo, 2004, p. 4). The activities aimed at solving public problems can take many forms. Students describe many kinds of community involvement: preparing food in soup kitchens, planting trees in community parks, participating in protest rallies, or being involved in local neighborhood associations. All these activities are considered civic engagement according to the above definition.

Forms of Individual Civic Engagement

To help educators consider the various forms of civic engagement students may engage in with their communities, we reviewed several sources that describe such typologies (Battistoni, 2002; Lawry, Laurison & Van Antwerpen, 2009; Lopez, et al., 2006; Patrick, 2003). The following eight categories represent a variety of forms of individual civic engagement:

- *Direct service:* giving personal time and energy to address immediate community needs. Examples include tutoring, serving food at a shelter, building or repairing homes, and cleaning up neighborhoods or parks.

- *Community research:* gathering and analyzing data related to a topic relevant to the community to help its members make informed decisions. This may include exploring a community to map the assets it can build upon, conducting a survey to describe how community members are affected by a certain problem, or collecting river samples to test for pollutants. This form of civic engagement provides knowledge on which other efforts can build.

Definitions

- *Civic engagement:* acting with a heightened sense of responsibility for one's communities, or "the will and capacity to solve public problems" (Ferraiolo, 2004, p. 3–4).

- *Engaged campus:* one that is consciously committed to reinvigorating the democratic spirit and community engagement in all aspects of its college life: students, faculty, staff, and the institution itself (Boyte & Hollander, 1999).

- *Campus-community partnership:* a sustained, mutual cooperation between an institution of higher education and one or more community organizations, in which both partners consider themselves "part of the same community, with common problems, common interests, common resources, and a common capacity to shape one another in profound ways" (Enos & Morton, 2003, p. 20).

- *Engaged scholarship:* connects the intellectual assets of the institution to public issues. "Through engaged forms of teaching and research, faculty apply their academic expertise to public purposes as a way of contributing to the fulfillment of the core mission of the institution" (Holland, 2005, p. 7).

- *Community-based research:* a collaborative enterprise between researchers (professors and/or students) and community members to validate multiple sources of knowledge and promote use of multiple methods of discovery with the goal of social action and social change (Center for Social Justice, Research, Teaching, & Service, Department of Sociology and Anthropology and the Community Research and Learning Network, 2008).

- *Education and advocacy:* raising public awareness of social issues by engaging in public debates or discourse, writing letters to the editor, posting links about an issue on social networking internet sites, distributing educational materials to the public, or speaking to community groups. This includes using various modes of persuasion (e.g., marches, writing letters) to convince government or corporate decision makers to make choices that will benefit the community.

- *Social innovation:* working with the diverse constituencies within a community and building on existing assets to solve problems and improve the community.

- *Political involvement:* participating in processes of government, such as campaigning, signing petitions, and voting. This includes: 1) Keeping informed about issues in the local, national, and global community in order to vote responsibly, and 2) Writing to urge certain actions of government representatives and holding them accountable to campaign promises.

- *Socially responsible personal and professional behavior:* maintaining a sense of responsibility to the welfare of others when making personal or professional decisions; using one's career or professional training to benefit the community. This includes personal lifestyle choices that reflect commitment to one's values: recycling; using public transportation; buying or not buying certain products to show support or disagreement with the practices of the corporation that makes them; and choosing to work for companies with socially just priorities.

- *Philanthropic giving:* charitable efforts such as donating funding or needed items, or organizing or participating in fundraising events.

- *Participation in associations:* joining community organizations that develop the social networks and trust that is the foundation for community-building efforts. This includes participation in civic associations, sports leagues, church choirs, and school boards.

Each form of civic engagement has a role in improving communities. No one approach is best; rather, the various forms work together to address problems from multiple angles. For example, *direct service* provides immediate assistance but rarely addresses the root causes of problems. *Advocacy* and *political involvement* are aimed at long-term solutions that target the causes of problems but offer little relief in the short term. When done intentionally, *philanthropic giving* can address both immediate needs and long-term solutions, but it doesn't necessarily help participants understand the underlying social issues or their personal or professional contributions to the problem or the solution. *Socially responsible behavior* includes the important element of personal commitment to being part of the solution but may lack the organized group effort to create meaningful change.

Habits of Civic Engagement
Keith Morton (1995) describes a model of service that includes a continuum ranging from *thin* to *thick* service. According to the model, the more that service addresses the root causes of problems and builds personal relationships in the community, the thicker it becomes. This model can also apply to the other forms of civic engagement.

In order for students to apply a thicker approach to their community activity, they need to develop the knowledge, skills, and motivations to act, which we call the *habits* of civic engagement. To fully engage with each habit, students must develop in all three areas.

The seven habits of individual civic engagement proposed here are:

1. *Critical thinking* is needed for civic engagement (Colby et al., 2003; Eyler & Giles, 1999; Jacoby, 2009; Kirlin, 2003; Musil, 2009; Patrick, 2003) in order to understand the complexity of community problems when multiple solutions are required, rather than simple, one-dimensional answers. It requires understanding that some approaches address immediate needs, while others address the network of problems that create those needs. This habit indicates the ability to deal with ambiguity, to evaluate conflicting evidence and integrate multiple perspectives. Critical thinkers understand how systems work together to create problems or to solve them. They are able to recognize how to frame an issue and to change their thinking, rather than twist the evidence to fit their rationale.

2. *Civil discourse* is the habit necessary for civil debate. Community members must be able to dialogue with those who hold different perspectives (Jacoby, 2009), listen to others, consider the merit of other positions, clearly communicate their own opinions, grounding them in evidence, and deliberate with others about the best course of action (Barber, 1998b; Colby et al., 2007; Musil, 2009). Discourse is included in all the forms of civic engagement but may look different in each. It includes public debate at a town-hall meeting, or a skillfully written letter to the editor.

3. *Leadership* is the ability to work with others to effect change. Civic leaders need the ability to participate in collective decision making, collaborate, build a sense of community, mutual respect, and common vision (Colby et al., 2007; Colby et al., 2003; Eyler & Giles, 1999; Kirlin, 2003; Musil, 2009; Patrick, 2003), and facilitate group problem solving (Jacoby, 2009). Sometimes this habit will also include the ability to work with others through controversy with civility, dealing with conflict, building consensus, and helping a diverse group work together (Colby et al., 2007; Musil, 2009). Being able to partner across organizational lines to effect change—often called coalition building—is an essential leadership skill.

4. *Multicultural awareness* is a habit that ensures all voices in the community are heard. Civic engagement requires the ability to build bridges across difference and to value the diversity in the community (Colby et al., 2003; Musil, 2009). It involves the ability and willingness to acknowledge another person's vantage point, as well as the awareness of one's own cultural values and how they shape interactions with others. Understanding social justice, being aware of systems of privilege and inequality (Eyler & Giles, 1999), and recognizing how communities can restrict and exclude some members (Musil, 2009) are also aspects of this civic habit.

5. *Understanding social issues* refers to one's awareness of current events (Lawry, et al., 2009; Colby et al., 2007), knowing how the community operates and the problems it faces

(Jacoby, 2009; Patrick, 2003), understanding how a community's history and political, economic, and social systems shape its needs and strengths (Colby et al., 2007; Musil, 2009). Knowing how to learn more about an issue and evaluate the credibility of diverse sources in order to develop an informed perspective is also related to this civic habit.

6. *Social responsibility* is the habit that includes developing empathy, concern for others, commitment to ethical action (Colby, 2003; Musil, 2009; Patrick, 2003), clarity about core values around equality, opportunity, liberty, justice (Musil, 2009), and concern for the rights and welfare of others (Jacoby, 2009). This habit is at the heart of one's awareness of the impact of decisions and behaviors on others and an understanding of the global effect of one's local decisions. It grows from feeling connected to the community, considering the community's social problems to be at least partly their own, becoming committed to do the right thing, and having a sense of responsibility to act (Colby, 2003; Eyler & Giles, 1999).

7. *Strategic competence* is the ability to work within various systems, to get things done within a bureaucracy and amid ambiguity. Effective civic involvement involves strategically transforming one's sense of responsibility into action (Colby et al., 2003). It includes being able to plan practical strategies for action, implement them, and reflect on them (Eyler & Giles, 1999; Musil, 2009). Community problem solving often involves figuring out what to do without a map or instruction sheet. Working within a political structure and also sometimes challenging that structure are imperative. This habit relies on finding answers, figuring out whom to talk with to get things done, and negotiating red tape.

Service-Learning for Civic Engagement

Service-learning is a powerful pedagogy to help students develop the habits of civic engagement and be prepared for more effective community involvement. Service-learning, however, is not currently reaching its full potential in this area. Research has shown that a large majority of young people who volunteer do not make connections between their service and social or political problems; rather, their intentions are just to generally help others (Lopez et al., 2006). Hollander and Hartley (2003) cite several research studies indicating that, although there are many proven civic outcomes associated with service-learning, including willingness to act on behalf of the common good and advances in multicultural understanding, service-learning as currently practiced has not resulted in increased interest in public affairs.

Some evidence indicates, however, that service-learning is leading students to broader civic engagement. The students who wrote *The New Student Politics* (Long, 2002) do not see themselves as disengaged from politics but as engaged differently. These students discussed their frustration at being misunderstood by those who measure civic engagement only as voting or attending protest rallies. They described their involvement in social change as *service politics,* a term indicating that their direct-service experiences help them understand the systemic issues that create community needs and recognize the need to address those issues through actions in addition to service.

Service-learning programs that aim to promote civic engagement should intentionally focus on using the pedagogy of action and reflection to foster the habits of civic engagement. They should broaden students' opportunities for involvement to include multiple forms of civic engagement, not only direct service, which is more typical of service-learning programs. Service-learning can help students become aware of the economic, cultural, and social systems that maintain inequality. It can help them see the complexities of communities and social problems. This knowledge can help them identify the benefits and shortcomings of the various forms of engagement and realize that no single form of civic engagement can meet all needs.

To help students engage more broadly, we recommend that they explore the questions in Worksheet 11-1 (beginning on page 249). Depending on the service activity and the students' readiness, some of the questions may guide pre-service discussion; others, post-service reflection.

Service-Learning and the Engaged Campus

Just as there are many ways to define civic engagement for individuals, multiple terms are used for *institutional* civic engagement, including the "engaged campus," "universities as citizens," and "civically responsible institutions." These terms highlight the institution's role in improving the community of which it is a part. Both individuals and institutions can commit themselves to developing partnerships with communities. The preceding section addressed the individual forms and habits of civic engagement; this section addresses civic engagement on the institutional level and service-learning as a catalyst for developing an engaged campus. Campus Compact (1999) defines the "engaged campus" as one consciously committed to reinvigorating the democratic spirit and community engagement in all aspects of its college life: students, faculty, staff, and the institution. This broader notion of campus engagement calls for faculty and students to conduct scholarship that is informed by and has an impact on local communities; for presidents and other institutional leaders to speak publicly about community issues and the importance of community engagement; for staff and administrators to actively make partnerships beyond the bounds of campus; and for institutions to share the physical and economic resources of the campus with community partners.

In 2005, the Carnegie Foundation for the Advancement of Teaching created an elective classification system in which institutions of higher education with a strong commitment to civic and community engagement could seek recognition. The classification includes three categories: curricular engagement; outreach and partnerships; and a category for institutions that excel in both curricular engagement and outreach. In 2006, 76 colleges and universities were selected as institutions of community engagement (Driscoll, 2008). In 2008, that number rose to 120. Creating an engaged campus involves more than supporting just a few isolated campus-community programs; it often involves a significant culture shift. Walshok (1999) describes ways campuses can create new institutional mechanisms for supporting civic engagement. She offers three shifts that are essential for campuses to make if they are to fully embrace the work of civic engagement: viewing the campus as one of many centers of specialized knowledge in a community rather than as the only center of knowledge; viewing the university as a convener rather than as the sole source of expertise on pressing social issues or problems; and seeking to establish an ongoing collaborative relationship with community rather than settling for episodic outreach.

Another way that campuses can transform their cultures to more explicitly address civic engagement is to rethink traditional notions of teaching, research, and service so that civic responsibilities and public contributions are more central to the work of the institution (Ramaley, 2000). Ramaley proposes a shift from viewing faculty as the sole transmitters of knowledge to instead valuing the centrality of *learning* and the role of students and community partners as co-creators of knowledge. Instead of limiting research by traditional disciplinary boundaries, she proposes we broaden the definition of legitimate scholarly work to include the process of *discovery,* in which faculty, students, and community members actively participate in the development, application, and integration of knowledge. Ramaley advocates for campus-community *engagement* in which knowledge and resources are shared reciprocally, rather than the usual campus outreach approach to the community.

Refocusing the academy on the processes of learning, discovery, and engagement leads to an examination of the habits of the engaged campus. Just as this chapter identified earlier seven habits of individual civic engagement, practices of engaged institutions that contribute to a rediscovery of the public purposes and civic mission of higher education can also be identified. Civic scholars have enumerated many of these practices in publications including, among others, The Kellogg Presidents' Commission on the Future of State and Land Grant Universities' *Returning to Our Roots* series (2001); The Carnegie Foundation for the Advancement of Teaching's *Educating Citizens: Preparing America's Undergraduates for Lives of Moral and Civic Responsibility* (Colby et al., 2003) and *Educating for Democracy: Preparing Undergraduates for Political Engagement* (Colby et al., 2007); and Campus Compact's *Presidents' Declaration on the Civic Responsibility of Higher Education* (1999). The following seven habits of engaged campuses are drawn from these resources:

1. *Develop sustainable partnerships.* The Kellogg Presidents' Commission on the Future of State and Land Grant Universities (2001) recommends that institutions foster partnerships across institutional, organizational, and academic boundaries to enhance quality, relevance of programs, and effective responses to issues. Jacoby (2003) agrees that partnerships are essential for "enhancing learning and bringing human and other resources to bear on addressing society's most pressing problems and meeting its greatest needs" (p.17). She articulates the benefits of sustained campus-community partnerships as providing fertile ground for service-learning and other active pedagogies, offering opportunities for faculty members to conduct engaged scholarship and community-based research, and allowing community members to engage with the institution as a whole, rather than just with individuals or specific programs.

2. *Offer institutional incentives and rewards.* Engaged institutions should design ways to honor civic engagement in hiring, tenure and promotion, development, and salary decisions. Incentives and awards should also extend to funding the work of civic engagement through increased acknowledgment of the social impact of research and partnerships. Colby et al. (2003) maintain that institutional support and rewards "need not always be formal" (p. 210). They enumerate strategies such as institutions offering public state-

ments of support for civic engagement and engaged scholarship, providing faculty development opportunities, developing a supportive infrastructure and logistical assistance, extending opportunities to non–tenure-track faculty, and considering civic engagement in faculty recruitment.

3. *Be innovative.* Changing times call for new methods and approaches to old problems. The Kellogg Presidents' Commission (2001) describes higher education's ability to innovate and create new ideas that are responsive to society's needs as one of the fundamental habits of an engaged university. Innovations in curriculum, organization and delivery of programs, and the adoption of new perspectives are all key to sustaining community engagement.

4. *Conduct meaningful assessment and evaluation.* How can we know if we are achieving important civic goals and objectives if we never measure the impact of our efforts? The Kellogg Presidents' Commission (2001) supports the development of measures for assessing public engagement as indicators of institutional performance. Cambridge (1999) suggests that "because the university exhibits its role as citizen through its students, faculty members, institutional practices, and relationship to other institutions and society," each of these constituencies must be examined in terms of "higher education's role in promoting a democratic capacity for citizenship at each site" (p. 176).

5. *Seek mission congruence.* Hollander and Saltmarsh (2000) describe how, as institutions of higher education reshape themselves to meet the needs of civic renewal, they often return to their founding mission of serving democracy by educating students for productive citizenship. The engaged campus does more than just articulate public goals in its mission statement; it seeks to live up to those commitments in its structure, values, and behavior (Ferraiolo, 2004). In many cases, market forces and increasing disciplinarity have caused institutions to relegate civic education to the margins of the curriculum (Colby et al., 2003). Efforts to educate engaged citizens will require a critical examination of "the opposing trends of commodification, specialization, and institutional competition" (Colby et al., p. 48) and an embracing of an emerging vision of moral and civic education.

6. *Promote public dialogue.* Ferraiolo (2004) exhorts presidents, trustees, administrators, faculty, and staff to "engage students, the public, and community partners in thoughtful, reflective, democratic dialogue and insist on respecting the diversity of opinions that result from that dialogue" (p.6). Campus Compact's *Presidents' Declaration on the Civic Responsibility of Higher Education* (1999) asks institutional leaders to create a campus culture where there is genuine, vigorous, open dialogue about critical issues of education and democracy. The Kellogg Presidents' Commission (2001) calls for civic engagement to be "emphasized explicitly and regularly by university officials . . . in communicating with the public and within the university" (p. 4).

7. *Leverage university capacity.* The Kellogg Presidents' Commission (2001) calls on public universities to utilize their substantial organizational resources as building blocks for the

engaged university of the future. Aligning existing organizations, stakeholders from the public and private sectors, and physical, technological, and financial resources can create a more powerfully engaged university. Trends such as social entrepreneurship, social value creation, and social responsibility are calling for multi-sector collaboration to address intractable public problems (Bornstein, 2005; Light, 2008). Universities should be key players in this shared work.

These habits may seem logical and even self-evident, but they can be challenging to implement on a systemic level. Though campus-wide community engagement is a noble calling, the U.S. higher education system traditionally has hierarchical and individualistic values. Hierarchical systems in which authority and power are proportional to one's place in the chain of command still exist on most college campuses. A tradition of individualism and competitiveness also pervades academia as departments and individuals are pitted against each other in the quest for scarce resources and recognition. To foster the habits of an engaged campus, the institution must identify ways in which the members of the campus community can work together across administrative and academic lines to address community needs.

If we examine constraining and empowering beliefs, we can see why different campus constituents may or may not perceive themselves as part of an engaged campus. *Constraining beliefs* are thoughts or ideas that limit a person's ability to effect meaningful change or get involved in the engaged campus. *Empowering beliefs* are those that help a person see possibilities and commitments he or she might make in order to work toward campus-community engagement.

For example, students may come to campus with the sole purpose of personal or career advancement. Involvement in community service-learning might transform their perspective from egocentric to seeing their responsibility to the larger community. Faculty may be focused on achievements within their discipline and the lack of reward for community work, and therefore fail to see the potential real-world impact of interdisciplinary approaches to complex social issues. They may not realize the power of community engagement to renew and motivate their personal research aims. Academic administrators may be hampered by tradition and institutional politics, although they are uniquely poised as campus decision makers to modify existing systems (i.e., promotion, tenure, rewards, funding priorities) to foster campus and community engagement. Student affairs staff may feel they are marginalized or not taken seriously by the academy. By drawing on their knowledge of student development and experiential learning, they can build bridges between community partners and engaged faculty, and between students, campus, and community, to teach the essential skills of civic engagement. College presidents may not appreciate the value of publicly articulating the value of the engaged campus. Yet they are positioned to focus resources on institutional and community transformation, and serve as models for others at the institution. Finally, community partners may feel they lack familiarity with campus policies and practices, or perhaps have a history of being "used" or ignored by campus entities. They are mistrustful and skeptical. Yet community partners can voice pressing local needs and mobilize community members toward shared goals.

Only by working with stakeholders to transform constraining beliefs into empowering ones can all members of a community see themselves as part of an engaged campus. Service-learning can be a powerful way to "re-envision relationships between campus and community, student and content, faculty and student" (Ward, 2003). Pigza and Troppe (2003) offer many ways that service-learning professionals can promote the engaged campus. CSLPs should link service-learning with other institutional priorities such as retention and diversity so that it becomes essential to campus policies and practices. They should scan campus publications for relevant people, research, and programs to identify allies for service-learning. CSLPs should ensure that service-learning and civic engagement are included in official campus documents such as mission statements and strategic plans. They should promote faculty research activities that connect with community involvement. Finally, they should use campus and local media to showcase substantive service-learning and civic engagement efforts in the community, recognizing that it is essential to "seek ways to describe more accurately and deeply the interdependency of campus and community partners so that partnership activities become more than photo opportunities" (Pigza & Troppe, 2003, p. 127).

If service-learning can be a powerful catalyst for broader campus engagement, it follows that engaged campuses are rich environments for sustaining community service-learning. Hartley, Harkavy, and Benson (2005) describe how institutions have embraced service-learning to varying degrees. On some campuses, service-learning has a "home" only in certain disciplines or happens in small pockets where isolated faculty or staff members "labor with meager support" (p. 205). At campuses that truly embrace civic engagement, however, service-learning has been incorporated into institutional life to a "striking degree" (p. 205). Hartley, Harkavy, and Benson characterize these campuses as places where faculty, staff, and institutional leadership have embraced service-learning as part of the fabric of the larger institution. In a broad commitment to civic engagement, these institutions recognize service-learning's legitimacy and offer institutional support in the form of funding, staffing, and roles and rewards that value community engagement. Additionally, new models of community service and service-learning have emerged that emphasize civic engagement, social change, and social justice (Welch, 2009). As institutions make intentional efforts to educate undergraduates for citizenship, service-learning emerges as "one of the most powerful pedagogies....for developing moral and civic responsibility" (Welch, 2009, p. 177). In 2007, the Association of American Colleges and Universities' National Leadership Council for Liberal Education and America's Promise (LEAP) identified service-learning as a "high-impact practice" that leads to a range of positive outcomes for students, as well as colleges and universities (Brownell & Swaner, 2009). These outcomes include gains in moral reasoning, in students' sense of moral and civic responsibility, and in the development of a social justice orientation, as well as an increased ability to apply class learning to real-world situations.

Service-Learning and Engaged Scholarship

Higher education institutions, particularly research universities, have been slow to embrace engaged scholarship because of their long tradition of supporting and investing in objective inquiry, with the primary purpose of adding to the knowledge base of a field or discipline. Traditional academic research is "pure, disciplinary, expert-led, hierarchical, peer-reviewed, and university or 'lab'-based" (Holland, 2005, p. 2).

In contrast, engaged scholarship:

- Is collaborative and participatory;

- Draws on many sources of distributed knowledge;

- Is based on partnerships;

- Is shaped by multiple perspectives and expectations;

- Deals with difficult, evolving questions—complex issues that may shift constantly;

- Is long term, in both effort and impact, often with episodic bursts of progress;

- Requires diverse strategies and approaches; and

- Crosses disciplinary lines. (Holland, 2005, p. 7)

Engaged scholarship comes in many forms and is defined differently by different disciplines. For example, public scholarship, community-based research, and action research are all ways faculty seek to develop an interactive flow of knowledge between the university and community. Some definitions and distinctions of engaged scholarship are:

- *Public scholarship:* research that seeks to make the university's knowledge into truly public knowledge utilized in public ways (Brown, 2005). It optimizes the extent to which university research informs and is informed by the public good, maximizes the generation and transfer of knowledge and technology, educates the public about the university's research, and listens to the public about what research needs to be done (University of Minnesota, 2006). The University of Minnesota has a long tradition of public scholarship. It offers public education efforts such as a "Mini Veterinary School," which offers community members like pet owners, pet feed producers, and agricultural representatives life-long learning about animal care integrated with the professional Veterinary School curriculum. University scholarship informs community practice, and community members communicate their animal-related needs to institutional researchers.

- *Community-based research:* a collaborative enterprise between researchers (professors and/or students) and community members that seeks to validate multiple sources of knowledge and promote the use of many methods of discovery, with the goal of social action and social change (adapted from Center for Social Justice, Research, Teaching & Service, 2008). Paul (2003) describes community-based research as functioning at the intersections of three core functions of higher education: research, civic engagement, and liberal learning. She offers the Trenton Youth Community-Based Research Corps (TYCBRC) at the College of New Jersey as one model of effective community-based research. TYCBRC students take a series of three courses that include preparation for community engagement; an eight-session program fostering youth advocacy skills around different community issues, complemented by an academic class designed to promote reflection and connection to course content; and a year-long community-based research partnership in which students "accomplish major research projects with and on behalf of their community partners" (Paul, 2003, p. 206).

- *Participatory action research:* seeks to break down barriers between the research enterprise and the process of social change by recognizing the interaction between the researcher and those being researched, by being sensitive to community needs, and by giving voice to community members (Nyden, 2003). It can require training and skill building so all involved can partner effectively. Stringer (2007) describes participatory action research as having the following characteristics: it is *democratic,* enabling the participation of all people; it is *equitable,* acknowledging people's equality of worth; it is *liberating,* providing freedom from oppressive, debilitating conditions; and it is *life enhancing,* enabling the expression of people's full human potential (p.11). The University of Richmond in Virginia offers a participatory action research class where students learn about participatory action research and liberation pedagogy, and then plan and conduct a participatory action research project in the community, such as working with inmates from a local prison to evaluate and improve the prison conditions.

When the principles of service-learning are applied to these forms of engaged scholarship, the efforts do more than just expand the knowledge base of the researcher's academic discipline. They also give voice to students and community members and build capacity for social change. Community-based research can benefit students by building on their service experiences and interest in social issues to provide a different form of civic engagement. Since community-based research involves working with community members, students develop relationships outside the traditional bounds of campus and learn to work alongside others to investigate and address relevant social issues. Community partners, including nonprofits, religious organizations, neighborhood associations, social groups, and individual community residents, can benefit from community-based research in that they can highlight their assets and strengths, are viewed as advisors and experts, can get their pressing questions addressed, and can develop sustained relationships with university partners.

Building on such principles of service-learning as sensitivity to community needs, acknowledgment of community assets, and collaboration with community partners can transform an applied research project into a true service-learning experience. For example, a faculty member who involves her sociology students in collecting life narratives of local residents who recently immigrated is an example of community-based research. If the faculty member involves both the students and the community of recent immigrants at all phases of the project—conceptualization, data collection, outcome analysis, and dissemination and application of results—then the project could also be considered community service-learning. The local community might decide to use the data to improve support systems for other immigrants. The students would benefit by developing empathy, civic commitment, and a practical understanding of the power of participatory research. The faculty member might be inspired, renewed, and feel a sense of public purpose for the work.

Conversely, imagine how an existing service-learning opportunity can be adapted into community-based research. For years, students actively volunteered at a local homeless shelter as part of a public health class that focused on adult development. Students kept reflection journals and participated in structured in-class discussions designed to link their service experience with their understanding of the course content. One semester, through their interaction with homeless individuals, several students in the class became concerned with the severe oral health needs of the residents and wanted to increase their access to dental services. With their professor, staff at the shelter, and some of the residents, the students conducted a survey to assess the level of access to free or low-cost dental services for homeless and low-income individuals. The report examined the oral health status and level of access and barriers among the adult homeless population in the area.

Conclusion

By situating service-learning in the context of civic engagement, each strengthens the other. The hallmarks of service-learning, including the focus on student learning and community effectiveness and the pedagogy of action with reflection, can be applied to other forms of civic engagement as well. One might think of it as bringing the "learning" of service-learning to civic engagement.

For its part, civic engagement brings to service-learning a broad range of ways for students to get involved in the community. These additional forms of engagement not only help students understand the multiple approaches needed to solve complex community problems but also make service-learning attractive to students interested in getting involved in their communities in ways other than direct service alone. At the institutional level, service-learning is inextricably interlinked with both the engaged campus and the scholarship of engagement. The community service-learning professional connects service to the broader spectrum of civic engagement so that students acquire public values and the knowledge, skills, and efficacy to act on them.

References

American College Personnel Association & National Association of Student Personnel Administrators. (2004). *Learning reconsidered: A campus-wide focus on the student experience*. Washington, DC: Authors.

Barber, B. R. (1998a). *A place for us: How to make society civil and democracy strong*. New York: Hill and Wang.

Barber, B. R. (1998b). The discourse of civility. In S. L. Elkin (Ed.), *Citizen competence and democratic institutions* (pp. 39–47). State College, PA: Penn State University Press.

Battistoni, R. (2002). *Civic engagement across the curriculum*. Providence, RI: Campus Compact.

Bornstein, D. (2005). *How to change the world: Social entrepreneurs and the power of new ideas*. New Delhi: Penguin Books.

Boyte, H., & Hollander, E. (1999). *Wingspread declaration on renewing the civic mission of the American research university*. Providence, RI: Campus Compact.

Brown, D. (2005). Public scholarship at Penn State: An interview with Jeremy Cohen. *Higher Education Exchange.* Dayton, OH: Kettering Foundation.

Brownell, J. E., & Swaner, L. E. (2009). High-impact practices: Applying the learning outcomes literature to the development of successful campus programs. *AAC&U Peer Review, 1* (2), 26–30.

Cambridge, B.L. (1999). Effective assessment: A signal of quality citizenship. In R.G. Bringle, R. Games, & E. A. Malloy (Eds.), *College and universities as citizens* (pp.173–192). Needham Heights, MA: Allyn & Bacon.

Campus Compact. (1999). *Presidents' declaration on the civic responsibility of higher education.* Providence, RI: Author.

Center for Social Justice, Research, Teaching, & Service, Department of Sociology and Anthropology and the Community Research and Learning Network (2008). *Faculty handbook: Community-based learning and research* (2nd ed.). Georgetown University, Washington, DC.

Colby, A., Beaumont, E., Ehrlich, T., & Corngold, J. (2007). *Educating for democracy: Preparing undergraduates for responsible political engagement.* San Francisco: Jossey Bass.

Colby, A., Ehrlich, T., Beaumont, E., & Stephens, J. (2003). *Educating citizens: Preparing America's undergraduates for lives of moral and civic responsibility.* San Francisco: Jossey-Bass.

Driscoll, A. (2008). Carnegie's community engagement classification: Intentions and Insights. *Change,* (January/February), 38–41.

Ferraiolo, K. (Ed.). (2004). *New directions in civic engagement: University avenue meets main street.* Charlottesville, VA: The Pew Partnership for Civic Change.

Enos, S., & Morton, K. (2003). Developing a theory and practice of campus-community partnerships. In B. Jacoby (Ed.), *Building partnerships for service-learning* (pp. 20–41). San Francisco: Jossey-Bass.

Eyler, J., & Giles, D. E. (1999). *Where's the learning in service-learning?* San Francisco: Jossey-Bass.

Hartley, M., Harkavy, I., & Benson, L. (2005). Putting down roots in the grove of academe: The challenges of institutionalizing service-learning. In D. W. Butin (Ed.), *Service-learning in higher education: Critical issues and directions* (pp. 205–222). New York: Palgrave-MacMillan.

Holland, B. (2005). *Scholarship and mission in the 21st century university: The role of engagement.* Unpublished white paper based on keynote address to the Australian Universities Quality Agency Forum, July 5, 2005.

Hollander, E., & Hartley, M. (2003). Civic renewal: A powerful framework for advancing service-learning. In B. Jacoby (Ed.), *Building partnerships for service-learning* (pp. 289–313). San Francisco: Jossey-Bass.

Hollander, E. L., & Saltmarsh, J. (2000). *The engaged university. Academe,* 86(4), 1–6.

Jacoby, B. (Ed.). (2003). *Building partnerships for service-learning.* San Francisco: Jossey-Bass.

Jacoby, B. (2009). Civic engagement in today's higher education: An overview. In B. Jacoby (Ed.), *Civic engagement in higher education: Concepts and practices* (pp. 5–30). San Francisco: Jossey-Bass.

Keeter, S., Zukin, C., Andolina, M., & Jenkins, K. (2002). *The civic and political health of the nation: A generational portrait.* College Park, MD: Center for Information & Research on Civic Learning and Engagement (CIRCLE).

Kellogg Presidents' Commission on the Future of State and Land Grant Universities (2001). *Returning to our roots: Executive summaries of the reports of the Kellogg Commission on the future of state and land grant universities.* Retrieved July 21, 2009, from http://www.aplu.org/NetCommunity/Page.aspx?pid=305.

Kiesa, A., Orlowski, A. P., Levine, P., Both, D., Kirby, E. H., Lopez, M. H. et al. (2007). *Millennials talk politics: A study of college student political engagement.* College Park, MD: Center for Information & Research on Civic Learning and Engagement.

Kirlin, M. (2003). *The role of civic skills in fostering civic engagement.* College Park, MD: Center for Information & Research on Civic Learning and Engagement.

Lawry, S., Laurison, D., & Van Antwerpen, J. (2009). *Liberal education and civic engagement.* New York: Ford Foundation.

Light, P. C. (2008). *The search for social entrepreneurship.* Washington, DC: Brookings Institution Press.

Long, S. E. (2002). *The new student politics: The wingspread statement on student civic engagement.* Providence, RI: Campus Compact.

Lopez, M. H., Levine, P., Both, D., Kiesa, A., Kirby, E., & Marcelo, K. (2006). *The 2006 civic and political health of the nation: A detailed look at how youth participate in politics and communities.* College Park, MD: Center for Information & Research on Civic Learning and Engagement.

Morton, K. (1995). The irony of service: Charity, project, and social change in service-learning. *Michigan Journal of Community Service Learning, 2,* 19–32.

Musil, C. M. (2009). Educating students for personal and social responsibility: The civic learning spiral. In B. Jacoby (Ed.), *Civic engagement in higher education: Concepts and practices* (pp. 31–48). San Francisco: Jossey-Bass.

National Leadership Council for Liberal Education and America's Promise. (2007). *College learning for the new global century: A report from the National Leadership Council for Liberal Education & America's Promise.* Washington, DC: Association of American Colleges and Universities.

Nyden, P. (2003). Partnerships for collaborative action research. In B. Jacoby (Ed.), *Enhancing partnerships for service-learning* (pp. 213–233). San Francisco: Jossey-Bass.

Patrick, J. J. (2003). Defining, delivery, and defending a common education for citizenship in a democracy. In J.J. Patrick, G. E. Hamot, & R. S. Leming, (Eds.), *Civic learning in teacher education: International perspectives on education for democracy in the preparation of teachers* (Vol. 2). Indiana University: ERIC Clearinghouse for Social Studies/Social Science Education.

Paul, E. (2003). Community-based undergraduate research: Collaborative inquiry for the public good. In B. Jacoby (Ed.), *Enhancing partnerships for service-learning* (pp. 196–212). San Francisco: Jossey-Bass.

Pigza, J. & Troppe, M. (2003). Developing an infrastructure for service-learning and community engagement. In B. Jacoby (Ed.), *Enhancing partnerships for service-learning* (pp. 106–130). San Francisco: Jossey-Bass.

Ramaley, J. A. (2000). Embracing civic responsibility. *Campus Compact Reader, 1*(2), 1–5.

Stringer, E. T. (2007). *Action research* (3rd ed.). Los Angeles: Sage.

University of Minnesota Report from the Public Scholarship Committee. (2006). Retrieved July 21, 2009, from http://www1.umn.edu/civic/archives/cholar.html.

Walshok, M. L. (1999). Strategies for building the infrastructure that supports the engaged campus. In R.G. Bringle, R. Games, & E. A. Malloy (Eds.), *College and Universities as Citizens* (pp. 74–95). Needham Heights, MA: Allyn & Bacon.

Ward, K. (2003). *Faculty service roles and the scholarship of engagement.* ASHE-ERIC Higher Education Report, 25(5). San Francisco: Jossey-Bass.

Welch, M. (2009). Moving from service-learning to civic engagement. In B. Jacoby (Ed.), *Civic engagement in higher education: Concepts and practices* (pp. 174–195). San Francisco: Jossey-Bass.

Additional Resources

Association of American Colleges and Universities (AAC&U) (http://www.aacu.org/resources/civicengagement/index.cfm)

American Democracy Project (http://www.aascu.org/programs/adp/index.htm)

American Psychological Association: Civic Engagement and Service-Learning (http://www.apa.org/ed/slce/home.html)

Campus Compact (http://www.compact.org)

Carnegie Foundation for the Advancement of Teaching: Community Engagement Elective Classification (http://www.carnegiefoundation.org/classifications/index.asp?key=1213)

Center for Information & Research on Civic Learning and Engagement (CIRCLE) (http://www.civicyouth.org/)

Civic Practices Network (http://www.cpn.org/tools/manuals/index.html)

Community College National Center for Community Engagement (http://www.mc. maricopa.edu/other/engagement/)

Idealist (http://www.idealist.org/)

The Scholarship of Engagement Online (http://schoe.coe.uga.edu/benchmarking/bei.html)

University of Maryland Coalition for Civic Engagement and Leadership (CCEL) (http://www.terpimpact.umd.edu/)

WORKSHEET 11-1:

Reflection Questions to Move Participants from Service to Other Forms of Engagement

To understand social issues:

- What do we know about the social issue being addressed and about how it has affected this community in particular?

  _____

  _____

  _____

  _____

- What are the symptoms of the problem, and what are the causes?

  _____

  _____

  _____

  _____

- What systems are in place that maintain the problem, and how can they be broken down?

  _____

  _____

  _____

  _____

- What social issues are connected to the problem addressed by the project (such as racism, class stratification, sexism, etc.)? Can a difference be made on this issue without addressing these social problems?

  _____

  _____

  _____

  _____

(continued)

WORKSHEET

To examine the service-learning project:

- What are the strengths and limitations of the project?

  _____

  _____

  _____

  _____

- Does the project address immediate needs or long-term solutions?

  _____

  _____

  _____

  _____

- If the project continued, would the problem go away eventually?

  _____

  _____

  _____

  _____

- If the project stopped in order to try another approach to the issue, would the community suffer?

  _____

  _____

  _____

  _____

(continued)

- Are there assets in the community that are not being tapped? Is our involvement so focused on the community's deficits that we haven't seen its assets?

  _____

  _____

  _____

  _____

To explore future action and other forms of civic engagement:

- Is enough known about the issue and this community, or is more research needed?

  _____

  _____

  _____

  _____

- Who needs to understand the problem better and be convinced to make a change?

  _____

  _____

  _____

  _____

- Have the voices of all members of the community been heard? What steps have been taken to ensure everyone agrees on the direction of the effort?

  _____

  _____

  _____

  _____

(continued)

WORKSHEET

- Is more funding needed? Who would receive the money and what would they use it for? Who could be approached for funding?

  _____

  _____

  _____

  _____

- What relevant laws or policies affect the issue, and how did they come to be?

  _____

  _____

  _____

  _____

- What stance do local and/or national politicians take on the issue?

  _____

  _____

  _____

  _____

- How are other individuals or groups working to address the problem? Discuss the strengths and limitations of those approaches and how a coalition might be able to coordinate efforts.

  _____

  _____

  _____

  _____

(continued)

- What campus or community organizations could be tapped to make the effort stronger? Should a new organization be formed to bring together people who are interested in this issue?

_____

_____

_____

_____

- What aspects of the students' personal behavior might contribute to the problem?

_____

_____

_____

_____

- How can students use the knowledge and skills they are gaining in college, particularly in their career field, to help address the issue?

_____

_____

_____

_____

- What other forms of civic engagement would be effective in addressing the issue?

_____

_____

_____

_____

WORKSHEET

About the Authors

Robert G. Bringle

Dr. Robert Bringle has been involved in the development, implementation, and evaluation of educational programs and is widely known for his research on jealousy and close relationships. His work as Executive Director of the Indiana University-Purdue University Indianapolis (IUPUI) Center for Service and Learning has resulted in numerous awards and national recognition for his campus and himself. For his scholarly journal articles, chapters, and books on service learning, Bringle was awarded the Thomas Ehrlich Faculty Award for Service-Learning by Campus Compact and was recognized at the International Service-Learning Research Conference for his outstanding contributions. He was the Volunteer of the Year in 2001 for Boys and Girls Clubs of Indianapolis. The University of the Free State, South Africa, awarded him an honorary doctorate for his scholarly work on civic engagement and service-learning.

Patti H. Clayton

Patti H. Clayton, Ph.D., is an independent consultant (PHC Ventures: www.curricularengagement.com), a Senior Scholar with the Center for Service and Learning at IUPUI, and a Visiting Fellow with the New England Resource Center for Higher Education (NERCHE). She was previously founding Director of the Center for Excellence in Curricular Engagement at NC State University. Clayton co-developed the DEAL Model for critical reflection and assessment as well as models for student leadership, faculty development, curriculum development, and institutionalization. Her work focuses on building the capacity of individuals, institutions, and the field as a whole for scholarly and democratic community-engaged teaching and learning.

David M. Donahue

David M. Donahue, Ph.D., is Associate Professor of Education at Mills College in Oakland, California. He works with teacher credential students preparing to teach art, English, and history in secondary schools and graduate students investigating teaching and learning with a focus on equity in urban contexts. He is one of ten Engaged Scholars for New Perspectives in Higher Education and a special consultant to the California Campus Compact–Carnegie Foundation Faculty Fellows Program for Service-Learning for Political Engagement. His research interests include teacher learning generally and learning from service-learning and the arts specifically.

Julie A. Hatcher

Julie A. Hatcher is Associate Director of the nationally recognized Center for Service and Learning at IUPUI. Her responsibilities include faculty development, research projects to assess the outcomes of service-learning and civic engagement, and management of a wide range of service-based programs. She was awarded the Dissertation Research Award by the International Association for Research in Service-Learning and Civic Engagement for her dissertation, entitled *The Public Role of Professionals: Developing and Evaluating the Civic-Minded Professional Scale*. Her published work and formal presentations have focused on civic engagement and service-learning in higher education, international comparative analysis, implications of John Dewey's philosophy for higher education, and reflective practice. She has consulted with numerous campuses on integrating service into academic study, including international projects with faculty from Egypt, Kenya, Macedonia, Mexico, and South Africa.

Barbara Holland

Barbara A. Holland, Ph.D., is Pro Vice-Chancellor Engagement at the University of Western Sydney, where she is implementing a university-wide strategic plan for partnerships relating to educational attainment in schools, environmental sustainability, cultural understanding, and economic development. Prior roles include Director of Learn and Serve America's National Service-Learning Clearinghouse and Senior Scholar at IUPUI. She is recognized internationally for her expertise on organizational change in higher education, with a specific emphasis on the implementation and assessment of service-learning, engaged research, and community partnerships. In 2006 she received the Research Achievement Award from the International Association for Research on Service-Learning and Community Engagement.

Carrie Williams Howe

Carrie Williams Howe, M.Ed., is the Associate Director of the Office of Community-University Partnerships and Service-Learning (CUPS) at the University of Vermont (UVM) and a member of the Vermont and National Campus Compact Consultant Corps. She regularly leads workshops in academic service-learning on her home campus and across New England, on topics ranging from curriculum development to facilitating reflection and managing effective partnerships. She is a lead facilitator of UVM's Faculty Fellows for Service-Learning Program and created the university's Service-Learning Teaching Assistant Program. In addition to her role in service-learning support and training, Howe teaches service-learning courses on topics such as civic leadership and nonprofit management.

Elaine K. Ikeda

Elaine K. Ikeda has served as the Executive Director of California Campus Compact (CACC) since 2000. For the last 15 years, Ikeda has contributed to the production of research knowledge related to service-learning and has co-authored several journal articles and book chapters on service-learning and student development, including a chapter in *Service-Learning and the First-Year Experience* (National Resource Center for the First-Year Experience and Students in Transition, 2002). She also has organized numerous conferences, institutes, and forums addressing service-learning and civic engagement in education. From 2005 to 2007, she directed the largest community partner research study in the nation, resulting in the research report

Community Voices: A California Campus Compact Study on Partnerships. Ikeda holds a Ph.D. in higher education & organizational change from the University of California, Los Angeles.

Barbara Jacoby

Barbara Jacoby is Senior Scholar for the Adele H. Stamp Student Union–Center for Campus Life at the University of Maryland, College Park. In this role, she facilitates initiatives involving academic partnerships, civic engagement, scholarship, and assessment of student learning outcomes. Jacoby is also Chair of the university's Coalition for Civic Engagement and Leadership. Jacoby received her Ph.D. from the University of Maryland in French Language and Literature in 1978. She is Affiliate Associate Professor of College Student Personnel in the Department of Counseling and Personnel Services. Among her many publications are five books, including *Service-Learning in Higher Education: Concepts and Practices* (Jossey-Bass, 1996), *Building Partnerships for Service-Learning* (Jossey-Bass, 2003), and *Civic Engagement in Higher Education* (Jossey-Bass, 2009).

Lacretia Johnson Flash

Lacretia Johnson Flash is the Assistant Dean for Conduct, Policy, and Climate at the University of Vermont. Prior to this role, Johnson Flash directed community service programs in the Department of Student Life at the University of Vermont, served as the Service-Learning Coordinator for College Park Scholars at the University of Maryland, and was an Artist-in-Residence at Studio G, affiliated with the Georgetown University Medical Center.

Susan Robb Jones

Dr. Susan Robb Jones is Associate Professor and Program Director in the College Student Personnel Program at the University of Maryland–College Park. Prior to Maryland she served as Associate Professor and Director of the Student Personnel Assistantship Program at The Ohio State University. She has published on topics such as service-learning and college student identity development, student resistance, the outcomes associated with required service, and university-community partnerships. She served as chair of the board of trustees of Project OpenHand, an AIDS service organization, and the After School Academic Partnership program (ASAP), both in Columbus, Ohio.

Mark N. Langseth

Mark Langseth is President and CEO of "I Have a Dream" Foundation – Oregon, which aims to significantly increase the college graduation rates of low-income children in the Portland metropolitan area. His past positions include Vice President for University Advancement and Executive Director of the Foundation at Metropolitan State University, Assistant Vice President for Development at Portland State University, Founding Executive Director of Minnesota Campus Compact, and Chief Operating Officer at the National Youth Leadership Council. Langseth is a former Kellogg Fellow and has produced several publications on campus-community engagement, including co-editing, with William Plater, *Public Work and the Academy: An Academic Administrator's Guide to Service-Learning* (Anker Publishing, 2005).

Pamela Mutascio

Pamela Mutascio served as Program Manager for seven years at Campus Compact, where she created and co-developed the prestigious Professional Development Institute for Community Service and Service-Learning Professionals. During her tenure she provided valuable resources, training, and technical assistance to member campuses; managed the annual membership survey and national student award programs; and led a variety of workshops on service programs and civic engagement in higher education. She also created the first national Leadership Award for Campus and Community Engagement for community engagement professionals, edited *Essential Resources for Campus-based Service, Service-Learning and Civic Engagement* (Campus Compact, 2004) and a number of fact sheets for the National Service-Learning Clearinghouse. Mutascio holds a Bachelor of Arts degree in women's studies and human services from Simmons College in Boston.

Billy O'Steen

Dr. Billy O'Steen's teaching and research focus on innovative curriculum design and professional development, with a particular emphasis on experiential education and service-learning. He received his B.A. in English and history from Vanderbilt University, and both his M.Ed. and Ph.D. from the University of Virginia (dissertation: *Experiential English: A Naturalistic Inquiry of Outward Bound in the Classroom*). Prior to his current position as a Senior Lecturer of Higher Education at the University of Canterbury in New Zealand, O'Steen was a faculty member in the Teacher Education Program at North Carolina State University, served as a Peace Corps administrator, worked as a legislative aide to a U.S. Senator, created and directed an intermediate school, taught English at a secondary school in Tennessee and two community colleges in California, guided whitewater raft trips in California, and facilitated multicultural education programs in Brazil and Tennessee.

Julie E. Owen

Julie E. Owen, Ph.D., is an Assistant Professor of Leadership and Integrative Studies in New Century College at George Mason University, where she teaches courses on socially responsible leadership and civic engagement. She is co-principal investigator of the Multi-Institutional Study of Leadership (MSL) Institutional Survey and the Leadership Identity Development (LID) project. In addition, she is co-editor of *The Handbook for Student Leadership Programs* (NCLP, 2006) and author of two monographs for the National Clearinghouse for Leadership Programs (NCLP).

Rev. Ann Palmerton

Rev. Ann R. Palmerton is Associate Pastor at the Broad Street Presbyterian Church in Columbus, Ohio, where the A.S.A.P. program brings students together with tutors from the church, community, and The Ohio State University. For 15 years Palmerton has served this downtown congregation in the areas of local mission and advocacy as well as in pastoral care. Prior to this downtown ministry she worked in congregations near The Ohio State University and in San Diego, California. She and her husband, Brad Binau, are the parents of Martin, Sarah, and Trevor.

Jennifer M. Pigza

Jennifer M. Pigza is Associate Director of the Catholic Institute for Lasallian Social Action at Saint Mary's College of California. She has been invested in engaged pedagogy and social justice education for nearly 20 years, beginning with 4 years of nonprofit work through the Jesuit Volunteer Corps. Currently, she supports both academic and co-curricular community service-learning programs, and her scholarship explores how faculty and staff sustain teaching and learning for social justice. Pigza holds a bachelor's degree in English literature (Loyola University Maryland), a master's of education degree in higher education and student affairs administration (University of Vermont), and a doctorate in the social foundations of education (University of Maryland).

Kathleen Rice

Kathleen Rice, Ph.D., of K L Rice Consulting (klriceconsulting.com), provides facilitation, training, and coaching services for nonprofit and educational social change agents. She specializes in higher education–university partnership building, leadership and organizational development, diversity and equity, and group facilitation. She draws from her experience, and from the many "teachers" she has had along the way, in academic and student affairs in six universities, as a Senior Trainer with the Corporation for National and Community Service, and as a teacher in The UNtraining: UNtraining white liberal racism, in the San Francisco Bay Area.

Marie G. Sandy

Marie Sandy is an Assistant Professor of Educational Policy and Community Studies at the University of Wisconsin Milwaukee, where she teaches courses on community participation and power, philosophy of education, and community organizing. A long-standing practitioner of service-learning and community-based research, she formerly directed California Campus Compact's Community Voices Across California Project, as well as a semester-long community-learning immersion program at Pitzer College. She is also the former deputy director of Wider Opportunities for Women in Washington, DC, where she worked as a community organizer and supervised service-learning students for several years.

Wendy Wagner

Wendy Wagner is the Director of the Center for Leadership and Community Engagement and Assistant Professor in Nonprofit Studies at George Mason University. She is the co-author of *Leadership for a Better World* (NCLP, 2009) and co-editor of *The Handbook for Student Leadership Programs* (NCLP, 2006). Wagner is a former coordinator of the National Clearinghouse for Leadership Programs and has extensive experience with civic engagement and service-learning programs

Marshall Welch

Marshall Welch, Ph.D., became the Director of the Catholic Institute for Lasallian Social Action (CILSA) at Saint Mary's College of California in 2007. Prior to this role, he was the Director of the Lowell Bennion Community Service Center at the University of Utah and a faculty member in the College of Education. He has taught numerous service-learning courses and has several publications, presentations, and workshops on service-learning, civic engagement, and spiritual development in education. He earned his doctorate in special education from Southern Illinois University in 1987 and completed his undergraduate work in education and sociology at Concordia College in Moorhead, Minnesota.